FRONTIER CITY

FRONTIER CITY

CITY

TORONTO on the VERGE of GREATNESS

SHAWN MICALLEF

SIGNAL
McCLELLAND
& STEWART

Grateful acknowledgement is given to the following
for permission to reproduce copyrighted material:

p. 38 – from ALL THE KING'S MEN © 2006 Columbia Pictures Industries, Inc.
All Rights Reserved. Courtesy of Columbia Pictures.

p. 208 – from SUBDIVISIONS. Words by NEIL PEART Music by GEDDY LEE
and ALEX LIFESON. © 1982 CORE MUSIC PUBLISHING. All Rights Reserved.
Used by Permission ALFRED MUSIC

Library and Archives Canada Cataloguing in Publication
is available upon request.

ISBN 978-0-7710-5932-2

ebook ISBN 978-0-7710-5933-9

Typeset in Galliard by M&S, Toronto

Printed and bound in the USA

Cover photograph: SoTeeOh / www.soteeoh.com

Published by Signal,
an imprint of McClelland & Stewart,
a division of Penguin Random House Canada Limited,
a Penguin Random House Company

www.penguinrandomhouse.ca

1 2 3 4 5   21 20 19 18 17

Dedicated to the memory of Dr. Martha Lee, for making things like this seem so vital in first year political science, and for encouraging me to pursue them.

CONTENTS

A CITY **ELECTION** is like a civic autopsy. The corpse lies bare, its internal workings exposed: the diseased tissue is isolated; the torn aorta inspected; and the organs' failure examined. Yet in this kind of post-mortem the body on the table isn't dead. The city moves onward, animated as ever, pausing only for a rare moment of self-examination while the competing pathologists offer theories to explain its damaged condition. During an election, we are free to talk openly about what's wrong with the city, and to look to a brighter future. Usually, when not compelled to pay attention to municipal affairs, residents are content to play ostrich, raising their heads only for the occasional issues that affect them directly.

Toronto is a place that everyone thought they understood. It was a little predictable, not prone to dramatics, maybe even boring. Its politics, like those of all Canadian cities, were overlooked in favour of provincial and federal intrigues. Cities took care of garbage collection and parking violations, not the really important or particularly interesting stuff. Toronto had always worked fairly well historically, so nobody really had to pay attention, it was just going to carry on as it always did. In 2010 Toronto suddenly was very interesting to the people who live here, and ones further afield. City hall became something not just policy wonks paid attention to, and was maybe a bit too interesting for those here. Toronto had never been the Jimmy Kimmel kind of interesting, but suddenly there was the mayor sitting next to him, taking jokes like a boxer takes punches as he goes down.

Research for this book began at the height of civic drama in Toronto during the last year of Rob Ford's mayoralty in 2014, before he dropped out of the race following his cancer diagnosis. It's a challenge to get back into the headspace of those days because it seems almost unbelievable now, like some wild, fictional potboiler on the city politics of some mercurial burg.

The city lurched from one leadership crisis to another and international news media were routinely camped out at city hall, their satellite trucks parked in a row outside. There was a sense here of things coming undone, that the foundation civil society had relied on for decades was unsound and that bedrock institutions no longer mattered. "Truth" even seemed under attack, and endless fact checking by reporters didn't matter much, foreshadowing the rise of Donald Trump.

How did Rob Ford arrive at the top of Toronto? What was happening in the city? What did Rob Ford mean? These are all questions Torontonians and others asked themselves over and over, most without receiving satisfactory answers. Into that void came crude caricatures of the kind of person who would vote for Ford: dumb people; selfish rich people; philistines; car drivers, suv drivers, suburban people, even. The city needed somebody to blame for Rob Ford.

Beyond Ford's personal tale, the details of which everyone knows too much about, there is a more complex Toronto story that's still vital and current. Somebody like Rob Ford, could become mayor again, and the cause, the thing to blame, is the city itself, not any one kind of person or particular political ideology.

That's why Toronto today is so hard to understand or to neatly put in a box. Mayoral election campaigns try to appeal to everyone and are reduced, by necessity, to focusing on a few issues. Sometimes an entire election can hinge on just one issue, such as a subway, taxes, or a bridge to an island airport. Mayoral elections suck up all the media oxygen too, and obscure the other hundreds of races going on, where the complex nature of this place is more readily apparent.

To get a read on the city close to the ground, I went for walks with ten people who ran for city council and with two who were vying for school board trustee positions. We walked and talked and looked. They showed me their Toronto: the streets, the parks, the shops, and the people they interacted with every day, the people and places that, in part, caused them to undertake something that would consume nearly a year of their lives without the celebrity that comes with the mayoral race. These conversations shared their intimate view of Toronto, and its issues right now, and showed why someone like Rob Ford could be elected again here or elsewhere if such problems aren't addressed. Like a good city walk, there were ample opportunities for diversion and to follow interesting side streets of thought and ideas to see where they led.

All the candidates I walked with were underdogs. As non-incumbents in local races, where name recognition is every-thing, they faced a considerable challenge. The underdog's view has value, though, an enlightened position at the street level that looks up and critiques power rather than trying to hold on to it. The cracks are always visible from below, and these candi-dates listened to people at the door every day, absorbed their worries and city views, and shared some of them with me while we were on the streets exploring. These candidates heard about the discontent in Toronto first-hand and knew why so many good and decent people voted for a Rob Ford.

Our walks also revealed the geography of this massive city. It's hard to fully grasp how big this place is until you spend a few hours walking just one or two neighbourhoods in a part of the city that doesn't get much attention. Each neighbourhood reveals another adjacent to it, and then another, and another. The city goes on and on. Then there were the unheralded ravines or oblique views of the downtown skyline we came upon, perhaps twenty-five kilometres away from the city centre. Hiding in all that geography is not only the beauty of this city, a place on the verge of its own version of civic greatness that's been building for decades as people came here from every corner of the globe, but also some less beautiful things that might prove to be the city's slow undoing.

Rob Ford was an early warning sign that things were not universally all right in Toronto. Populist politicians have always been around and always will. But the particular kind of grievance-based, reactionary politics that give a middle finger both to institutions and the chattering classes who have for so long felt comfortable in this city came when there was still time to find ways to fix what's wrong. The post-mortem need not end when the election is over, and to ignore what Toronto learned about itself during these past few years would be perilous. I hope this book provides a reminder of some of those things, but also an abundance of reasons why this place is worth fighting for.

Let's go for a walk with some Torontonians.

CHAPTER ONE

A POPULATION OF POPULATIONS

ALL CITIES have their magic moments, when they feel like a picture postcard or film set, with clichéd scenes of idyllic urban life that seem too perfect to be real. One of Toronto's has got to be the ride on the ferry from the Toronto Island park at the end of a summer's day.

For some, the island means the beach – the water is clean and clear, if a bit on the cold side – or a family picnic, on one of the great island lawns or at the mid-century modern concrete pavilions, with their display of some Expo '67 flare that trickled down to Toronto from Montreal. There are cute rides at the Centreville Amusement Park, and animals to pet at the Far Away Farm next door. Charlotte, the farm's Landrace pig, is always a big hit. Some interloping islanders might slip out to the less-frequented nooks on the island for other extracurricular activities unlisted in the official city manual of how to have fun, but there's space for everyone. The sun seems to move slower across the island sky too, with the speed and urgency of city life temporarily put on hold.

People visiting the island *look* like Toronto. The ethnic, social, and cultural mix of people found there on a peak weekend day matches the city's multicultural demographics that

Torontonians are proud to tout whenever they have the chance. These peak weekend days are also when certain parts of the city seem downright empty, as a mass middle-class exodus to hinterland redoubts causes hours-long traffic jams in the middle of rural nowhere on Sunday evenings.

"Going to the cottage" is a Toronto tradition that looms large in the psyche of the city, but most Torontonians don't have access to this getaway. The island, then, is cottage country for the uncottaged, a communal backyard that can handle many dozens of hibachi barbecues at a time. It's egalitarian Toronto at its best, a place where the ideals fundamental to its self-image can be seen.

The island and ferry back are also the best place to look at the city itself. It's quite a thing to approach on the water: an Oz-like skyline that changes each year as more buildings and skyscrapers are added to the composition in an ever-widening mass of concrete, glass, and humanity spreading east and west along the waterfront, with construction cranes indicating more is coming. Kids from a different generation might have counted Volkswagen Beetles to pass the time, but in Toronto kids have been overheard on the ferry counting the cranes, a challenge as there's always another one hiding behind a building, appearing only as the ferry shifts perspective. It's been like this for a decade and a half now, a steady expansion that even the 2008 financial crisis couldn't slow down.

Viewed from the ferry, all is well, or so it seems. Even on dry land there's a stunning new waterfront, with public spaces conjured up by some of the world's best designers. Across from the Redpath Sugar refinery, one of the last remaining vestiges of what was once a working, industrial waterfront, is Sugar Beach, a human-made place with perfect white sand, Muskoka chairs, and painted chunks of rock that look like candy-striped chunks of the Canadian Shield.

You can't escape the idea of cottage country anywhere in Toronto. There are other new parks like this around this city, marvels that will be written up in glossy landscape architecture magazines alongside similar places in other cities. Even the dirty underbelly of the Gardiner Expressway – the 1950s carbuncle that some would say has plagued Toronto, cutting it off from the lake – got a $25 million boost in 2015 from a local philanthropist to turn it into a linear park. This project is the flip side of the High Line in New York, an abandoned, elevated rail line that became a showpiece that people can promenade along for kilometres while regarding a New York that has also scrubbed itself up, losing the filth and decay it had come to be associated with in the dark days of the 1970s. A tourist in New York today can spend days exploring a transformed city at places such as Brooklyn Bridge Park, which took a few kilometres of industrial waterfront and installed public art and sports fields and landscape architecture worthy of that city's Frederick Law Olmsted tradition.

In Boston they buried their elevated highway with the Big Dig, a multi-billion dollar project that turned the scar that was the city's Central Artery running through its downtown into a chain of beautiful public spaces. Chicago installed a stainless-steel bean, "Cloud Gate," by sculptor Anish Kapoor, in Millennium Park, the backdrop for millions of selfies a year. Next to it is the Pritzker Pavilion, an outdoor concert theatre where Chicagoans can drink a bottle of wine underneath a trellis designed by Frank Gehry while listening to the symphony in a location that was once dominated by railways until the park was built overtop. This is how prosperous cities demonstrate their wealth today.

Toronto has other equivalent spaces, like the new Corktown Common, a stunning park a few kilometres east of downtown, the centrepiece of a new dense neighbourhood built on reclaimed industrial land. The park also doubles as a flood-control barrier that could save downtown from the ravages of a one-hundred-year flood – a big one that ecologists warn is probable every century – that might rise from the adjacent Don River. Form and function together, in a city that sometimes had the latter but too little of the former.

This city, despite a deeply entrenched cynicism after years of project delays in transit and waterfront development, appears to be firing on all cylinders. Neighbourhoods that were once down on their heels are suddenly hot, written up in the *New York Times* and *The Guardian* and magazines, helping boost average property values into the seven-figure range. A new crosstown light rail project is being built. The subway is being extended to York University and beyond the city limits into Vaughan. Queens Quay, the waterfront's grand avenue, was recently redone to standards so high it no longer feels like Toronto. Bloor Street, in the summer of 2016, even got a two-and-a-half kilometres-long bike lane, the first part of a dream so many cycling activists held on to for years. All that and more, but most importantly, people keep choosing to move to Toronto. Their reasons may vary, but the city remains a destination for human migration of all kinds.

TORONTO'S SUCCESS is part of an urban renaissance across North America and beyond, and a rediscovery of urban living. The transformation of neighbourhoods such as Prenzlauer Berg in Berlin, Hackney in London, East Liberty in Pittsburgh, or even Midtown in Detroit are not unlike what Parkdale, the Junction, and Leslieville have gone through in Toronto over the last decade. It isn't just neighbourhoods that are generating excitement, it's cities themselves.

The emergence of de facto city states that power national economies and operate almost like international actors, competing with each other to attract talent and capital while managing their own kind of foreign policy, is redefining how the world works. "The world is watching cities," proclaims the C40 Cities Climate Leadership Group. C40 is a network of eighty of the world's megacities, including Toronto, committed to addressing climate change. "Cities are where the future happens first," is another of the organization's mantras, one that rings true, because many cities were taking action on climate change before their national governments were. Cities lead, and this will be an urban century. The global migration to cities in this era is unprecedented, and the cities that harness that energy will be the leaders in this urban century, studied and emulated by the others.

Toronto looks like it's destined to be a leader – all those cranes in the sky, with growth levels the envy of many, if not most, cities. Even well away from the gorgeous view from the ferry, there's prosperity in well-to-do neighbourhoods connected by kilometres-long stretches of main streets such as Yonge, Bayview, Avenue Road, or College that give little indication that the story of Toronto's prosperity isn't universally shared throughout the city.

The relatively wealthy part of the city is big, so big that it's easy for its residents to live out their entire days in a bubble of relative affluence, seduced into the idea that, as the late former Mayor of Toronto Rob Ford often said, "Everything is fine." But it isn't fine.

Toronto is a Los Angeles-sized place, forty-four kilometres wide along the lake and sprawling north until Steeles Avenue, where the suburbs, generalized as "the 905," named after the change in area codes outside of the city limits, continue on in what was until recently some of the best farmland in Canada.

Torontonians could save a lot of money at vacation time by being tourists in their own city, as it would be a life-long effort to explore every pocket of this place, to understand its varied geography and nearly 150 officially recognized neighbourhoods. Most people living here don't have a grasp of how big it is, the idea of the city fading into a kind of urban haze at the periphery of their imagination. They know there's more out there but have no reason to go visit it.

With nearly three million people inside Toronto, and seven million in the region, and more coming, there are entire populations in Toronto that exist in separate social, cultural, and economic spheres. Getting to know the city, to truly know it, is a task most people don't have time for. What that vast geographic spread does is allow the parts that aren't doing so well to drift under the radar – or rather, out of the radar range – of the prosperous parts, the parts on all the postcards and the neighbourhoods that the *New York Times* occasional raves about. Not knowing the city's geography also contributes to not thinking it's a place worth fighting for.

CONTRAST THE view from the ferry with that at the corner of Albion Road and Kipling Avenue, at the northwest edge of Toronto, some thirty kilometres by car, or an-hour-and-a-quarter transit ride, in good traffic, from the ferry docks. There are no postcards of this intersection, but on the face of it, there's nothing wrong here either.

On one corner, past a gas station and across a sprawling parking lot, is the Albion Centre, a neighbourhood mall. Kitty-corner is another, repurposed gas station, the mid-twentieth-century bungalow-inspired design suggesting an old Texaco, functioning now as a used-car lot and garage, with vehicles parked haphazardly on the property. Behind it is a mid-rise apartment tower. Across the street, the third corner is lined with backyard fences of a housing subdivision. It's a typical North American landscape. On the fourth corner, there's a City of Toronto community centre: the Albion Pool and Health Club. And back at the first corner, inside the Albion Centre, the mall, there's a branch of the Albion Neighbourhood Services, an organization that helps with housing, immigrant settlement, and employment.

Despite everything seeming average, typical, non-descript, ordinary, and fine, this intersection is one of many at the core of a "nation" that elected one of the most extraordinary mayors of any city anywhere, one of many in the unexpected heartland of a movement that would shake Toronto to its foundation and induce a radical questioning of what the city thought it was, at least for a while.

A few blocks south of here, across a branch of the Humber River, is the City of Toronto's Ward 2 where, for the first time in 2000, Rob Ford had been elected city councillor. In 2010, with the help of people throughout the city from corners like Albion and Kipling and elsewhere, Ford would become the mayor of Toronto, a city that became the fourth-most-populous municipality in North America during his tenure. This was the homeland of Ford Nation, and what's most remarkable about it is that it is wholly unremarkable. It is not a ghetto, or a slum, or any of the pejoratives that are often dumped on lower-income neighbourhoods; nor is it a pocket of libertarian wealth. It simply isn't glamorous, not in the way the postcard neighbourhoods are, the ones that get all the chatter and the bulk of the prosperity, and the ones that came to represent Toronto's renaissance in the first decade of the 2000s and beyond.

IN 2001 the City of Toronto created the position of Poet Laureate whose job was to talk and write about the city in ways that people usually don't. The civic poet writes about the spirit of the place, the things that can't be quantified in policy. The city's second laureate, installed in 2004, was Pier Giorgio Di Cicco, a Catholic priest who wore black turtlenecks, smoked cigarettes, and held mass regularly at an Etobicoke parish. His enthusiasm for the city matched that of the mayor he served under, David Miller.

Di Cicco and Miller helped whip up the civic euphoria over "Torontopia" – a movement that began in the early years of the twenty-first century as Toronto found its legs after both a disastrous recession and a radical amalgamation that transformed the way the city was governed and run.

Di Cicco most certainly didn't describe the city in conventional terms. During his tenure as poet laureate he put out a slim volume of his verse-like prose called *Municipal Mind: Manifestos for the Creative City*, writing that a city is a poem in progress and that citizens are the authors of the poem, and that a city must look glamorous in its own eyes to love itself. He wrote of the civic buzz and asked if there was a place for conviviality, joy, delight, play, laughter, and serenity to exist in the city.

For the poet, the city was, or should be, lush and attractive, and it should provide not just a living, a mere existence, but the good life – the kind of life that comes along with economic prosperity, something Toronto had, and has, in abundance. The notion of "creative cities," made popular by Richard Florida's 2002 book *Rise of the Creative Class*, considered the changing ways in which people in cities worked, but the phrase took on a life of its own. Di Cicco's book, in part, interpreted that notion as meaning each citizen in the city has the wherewithall to make it better, to create the city they want.

Although Torontonians did not cheer themselves on in the way that, say, New Yorkers, Chicagoans, or Bostonians might – though that is changing with the likes of Drake singing about the city at international pop star heights, and all manner of Toronto-inspired swag being produced at the independent artist and designer level – Di Cicco did and was the poet in residence of Torontopia – a term first used by the city's indie rock community during the early 2000s cultural renaissance and later by those celebrating the city's general evolution – showing up to all the civic-minded events and evoking the kind of city Toronto was striving to be. Di Cicco was never specific about the parts of Toronto he was writing about in *Municipal Mind*, although he did point out that "it is in the edge cities and in the suburban archipelagos that the creative agenda is desperately needed."

Di Cicco had concerns about gentrification and diversity, but his writing embodied the can-do civic spirit that flowed through some parts of Toronto, fed by those who were engaged in local politics and city planning processes, and by people who were simply getting excited about living here and engaging with it in various ways – a spirit that slowly trickled out into wider and wider circles. Di Cicco and his voice were what Toronto needed at the time and he described the book, his legacy project from his time as poet laureate, as an effort toward the rehabilitation of the civic dream.

"How do we align our dreams of the city with the economics of the city and official 'civic aesthetic'?" was the question Di Cicco asked on behalf of residents. "There is at the centre of the urban discussion a realm called 'civic aesthetic,' where the city must be re-aligned to the dreams of citizens and where the building is measured in compliance with, or by transgression of, the civic dream."

This belief was the social contract of both Torontopia and civil society in Toronto, that the ideal Toronto they imagined could reasonably be achieved, and that when something was in the way of that progress, it could be overcome. It was, at its heart, an optimistic view, but it was also an optimistic time. Toronto was the envy of so much of the world, and it seemed to be getting so much right.

It was a bit of an illusion, though: as shiny Toronto grew even brighter, there were parts that didn't have the means to participate, that didn't feel the euphoria, or even a connection to the mechanisms for change. As necessary as the vision of Torontopia was to get the political class engaged in this place, it was limited. It couldn't lift the spirit of the whole city, and large parts were waiting for somebody who could.

BACK AT the Albion and Kipling intersection – and in many square kilometres or pockets like it – discontent was growing. The buzz here was different than in Torontopia. It had its own art, loves, passions, and everything a good city has, but the citizens of this would-be nation felt left out of the spirit of the place that the poet wrote of, left out of that civic aesthetic.

Because it's an aesthetic, something ephemeral, a feeling, it's easy to overlook the differences between the prosperous and not-so-prosperous areas of the city: they don't look that different from each other. There are differences in built form, of pre-war and post-war design and sprawl and density, but taken as a whole Toronto is a melange of urban and suburban styles typical of many North American cities. The real differences can hide below the surface, tucked into pockets of townhomes on culs-de-sac and apartment towers next to ravines. It's where discontent simmers.

This discontent didn't happen overnight, of course. Toronto is a learned city, filled with universities and civil society organizations that study it and regularly check its pulse. One organization, the Toronto Foundation, even puts out an annual comprehensive study called "Vital Signs," and in the urban affairs section of the Toronto Reference Library there are dozens of shelves holding reports from scholars who have studied Toronto in minute detail. "Alarm was sounded in various ways," says University of Toronto sociologist David Hulchanski. "The 1979 *Metro Suburbs in Transition* report identified the inner suburbs as a trouble area, but political leaders scoffed at it."

The report, from the Social Planning Council of Metropolitan Toronto, looked at neighbourhoods, services, and equity in Toronto, but apart from appealing to those people who pay specific attention to these things it failed to light any fires. And there wasn't then a political reason for anybody to care. Toronto had just come off what some still call its first great era, coasting into the 1980s on its massive growth since World War II. However, worrisome trends continued.

A couple of decades later, the United Way looked at Toronto's troubles, in their 2002 report titled *Decade of Decline*. It tracked wages through the 1990s and found that the financial situation of Torontonians had worsened, even during the latter half of the decade when the city had pulled out of the recession and was experiencing the beginnings of its next economic boom. The income gap was widening, and poverty increasing, at both individual and neighbourhood levels.

In 2004 the United Way released a study called *Poverty by Postal Code*, which examined the geography of neighbourhood poverty in Toronto between 1981 and 2001, and in 2011 they published a second study, this one looking at a decline in income, housing quality, and community life in Toronto's inner suburban high-rise apartments. Now even the city itself was starting to map the poverty of its citizens. But the dominant urban narrative was so much about those cranes in the sky and the escalating real estate market that these reports' message was one few wanted to hear, although the numbers come as a shock to many in Toronto's bubble of prosperity.

Between 1980 and 2010, income inequality among Toronto neighbourhoods increased by 96 per cent, and the number of low-income neighbourhoods increased as well: in 1980, low-income neighbourhoods made up 28 per cent of the city's neighbourhoods, but by 2010 *half* of Toronto was low-income. Considering that incredible skyline view, that is a staggering percentage that should have everyone worried.

"*Poverty by Postal Code* gave way to the Building Strong Neighbourhoods' task force and a place-based strategy for the city and United Way," says Pedro Barata, Vice President of Communications and Public Affairs at the United Way. "We have been able to bring out the geographic nature of poverty by identifying neighbourhood improvement areas we called priority neighbourhoods. It's a platform for us to focus investments."

In the mid-2000s, the United Way and City of Toronto identified thirteen priority neighbourhoods in the city. Many Torontonians had likely driven past these neighbourhoods – such as Dorset Park, the cluster of high-rises at Kennedy Road and Highway 401 – and not known they were low-income or in trouble. The modern apartment towers look rather beautiful rising from the leafy park and are indistinguishable from ones found in wealthier neighbourhoods. In Toronto, neighbourhoods in trouble rarely, if ever, look like those portrayed in film and television. Toronto doesn't look like *The Wire*.

"The built form, in terms of poverty, may also hide what's living behind the walls," says Barata. "You may drive by a neighbourhood and the street life may belie what's actually happening, like poor access to child care, job prospects, and repairs needed in aging towers. All of these will not be readily apparent."

Another key warning sign, and one that dramatically helped people worried about these issues get a handle on this geography, is Hulchanski's groundbreaking *The Three Cities Within Toronto* report that looked at income polarization by neighbourhood from 1970 to 2005. "We weren't surprised by the inequality," says Hulchanski. "But we wanted to show it on the map, to show those trends."

Hulchanski and his team grouped income trends in Toronto into what they called "three cities": a city where income was rising, one where it's staying the same, and another where people were getting poorer. While the city with stable income, what we might call the middle class, was shrinking, both the very rich and very poor cities were growing, with the latter growing the fastest. The map of it is startling, showing what Barata describes as an inverted U of increasing poverty that goes up through Etobicoke, across the top of the city, and down in a cascade across all of Scarborough. Precarious employment, inadequate access to social services, poor affordable housing choices, and lack of jobs are all problems here.

Other than out of concern for their fellow humans, why should people in wealthier parts of Toronto care about the geographic and social inequity in their city? Barata says there are many reasons why, beyond any moral imperative, and the first is economic. "If we are going to be a competitive city that will attract investment, a city that is known for a really strong workforce, we have to make sure everybody is at their best," he says. "Being a livable city is an economic advantage: [it makes] people want to live here, raise their families and start their businesses."

Barata points to another fiscal reason: if we don't invest in these communities now and stem these trends, we'll pay much more later on. "Poverty is expensive," he says, citing unemployment and criminal justice costs down the road if trends continue. Other cities, like London and Paris, have experienced civil strife when they allowed conditions to deteriorate too far.

The policy areas that need attention include quality affordable housing, availability of community services, income security, and what Barata calls workforce development. "With precarity, people aren't going to get training through work, it'll be out of pocket, but the market demands it. [The money for training has] got to come from somewhere and it should be a lot easier for people." How did we get to such a state? Hulchanski says that by ignoring early signs of trouble, Toronto did this to itself. "It wasn't an earthquake," he says. "Invest in another direction and the maps will change."

IT ISN'T just these priority neighbourhoods that are feeling the pinch. Prosperous Toronto is getting harder to live in, too. Torontonians' conversations compulsively turn to real estate. This is a city obsessed with property and a market that has steadily increased for two decades, squeezing more and more people out of it. At the same time, rents in Toronto, whether downtown or on the periphery, continue to rise. Toronto is not yet a New York or London, where even people making six-figure salaries often need roommates to make the rent, but the city is moving in that direction.

Beneath these pressures is an ongoing battle to add density to the city, to create space for the people already here who need to find affordable places to live, and for others who are on their way. Neighbourhood-level skirmishes flare up regularly – pitched battles between homeowners who've achieved a foothold, and condo buyers or apartment dwellers trying to get in.

In North America, San Francisco offers perhaps the most fraught example of a battle for space. In the past few years the Bay Area has been experiencing a kind of class war, between well-paid technology workers who were being bused from San Francisco to jobs at Google and other companies in nearby Silicon Valley and those who found they were being priced out of their city. In this dynamic, the tech workers serve as scapegoats for economic inequality.

A widely read article from April 2014 by Kim-Mai Cutler on TechCrunch, "How Burrowing Owls Lead to Vomiting Anarchists," explained the roots of San Francisco's housing crisis as being thirty to forty years of NIMBYism (or Not-In-My-Back-Yardism) that kept the San Francisco peninsula from growing denser to accommodate more people, creating an acute housing shortage. People resisted change, resisted developments a few storeys higher than the houses already there, and the pressure grew.

"It doesn't have to be this way," wrote Cutler, a keen observer of California's tech industry and culture. "But everyone who lives in the Bay Area today needs to accept responsibility for making changes where they live so that everyone who wants to be here, can. The alternative – inaction and self-absorption – very well could create the cynical elite paradise and middle-class dystopia that many fear."

Although some details of Toronto's story differ from San Francisco's, what's happened there should be a warning for this city, as they share many similarities. Toronto architect and former dean of the University of Toronto's John H. Daniels Faculty of Architecture, Landscape, and Design, Larry Richards, has referred to Toronto as "San Francisco turned upside down," meaning Toronto's ravines are the inverse of that city's hills and both are defining features of their cities' topography. Consider also that both cities have many central neighbourhoods built around the turn of the last century that have become incredibly desirable places to live, where the cheapest houses can't be had for much under six figures.

The sprawl of the seven million people in the Bay Area and the more than six million in the GTA has consumed vast tracts of agricultural land. Both cities have large numbers of commuters who cycle and take transit, yet the car is still an enormous part of life, with 46 per cent of San Francisco residents driving, and 56 per cent of Torontonians driving, based on most recent numbers. Like Toronto, San Francisco has a strong tradition of citizen activism born in resistance to destructive freeway and urban renewal schemes in the 1950s through the 1970s. Yet that resistance has morphed into a profoundly conservative culture of "no" in both cities, regardless of political affiliations.

In Toronto, where lots of new construction goes on, there are near-bloody battles on main streets over condo buildings six to eight storeys high that are opposed by nearby residents living in single-family homes that cost, at the very least, double what the condos would. This means the barrier to neighbourhood entry is many hundreds of thousands of dollars, rather than a few hundred thousand – not cheap, but open to more buyers and, most importantly, buyers on the first rung of property ownership. Some Toronto councillors take principled stands on the side of more people, such as Mary-Margaret McMahon in the Beach, during the fight over the six-storey condo building planned for a site on Queen Street where a one-storey restaurant previously stood, a battle so relentless she's said it gave her grey hair.

Not all councillors muster the same courage when needed. Most of the condos built in Toronto are not "luxury" but rather the only places many people with standard-issue, nine-to-five jobs will ever be able to afford to buy. Want more affordable housing? Make no mistake: this kind of NIMBYism doesn't much care if new residents are paying the market price or one geared to income. The message regardless is "This neighbour-hood is closed to newcomers."

The thing at stake if Toronto continues down the San Francisco path is the very idea that it's a place for everyone. One of the recent official city mottos was "You Belong Here," but the reality is much less friendly. Do we give up that welcoming idea of the city to match the city's demonstrated conservatism? Or do we find a way to change the culture of "no" into one more concerned with figuring out how to fit more people into this city, in buildings that are well designed and at various levels of affordability?

In Toronto there's still some breathing room, time to get it right, and it's been that way for a while. It's one of the reasons the Pennsylvania-born writer and urbanist Jane Jacobs found Toronto so attractive decades ago.

Jacobs and her family arrived in Toronto in 1968 with their daughter and two draft-age sons, first settling in a rented house on Spadina Road in the Annex, then as now an intellectual neighbourhood, near the University of Toronto and populated by students and professors. It was also a neighbourhood of rooming houses carved out of once-grand homes and a place some of the 40,000 American draft resisters who fled to Canada settled. Almost immediately, embracing her new city with vigour as both an advocate and a critic, Jacobs was caught up in an ongoing battle against an expressway plan that was to drive a vast gash through the neighbourhood,.

"Those were exciting times," says Jim Jacobs, her son, who still resides in Toronto. "Toronto had a major growth spurt between 1956 and 1966 and was an amazing and exciting place, not stagnant. We get used to it living here but if you've lived in a place that's stable, not stagnant, it may be a fine life, but that spark is missing. That's the essence of what she appreciated the most about Toronto." In *City Limits*, a National Film Board of Canada documentary produced in 1971 about Jacobs, she said that Toronto "is a city that still has options . . . it hasn't made so many mistakes that it's bound to go downhill." Forty some years later, there are still options, although they are diminishing.

Jacobs's legacy in Toronto often centres on her role in stopping the Spadina Expressway in the early 1970s, but those who worked with her are careful to say she insisted she was just one of many, and that momentum was already there when she arrived on the scene. The narrative is too delicious to resist, though: Jacobs, hot off her underdog win against Robert Moses in New York, where she played a roll preventing an expressway from destroying parts of Greenwich Village, moved to Toronto and settled first on Spadina Road, the very place Toronto's version of the Lower Manhattan Expressway was planned to obliterate. For many, the strength of that narrative led to sometimes exaggerated and wrong-headed claims of her influence on Toronto.

In some quarters of Toronto – if municipalities were given the power of canonization – the first local to be put up for sainthood would be Jacobs. The city takes prideful ownership of her and her ideas. She's championed by all sides of the spectrum, from free-market developers to left-wing urbanists, and it isn't uncommon to occasionally see both sides of some development squabble use Jacobs's writing, or rather, a high-level interpretation of what they think she wrote, to defend their position. She wasn't a fan of ideologies, and instead took each issue she wrote about on its own terms, which perhaps accounts for the wide interpretation of her work and speculations on what she might think about a particular contemporary issue.

During her nearly four decades in Toronto she was an activist, and a mentor to politicians and city builders of all stripes, often called on to consult on projects. "Everything was a big R&D lab for her; it was trial and error, seeing what succeeded, admitting when there was failure," says her friend and urban designer Ken Greenberg. Although she died at age eighty-nine in 2006, she was engaged with the city right until the end, occasionally seen at public events with the Victrola-like horn she would place up against her ear.

Her final book, *Dark Age Ahead*, was a sometimes hopeful but often desolate warning of the decay in the foundations of modern society and culture, including the roles of taxation and government. The book was released in 2004, in the heady days of Toronto's renaissance, and although Jacobs saw fit to include a fair amount of the city in the book, what she saw, as the title indicates, wasn't so great. In a chapter called "Dumbed-Down Taxes," she recalled that Peter Ustinov in the late 1980s had described Toronto as "New York run by the Swiss." "No longer does the description ring wittily true," she wrote. "Toronto's former neatness and cleanliness have so much degenerated that a visitor (me) to Richmond, Virginia, and San Francisco now enviously notices how clean, in comparison with Toronto, those cities are."

She went on to describe a city in decline: a homeless population overflowing in church basements and shelters, a transit system starved of operating funds and chronically overcrowded, high smog levels, and an ever-tightening rental market where little affordable housing was built. She also mentioned a change in the sensibility of the place, what she described as "a disquieting surliness or public sullenness: impatience, impoliteness, rage. These are more subtle signs that Toronto has become a city in crisis, indeed in multiple crises."

The city was caught up in its renaissance, but Jacobs and others saw the mounting threats to its success. There were two competing narratives in the city – the one, seduced by the growing skyline and wealth that was impossible to ignore, and the other, tuned in to all the warning signs. Some with means, who already felt connected to the city and part of civil society, ignored the latter narrative entirely; others who noticed immersed themselves in the civic scene, reasonably confident that the city was a work in progress that could be fixed by, as Hulchanski put it, investing in the other direction.

"Some people think optimistically that if things get bad enough, they will get better because of the reaction of benefit pendulums," wrote Jacobs in *Dark Age Ahead*. "When a culture is working wholesomely, beneficent pendulum swings – effective feedback – do occur. Corrective stabilization is one of the great services of democracy, with its feedback to rulers from the protesting to voting public."

Feedback and protest come in varying forms, and that disquieting surliness Jacobs noticed might have been her prescient senses at work again, seeing and hearing a rumble building in Toronto that would eventually burst forth in a blunt-force wake-up call in 2010, one that wasn't about strategic investment, long-term plans or city building.

Rob Ford, the outsider candidate from the farthest corner of the city, connected with people who felt they had been left out of Toronto's dominant political and economic narrative. It is no surprise, then, that the geographic location of the bulk of Rob Ford voters in the 2010 mayoral election corresponded directly with the third, poorer city that David Hulchanski's research mapped, that inverted U Pedro Barata spoke of. Ford won the election by forging an emotional connection with the people in that U, and quite a few elsewhere, telling them they, and the struggles they face daily, matter. He was the one person in Toronto who articulated their grievances in a way that connected with them, in the way the notions Di Cicco wrote about resonated with urbanists and others. The emotional bond Rob Ford was able to forge with voters – his nation – was incredibly strong.

That he didn't offer them many workable solutions, and that the chaos of his mayoralty further distracted the city from its problems, is arguable, but most important is that the 20,000 watt klieg lights Rob Ford inadvertently pointed toward a Toronto that had been in the shadows aren't turned off. The dark age ahead is fraught not just with inequality, and dimmed prospects for large populations here hoping to someday live the good city life, but it risks civil unrest and self-sabotage if not addressed. The riots in London and Paris suburbs a few years ago were also spotlights on inequality, a kind of protest that Toronto has blessedly not experienced yet. More troubling are the potential dangers of extremist dogmas that can take root when long-term inequality like this exists.

Toronto still has a chance to avoid it. What the city experienced is not unique; it repeats in cities around the world, and on national levels, with charismatic figures channelling the anger of inequality. The rise of Donald Trump in 2015 and 2016, and the fever pitch of his rallies in arenas and auditoriums across the United States, seemed eerily familiar to Torontonians: we had seen it all before.

Rob Ford's tenure as mayor ended in scandal and a cancer diagnosis that would claim his life in 2016 at the young age of forty-six. There will be others like him in Toronto and in other cities, populists who connect with people in ways that talk of policy or planning cannot.

Toronto remains a success story. The dark age is before us but we are not so far into the pitch we can't reverse course. Understanding the dynamics behind the rise of Ford is critical to reviving and healing the city body on the coroner's table. And if any place can turn itself around, it's Toronto, a city that's always been carried along by its people.

CHAPTER TWO

THE FRONT LINES OF DISCONTENT

IT FEELS like a long time ago, eons ago. But it was the beginning of a discussion that is still vital today and will be for years to come. It was the moment when aspects of Toronto that had been hidden, suppressed, or ignored came to light.

WE WERE all jammed at the front of the stage when the high-pitched bagpipe drone started up at the back of the big hall. The mayor was coming. Rob Ford was in the house.

The mayor's brother, Doug, had just revved up the home crowd with a defiant and unapologetic introductory speech. "You know Rob Ford returns phone calls," he said to great cheers. "Rob Ford cuts spending. Rob Ford challenges the elites." More cheers. People had waited hours to see Rob Ford. Rob Ford knew how to enter a room.

As the pipes got closer the crowed turned and necks strained to catch a glimpse of the mayor. The entourage moving through the hall was led by the bagpipers in full kilt, followed by a Canadian flag held aloft by a young woman in a FORD MORE YEARS T-shirt and standing on the shoulders of other girls, all exuding pep rally enthusiasm. The pipes moaned, the crowd screamed, as this entourage of volume and acrobatics made its way to the stage.

"You've got to cheer extra loud now because the media will turn the volume down," said a kid in his late teens to his friend standing next to me. The elite conspiracy to keep Rob Ford down ran deep. The crowd surged as Ford appeared, a flushed face in a sea of euphoria. "Keep cheering," the kid next to me yelled as he pushed to get closer to the mayor. Dozens of smartphones were held up. Arms reached for the mayor. Was this Beatlemania, Trudeaumania, or Kardashianmania? These screams were not the typical cheers of political partisans but those of disciples at a tent revival in full rapture. Being in Rob Ford's presence in 2014 was a modern celebrity experience, a tempest of TMZ and CNN all at once.

As the flag and pipers made it on stage Doug yelled into the mike, "Ford nation rocks!" The brothers hugged and Rob Ford took the podium. "Thank you, Ford Nation."

The crowd hadn't yet stopped cheering.

"This is just the beginning, folks," said Ford.

"Ford More Years," the crowd chanted.

The stage filled in with people wearing FORD NATION T-shirts, waving little Ford Mayor flags, and holding FORD FOR MAYOR placards. Rob thanked brother Doug, saying he'd been there for him "through thick and thin." He thanked his late dad, saying he "knew he would be proud." He introduced his wife, Renata, who had crowded on to the stage next to him with his daughter and son. Renata had called the police on Rob numerous times, and Rob had said vile things about her in front of rolling television cameras. She waved a little FORD NATION flag and smiled next to Rob's mom, Diane, the Ford matriarch. She got a shout-out too. They were all on stage. This crowd knew the family in this political saga like America knew the Kennedys, and each mention of a family member got more wild applause. At a Ford rally, this family is Toronto's family, Camelot in oversized T-shirts.

"Friends, I love this city, and I love being your mayor."

As the mayor started into his speech, a woman in an orange-striped dress began banging her wooden cane on the stage like a violent punctuation mark whenever Rob Ford finished one of his emphatic sentences, which means every sentence. The crowd behind had pressed her up to the thigh-high stage like she was at a rock-and-roll show, but one without front-of-stage security.

"Torontonians are strong, and fair, and resilient, and diverse. There's no better job than representing you folks in this great city."

Bam bam bam – the cane hit the stage.

At one point the woman half-crawled out onto the stage, and lay prostrate in front of Rob Ford speaking at the podium, a few dozen family members and supporters behind him onstage. Nobody disturbed her and she stayed there for a spell with her cane while Ford continued to speak.

"You'll always know your tax dollar will be used towards the good of all and not just the good of a few." *Bam bam!*

Somebody at the front of the stage had a giant foam #1 finger and was waving it around. This was more than a tent revival – it was a rock-and-roll show and *Monday Night Football* rolled into one.

"The people of Toronto will be represented by a mayor who gets it. A guy just like them."

Ford spoke for half an hour using a teleprompter, the speech a mix of self-congratulation and a list of achievements, such as abolishing the vehicle registration tax and saving Toronto a "billion dollars." Toward the end, though, he started to play on why there was such electric support in the room: this was a mayor people could emotionally connect with. He spoke to them with a directness every politician strives for but few ever achieve. Rob Ford was the Bill Clinton of Etobicoke, but also an everyman whose personal and public difficulties were seen as moot, if not an asset, to his supporters. He faced hurdles and setbacks just like them.

"I've come to appreciate how much it matters to people that their mayor has lived through life's ups and downs, working hard to support his family, run a business, and meet a payroll," he told the crowd. "Friends, the people of Toronto know I'm just like them. The people know when you call Mayor Rob Ford that Rob Ford will personally return their call."

Bam bam bam!

"Friends – they know they can approach me anywhere, anytime, because I always make time for people who approach me. The people of Toronto know that I understand them, that I stand up for them and I won't back down when I'm fighting for them. It's been an honour to serve this great city."

Bam bam BAM!

Rob Ford had a particular ability to pivot from running down the running of Toronto by people at city hall – even when he was at the helm – to boosting it as the greatest, most phenomenal place on earth. The Ford brothers liked the word *phenomenal.*

"There is no better city in the world than Toronto. Sorry, Jimmy Kimmel, Toronto's better than L.A."

Bam bam.

"As your mayor, friends, I continue to pledge honesty, transparency, accountability, and accessibility, because we are all in this together." These are words that had lost all meaning in Toronto, or anywhere contemporary politics are practised, although they're said over and over as if they'll come true if repeated enough. Ford spoke in the third person, as if he were the final judge of his own actions. Ford was fond of saying the past is the past and it's time to move on, then demand more accountability.

"Folks, if you have my back when they start throwing mud, if you have my back when I'm standing up to the special interests, if you have my back no matter what the weather is election day, I promise you Rob Ford will have your back for the next four years. Thank you."

With that the stage was instantly swarmed by fans as the early 1980s hair-metal anthem by Twisted Sister "We're Not Gonna Take It" started playing over the public address system, loud. Ford campaign staff tried to keep people off the stage but the event was out of control. Out of control the way Las Vegas is out of control, where bad behaviour is tolerated and managed: fall out of a chair and you'll be helped back into it, not asked to leave.

Balloons began to drop from a net hung from the celling but they got stuck so the mayor's other brother, Randy, wearing his trademark cowboy hat, began to pull at the net to get the balloons moving. Ford's security detail managed to bring the mayor through the crowd and escort him to the back of the room quickly with a throng of mostly men who were in the crowd chasing him until he was through a door into a private part of the building.

It was over, the campaign was launched, and the room quieted down to its previous state – but then Ford raced back into the room. Heads turned, people ran; *the mayor is back!* Rob made his way back up to the stage where he sat for the rest of the event greeting admirers and signing bobbleheads, fashioned in his image.

ON APRIL 17, 2014, the Ford Mayoral Machine was operating at a high torque. This was campaign launch day, the day that began Toronto's great reckoning: after four years of political drama, Rob Ford was asking Toronto to vote for him again. He promised many times this would happen, that the voters would decide if what he had done warranted being thrown out or not. It's what he wanted. It's what his opponents wanted.

It would be fair to speculate that the parking lot of the Toronto Congress Centre on Dixon Road could be empty on that day. After all, the mayor lied about crack smoking, then admitted to it; disparaged his wife; disrespected municipal conventions; racked up a list of ethics and conflict of interest violations; and uttered various threats and homophobic, racial, and misogynistic slurs – all while making Toronto an internationally famous punch line. Yet, the Congress Centre was the place to be that night. Pulling into the lot for the 2014 launch a few hours before his scheduled speech, I found Ford campaign workers directing cars to open spots halfway down the massive expanse of asphalt, and a steady stream of people walked through the lot to the main doors of the aircraft hangar-like building. Satellite news trucks were clustered nearby. There was a feeling of pilgrimage, of coming to an unlikely place to see an exceptional thing.

A FEW blocks west of Pearson International Airport, the area around the Congress Centre is a landscape of parking lots, light industrial buildings, and hotels for travelling business people. It's anonymous Toronto; never written about, with an interchangeable architecture that could be in Houston, Surrey, or the periphery of Orlando. The nearest residential neighbourhoods are a few kilometres away.

An international nowhere, it's also directly in the flight path of Pearson International's mighty runway 24R, and planes pass just overhead every few minutes. The high-tension power line towers a block east have red blinking lights that warn planes they're there. The low-rise industrial buildings with mirrored windows house mostly businesses with names of little renown: import-export businesses, customs brokers, and for-lease signs promising large amounts of commercial space. Transient and anonymous corporate Toronto, a cylinder in the city's economic engine, a place where liberal capital is most free and out of view in a highly regulated city. It's fitting that Ford, a mayor in the "government must be run like a business" mould, held his launch here.

This sprawling Dickensian landscape of the twenty-first century, where land is used and consumed without a plan, a place where the scale isn't entirely human, has never been a centre of political power. Until Rob Ford, that is. In 2010 the Congress Centre was the place where he stormed onto stage as the newly elected mayor with a near majority of the vote share, an event that just a few months earlier would have seemed like the work of a creative civic fabulist who assumed a too-robust suspension of disbelief. Rob Ford was supposed to remain a sideshow in Toronto politics, not the main event. This was *Toronto*, a city whose traditional self-image was neither Ford nor this Congress Centre nor Dixon Road.

Rob Ford added new geography to Toronto's political story, and many seasoned city reporters, used to going to the usual places, mostly downtown, likely used a GPS device to find their way to the Congress Centre. Inside the lobby, way-finding signs direct visitors to rooms named after famous Canadian artists, writers, and patrons, a who's who of elite society, such as David Mirvish, Donald Sutherland, Sylvia Safdie, Gordon Pinsent,

Charles Pachter, Pierre Berton and Alice Munro – all names that clashed with Ford's anti-elite rhetoric and the big-box surroundings (except, perhaps, David Mirvish, who owns downtown's most lovable big-box anomaly, Honest Ed's). It's arguable that in the four years he was mayor, Rob Ford surpassed every one of these people in notoriety and fame. And on campaign launch day, there was an army of volunteers decked out in Ford regalia – citizens of Ford Nation – on hand to work the event.

ROB FORD was a rich man who had a history of saying racist things, so the multicultural and varied class makeup of his campaign workers and volunteers was curious: they look like the idealized Toronto mix, abounding in people of various ethnicities and accents, just like those found on Toronto Island on a summer's day. Those who attend Ford events know they can be more multicultural than other events in the city, like hockey games, book readings or art openings. Which points to another surprising thing about the Fords: they brought out a side of Toronto that's been hidden in the background and often only celebrated on paper or in the city's motto, *Diversity Our Strength.*

The Ford Nation army was a happy lot on election launch day, putting people into lines to be processed before entry into the big hall. The atmosphere was celebratory and the lobby was turned into a kind of electoral Ellis Island before entry into Ford Nation was granted, with FORD FOR MAYOR signs covering the far wall. Everyone had to fill out forms: names, phone number and email. Each would be added to Ford's famously long list of contacts he had compiled during his decade as the consummate service-based city councillor, where he "returned every phone call" made to his office from constituents who had a problem. Everybody who filled out a form got a ticket for a T-shirt. The nation had its uniform. Once the promise of a T-shirt was in hand, people were free to walk through the door into the big room.

"Big room" is an understatement, and aircraft hangar not a cliché here: with bare steel rafters and a polished concrete floor with painted markings, an Airbus 330 would have comfortably fit inside. The room was set up banquet-style on a gargantuan scale. A rock-and-roll cover band played the stage at one end, the familiar red-and-blue "Ford for Mayor – Respect for Taxpayers" banner at the back of it with a massive video screen on either side. A red carpet ran back from the stage through dozens of round banquet tables, past a media platform crowded with cameras and equipment, and back through even more dozens of empty tables to what seemed like the horizon, with FORD banners hung above throughout.

The Fords rented a room prepared for Woodstock but got a much smaller crowd. There were estimates of around two thousand people at the event, large for any political event, but the size of the room is an indication of the hubris with which the Ford family viewed the perceived size of their nation, a group of people so numerous and so fierce that Doug Ford characterized them a month earlier in the most cinematic of terms regarding what they'll do to the other mayoral candidates: "Have you ever seen *Braveheart* when the guys are coming over the hill? That's going to be Ford Nation coming at these guys."

While waiting for the event to start, the crowd alternated between moments of excitement and boredom. Every twenty minutes or so somebody would climb into the full-sized fire truck inside the hall and pull the air horn, causing everybody to jump as it echoed around the hard-surfaced room. It was the audio exclamation point to the scene – honk if you're into Rob Ford – and each time a Ford campaign worker would amble over and get the person out of the truck. Nobody was chastised much. As the mayor would intone about his own antics, what's done is done.

The firefighters were upset though. Written on the side of the truck were the words SAVING THE TAXPAYERS FROM GETTING BURNED and SAVED THE TAXPAYERS A BILLION DOLLARS – FORD MAYOR. There were no lowercase letters in Ford Nation.

In a release issued after the event, the Toronto Professional Fire Fighters' Association said, "Rob Ford's decision to use a fire truck to trumpet his false claims about taxpayer savings Thursday is a slap in the face to tens of thousands of Toronto residents whose fire protection levels will decrease Monday when four actual fire trucks are taken out of service." The mayor's brothers said they bought the truck from outside of Toronto for $4,000. Everybody loves a fire truck.

The occasional honks were a distraction for the people waiting in lines. There were a lot of lines. One was to redeem the FORD NATION T-shirts; the volunteers did a brisk business before they finally ran out, after opening and distributing box upon box of T-shirts. Next to that line was the line for bobble-heads, objects that became a kind of Ford Nation holy relic during the latter part of the mayor's first term. Blessedly, the bar line was much shorter than the ones for T-shirts and bob-bleheads. The local Ontario wine was not cheap at eight bucks a glass, elite Toronto prices to be sure, but the cookies and potato chips set out on the tables were free and plentiful.

Spectacle at a Ford event came in big and small forms. A man marched around the tables throughout the evening with a big Canadian flag attached to a pole slung over his shoulder, as if waiting for his Iwo Jima moment. Another man wore a custom-made white-and-red suit with "Mr. Canada" embroidered on the back under a large maple leaf. Occasionally somebody shouted a Ford Nation salute or ranted about a particular issue, but the crowd was mostly bored, waiting for the event to start, waiting to see the celebrity mayor, while listening to the cover band play classic rock tunes like *Ride Sally Ride*.

The Fords ran a populist campaign and it attracted the predictable eccentrics. Municipal politics, being the level closest to the ground and affecting people more on an everyday basis, get an abundance of sideshow action at events. Provincial and federal politics fly much higher and get less of this. The Fords took it further, and it was uncanny how many times their campaign resembled fictional depictions of populism gone wild.

In the fall of 2014 an RV christened "The Taxpayer Express" in big letters above the windshield was added to the Ford campaign fleet. "Ford for Mayor – For the People" was written on the side, with a picture of Doug instead of Rob, as this was after the last-minute switcheroo in September when Doug took over after Rob's cancer diagnosis. FORD is what mattered, not the first name. The RV would appear at events, sometimes parking in inappropriate locations, blocking bike lanes or accessible parking spots.

The RV was reminiscent of the loudspeaker-equipped van that drove around in Robert Altman's 1975 film *Nashville* broadcasting homespun political aphorisms of populist presidential candidate Hal Phillip Walker. That campaign attracted a menagerie of oddballs and seemed a work of satiric post-Watergate fiction. Not so in Toronto, and although there was no loudspeaker on the RV, the Fords' rhythmic clichés and repetitive use of the word "folks" would have not been out of place in *Nashville*.

Being at a Ford event and watching him speak evoked memories of the 1949 film *All the King's Men*. In it a slovenly everyman, Willie Stark, is running for governor, a character based on Huey Long, the real-life governor of Louisiana in the 1930s. In the film, Stark, played by Broderick Crawford, addresses the Upton Fair Grounds during his campaign. It's a speech that could have been made by either of the Ford brothers.

> Naw, I'm not gonna read you any speech. But I am gonna tell you a story . . . It's about a hick, a hick like you, if you please. Yeah, like you. He grew up on the dirt roads and the gully washes of a farm. He knew what it was to get up before dawn and get feed and slop and milk before break-fast, and then set out before sunup and walk six miles to a one-room, slab-sided schoolhouse. Aw, this hick knew what it was to be a hick, all right. He figured if he was gonna get anything done, well, he had to do it himself . . . Now, listen to me, you hicks. Yeah, you're hicks too, and they fooled you a thousand times, just like they fooled me. But this time, I'm gonna fool somebody. I'm gonna stay in this race. I'm on my own and I'm out for blood. Now listen to me, you hicks! Listen to me, and lift up your eyes and look at God's blessed and unfly-blown truth. And this is the truth. You're a hick, and nobody ever helped a hick but a hick himself!

Replace "hicks" with "taxpayer" and the farm jobs with something a little more urban or industrial and the Ford campaign ran on the same blended octane of aggrieved underdog and self-reliance. Cities, by their nature, are not libertarian entities, and although often a conservative city, Toronto historically leaned in the Red Tory or centre-left direction. Before the Fords, this kind of rhetoric was heard on the fringes – one assumed nobody was left out, and certainly we were all in this together – but the Ford family managed to make this new kind of politics resonate with a large part of Toronto.

Being back at the Congress Centre for the 2014 launch brought the four years around full circle: the 2010 win was the real beginning of the 2014 campaign, as Rob and Doug never stopped campaigning and the next race started as soon as they won. Rob never embraced the leadership role that candidates who win generally do: governing everyone. Instead, the language and attack of the 2010 campaign did not stop; the Fords were forever talking about taking back the city from somebody else, even when they were the ones running the city. The idea of who the Mayor of Toronto was quickly became plural as well: "the Fords" became shorthand for the unique partnership Rob and Doug had, right and left hands that were sometimes perfectly coordinated and other times did not seem to know what the other was up to. Toronto had a co-mayoralty. Sometimes Doug would be sitting next to Rob during important interviews, almost as his minder. Other times, Doug would speak for Rob. A quote from Doug was as good as a quote from Rob. The notion of an autonomous mayor making decisions no longer held in Toronto.

To most Torontonians, if they thought of him at all prior to 2010, Rob Ford was a councillor from somewhere vaguely around the top-left corner of Toronto. He was the oddball on council, representing Ward 2 Etobicoke-North since 2000. Ford was thought of as the clown from somewhere "out there" who said funny, often offensive things that enraged city hall watchers and amused those who only heard about municipal politics when something exceptional happened, like a garbage strike, major transit issue, or when outrageous things were said. Ford supplied a lot of that, for years.

Few people took him seriously when he announced he would run for mayor in 2010. Toronto was not the kind of town that would elect a mayor that came from outside of civil society.

Over the course of the spring and summer of 2010, polls showed that Rob Ford was a real contender, and that former provincial minister George Smitherman might not walk away with the mayoralty as easily as some predicted. But to most people, Ford was still a freakish fringe candidate. His impressive polling numbers and their upward trend weren't able to overcome what people had seen over the last ten years, and it wasn't until Ford started holding events known as "Ford Fests" that there were tangible indications something else was afoot.

In September 2010, on the Friday evening when the Toronto International Film Festival began and the parties that the chattering classes were most excited about were all downtown and film-related, a friend and I decided to head to Etobicoke, far from the glamorous TIFF Bell Lightbox on King Street. We headed to Royal York Road where Rob Ford was holding a barbecue in his mom Diane's spacious backyard. What we found on this trip into Ford Nation was no trip upriver into the heart of darkness, but rather a visit to the very middle of Canada – where the meat is plentiful, the bar is open, and the Rob Ford voters friendly.

ROB'S DAD was the late Doug Ford Sr., a backbencher in Mike Harris's provincial Ontario government from 1995 to 1999. The patriarch of the Ford clan, he founded Deco Labels and Tags, the printing company that made the family wealthy. Doug Sr. was the first in the clan to enter politics, launching what would become a family dynasty of sorts. Once a family has had at least two generations involved in politics, they can call the family home a "compound," the place they go to recharge, plan, plot, and incubate new generations. Unlike the Bush and Kennedy families, with their famously private compounds on the Atlantic Ocean, the Fords opened theirs up to the public.

This is a family that pleaded for privacy and complained of an invasive media but invited everyone into their inner sanctum routinely, to sit by their pool and tramp around their backyard lawn. Throwing his door open was one of the ways the Fords portrayed themselves as a "regular guys," everymen just like the average voter – even though the family compound was much bigger than the homes most working and middle-class people in Toronto could hope to afford.

Yet no effort was made to hide the wealth. The Ford money and privilege has always been in plain sight. The Ford compound is landlocked at the end of a short cul-de-sac off of Royal York, north of Eglinton. Instead of being partially surrounded by the Atlantic, as are the presidential compounds, two-thirds of the property is bordered by parkland that follows a small tributary of the Humber River. The front of the house is unassuming and blends into the neighbourhood: a two-storey 1970s bungalow with a second empire roofline that makes it seem smaller than it is; around back, the large yard slopes down to the creek, exposing the true size of the three-storey house. The house matched Rob Ford's mystique by appearing more like a little guy than its true scale warranted.

Our expectations were low as we headed to the barbecue that night; political events tend to be sedate affairs, attended by partisans of the organization sponsoring the event, whether they be members of an ethnic club or some community group. But rolling up Royal York it was immediately clear this would be an altogether different kind of event, because there was traffic blocks away from the cul-de-sac.

Unlike the 2014 launch, this scene in 2010 was reminiscent of the original Woodstock festival, where hippies abandoned their cars in the rural gridlock and walked to the festival. Dozens of pedestrians were making their way along the sidewalks or trying to cross the street with no light or crosswalk in the early evening dusk.

Near the entrance to the Ford street teenagers held big, handwritten NO PARKING signs, directing cars to move along. We pulled into the big but nearly full Royal York Plaza stripmall parking lot opposite, a spot – so the *Globe and Mail* would later claim in an investigative report – where Doug Ford dealt hash in his younger years, when he hung around with a crew known as the Royal York Drifters.

This plaza, known as "The Drift," according to the *Globe* story, is the topography of Toronto *noir*, a mid-century modern drama well lit by sodium vapour lamps, at once both more affluent and suburban than the usual dingy settings of *noir* tales. Royal York Plaza has been the setting of a few decades' worth of Ford family drama, but the dooziest of the years still lay ahead.

Just two weeks after the 2014 launch, Mayor Ford would suspend his election campaign and seek help for his substance abuse problem after he was surreptitiously recorded ranting and swearing in Sullie Gorman's, a pub in Royal York Plaza. The targets of that particular tirade were wide: raising the rainbow flag at city hall, the problem of Italians, or "dagos," as he called them, and another mayoral candidate, city councillor Karen Stintz. "I'd like to fucking jam her but she don't want it," said Ford of Stintz, a phrase that was so over the top for even Ford's enablers – a group of people who seemed, from the outside, like the Memphis Mafia who escorted Elvis Presley to an early death – that the campaign was halted. Ford entered a Muskoka rehab clinic.

We found one of the last spots in the plaza lot and crossed Royal York Road over to the park named after Doug Ford Sr.

It's a city park but Ford Fest goers were parking on the grass, and Ford election signs festooned the grounds. This use was but one of many displays of the Ford family's assumption of entitlement in this city, especially in Etobicoke.

We approached the house with dozens of other people walking up the street, a Spielberg kind of scene where a typical suburban street becomes the site of something exceptional. The sound of the emcee riling up the crowd over the loudspeakers in the backyard was echoing through the neighbourhood. Anticipation was growing, and panic flickering. *Had we left it too late and missed the main event?* Maybe we should have taken Ford more seriously.

There was a long line in the front yard to get around back. Standing here in the dark in a spot where line-ups didn't usually form felt a little reminiscent of going to clandestine rave parties in the 1990s. The line was not to pay – although there were large donation jugs – but to get a personalized Rob Ford nametag and to have our names and numbers solicited for the ever-growing Ford Nation voter list. Even then, when his campaign was still considered a joke, Ford had an efficient machine at work.

Just as we entered the backyard, the sound system volume went way up as "Eye of the Tiger" played and Ford took to the stage erected in the backyard. We hadn't missed him after all. The compound was packed with hundreds of people. Five-hundred-watt portable lights lit the grounds, now dark around eight o'cock, and I got my first glimpse of the now familiar ROB FORD: RESPECT FOR TAXPAYERS banner behind him. His speech included his already established hits – tax, waste, tax, waste, taxpayers, gravy train – and the crowd met everything he said with an enormous roar of approval. That evening was the first time I heard that roar – the moment when Ford supporters became real. Ford was passionate, and people were relating. He was Willie Stark.

As he gave his speech little kids climbed the berms by the pool and hoisted ROB FORD FOR MAYOR signs bigger than their bodies into the air. People raised their burgers and beers and shouted. When Ford was done, a full big band started playing and people started dancing on the patio by the pool. My consort was hungry so he got in the meat line, which was at least seventy-five metres long.

Figuring there was no Ford vegetarian option I stood in the shorter bar line and got a Coors Light and watched the happy scene play out by a Venus-like statue that sprayed water into a smaller pool. Such statuary could be found all around the professionally landscaped backyard. Later, starving, I put ketchup and mustard on a bun and ate it. It's hard to be a vegetarian in Ford Nation.

This early Ford Fest party was fun – off-the-hook fun. People partied like it was a wedding, or Canada Day. People were nice. Nobody was ranting or mean-spirited, bicycles weren't being burnt in effigy, and the crowd, while fairly white, wasn't exclusively so, running at perhaps 15 per cent visibly multicultural, by rough estimation, a proportion that would grow at later Ford Fests. Rob's mom was running around taking pictures with people, as if they were friends hanging out in her backyard. Despite being richer than most, the Fords have an instinctive talent at bringing people into their family, even if the house itself was off limits during this party (port-a-johns were provided).

The friendliness of attendees was also a notch or two higher than most events in Toronto, whose coolness to strangers is legendary. While sipping my Coors a woman a decade or so older than I am jumped in front of me and asked, "Who are you texting?" I was tweeting. My friend and I were the only jerks buried in our phones at this 2010 event, just a little before tweeting and Instagramming everything became a widespread practice. I thought she was going to tell me to get out, that I didn't belong, but instead she grabbed my hand and led me to a table, then introduced me to her sister, who was holding a Rob Ford sign in one hand and glass of wine in the other. Then I met her brother-in-law and other family members. They asked, "Are you working for Rob?"

"No, I'm just here to see what he's all about," I said.

"Great," they said.

Then she asked me to dance – the first time a stranger asked me to dance in the ten years I had lived in Toronto, and it was at a Ford political event. Former downtown city councillor and current Member of Parliament Adam Vaughan would often say, having grown up in a political household, you've got to have fun while fighting a political fight or it isn't worth it. The Fords, at least at Ford Fest, embodied this more than anyone. Even as the rhetoric on stage was about haves and have-nots, and divisions between elites and real people, *people just like the mayor*, the party was fun. More fun than a TIFF party, even. People talked to each other without looking over their shoulders.

I liked being there. The Ford supporters at the barbecue reminded me a lot of the working-class crowd I grew up with in Windsor, Ontario, the same kind of "regular folk," but here in Toronto they were without Windsor's long tradition of organized labour membership and NDP voting tendencies to swing general sentiments in a leftish direction. Ford Nation was utterly familiar to me, a life where a *Reader's Digest* sat by the toilet; where people cut their white wine with 7UP, and where wood-panelled basements were standard – comfortable territory, but not highly politicized.

In Toronto this was a population that hadn't yet become a political constituency; nobody spoke to them with the passion and directness Ford did, except perhaps the local NDP politicians, although rarely with strength enough to make them partisans. It's a scene where money is always an issue, though, and where the whiff of waste isn't taken lightly, and the Fords knew that. Theirs is a kind of apolitical politics. In Windsor, the left filled this space. Ford's camp tapped into it and swung people to their side, people who would be called "Reagan Democrats" in the United States – working-class voters who opted for Ronald Reagan in 1980 in landslide numbers.

AN ODD thing happened as I was tweeting from the party, snapping pics and reporting on interactions I had with people and the things I saw. At first, the responses were in the spirit of our fun and somewhat gonzo act of crashing a party we weren't exactly part of. But when it became clear we weren't going to tweet about how awful Ford supporters were, I got some hostile pushback.

This was a time when Ford Nation was an unknown quantity, faceless voters routinely characterized as rubes or philistines. Right around the time of this party, retiring long-time city councillor Howard Moscoe, who represented a ward in the general geographic direction of North Etobicoke, suggested Ford supporters were illiterate. "With all these tax cuts and everything they are going to have to close libraries three days a week to pay for it. Rob Ford's supporters won't mind, because they can't read," he said.

This was the unquestioned common assumption. Ford, on the face of it, appeared to be unlike any political entity Toronto has ever produced and at odds with the civic self-image held by people who think about these things, ergo his supporters must be heathens and philistine. By simply going to Ford's barbecue, and not describing them as freaks or dingbats, it seemed to some folks on Twitter that my companion and I were endorsing him.

Neither of us was toeing the narrative line we've been told to believe about Ford supporters since he had started to run. But now that he was starting to lead the race and the threat was real, that narrative was dangerous.

EVEN AFTER Ford won in 2010, and to this day, people who should know better will fall back on common assumptions about the kind of person who voted for Rob Ford. In tolerant Toronto, it was okay to refer to Ford Nation as illiterate, stupid, or careless, just as Ford himself became the target of abuse from progressive, socially conscious people making rude reference to his weight.

Of course, Ford's own behaviour and nasty side opened the door to this name-calling, by setting the bar extremely low. Nonetheless, in 2010 an ugly side of Toronto was just beginning to show, and the next four years leading up to the election of 2014 would be a slow reveal of other sides of Toronto that had been hidden, suppressed, or ignored. The Fords, in their clumsy, angry way, forced Toronto to reckon with itself.

Now that Rob Ford is gone it's a mistake to think Ford Nation went to the grave with him. At his 2016 funeral thousands waited in long lines to pay their respects as he lay in repose in the city hall rotunda, and thousands more followed his funeral procession along Queen Street to St. James Cathedral. The discontent is still there, though much of it hidden again, spread throughout Toronto's vast geography. Somebody with Rob Ford's charisma could exploit it all again, for good or ill. It's at this city's and others' peril to ignore that discontent. The twelve people in the following chapters can help us remember why Toronto is either on the cusp of greatness or, as Jane Jacobs might put it, facing a new dark age ahead.

CHAPTER THREE

THE FOLKS OF FFOLKES AND THE POLITICS OF POTHOLES

"POTHOLES ARE politics," said Idil Burale as we looked at the new sign for Ffolkes Crescent, a dead-end street in a small subdivision about as far from city hall as possible without crossing the city limits.

Beyond here, in the northwest corner of Toronto, the residential neighbourhoods give way to an industrial landscape and eventually the municipalities of Mississauga and Vaughan. This is the edge of Toronto, but as Ward 1, it's also the bureaucratic beginning of the city. Residents of Etobicoke North told Burale that although this is Toronto's number-one ward, it took a long time to replace the sign when it went missing. That bothered them; something as essential as a street sign would likely not be a lingering problem if it disappeared in a part of the city more central to where Toronto's political and civic life plays out. A missing sign would just not stand; there's Indian takeout to deliver, dinner parties to find, eBay purchases to receive. And police and ambulances can't rely on GPS alone in an emergency. Folks on Ffolkes felt left out, as if they didn't matter. Sometimes all it takes to generate that feeling is a missing street sign. But then there are the potholes.

A few times each day, residents of these driveway- and

garage-lined streets felt and heard a *kerthunk* as their cars bounced in and out of the potholes that went unfilled for months. Over and over, *kerthunk, kerthunk,* another reminder their street was forgotten, lost in a vast megacity of nearly three million people, a city where new libraries open and stunning waterfront parks with pink umbrellas are heralded, but where their street keeps eating tires and the bodies of drivers brace for the thud every day. There are unfilled potholes downtown too, lots of them, but a vibrant downtown like Toronto's tends not to feel left out of anything; in Petula Clark's 1964 hit anthem *Downtown* there is no resentment, just a deep understanding that this is where it's all at and that downtown matters, potholes and all.

Feeling left out, far down the civic list of priorities, is a recipe for disengagement. Burale pointed out that Poll 22, the area around Ffolkes, had Ward 1's lowest voter turnout in the 2010 election. "People say, 'I'm happy with my life, I don't need to vote,'" says Idil of why municipal politics fall off the priority list for many citizens. It's a sentiment she often found at the door when she ran for city council here in 2014. But when she started talking about how to get the potholes on Ffolkes fixed, people here became engaged. Not about notions of city building, walkability, or livebility, but about the delivery of services, services they felt they had paid for. During her campaign, Burale walked a line between heady ideas of what makes a great city – all things that don't fit very well into sound bytes – and issues of everyday service delivery that resonate with many voters in Toronto. It's a difficult balance to negotiate, especially in this part of town.

FFOLKES CRESCENT is, or was, part of Ford Nation, a constituency with no formal borders but ample geography. It was fitting to begin a tour of the neighbourhood with Burale here, as the Ford brothers used the word "folks" a lot when talking about citizens of Toronto. This corner of the Nation is about six kilometres north and slightly east of the Congress Centre where Rob Ford kicked off his 2014 campaign. Unlike neighbourhoods in other parts of the city that are contiguous, one blending into another, the neighbourhood around Ffolkes is an island, with the industry to the north, and the Humber College campus and the Humber River to the south, and the vast Woodbine Racetrack property beyond that. Pearson International Airport is just west of here.

A walk between neighbourhoods would be on wide arterial roads with fast-moving traffic. It would be a long walk too, with little commercial activity to make it interesting for the pedestrian.

This neighbourhood is typical of many in Toronto's inner suburbs where there isn't a continuous urban flow from one to another. However, as much as Ffolkes might seem to be an island, it's not a deserted one. Humber College around the corner is a busy place, attracting students from the entire region. Some of them live in basement apartments in the Ffolkes neighbourhood, just as students of the downtown universities do in older parts of the city.

The college is one of the many nodes around Toronto that have become satellite centres, essentially miniature downtowns regardless of what their built forms look like. Closer to Brampton's city hall than Toronto's, the area feels like the connective tissue between the area codes 416 and 905, the numbers that mark their holders as from inside or outside Toronto's borders. With all Brampton and York Region buses passing through the ward to get to Humber, this part of Toronto defies old ideas of what the suburbs are and is one of the many places around the Greater Toronto Area where political borders don't mean much.

Ford Nation's stomping grounds have often been characterized as a suburban wasteland, bereft of beauty or culture. A wander through the halls of Humber College reveals a student body that quickly puts such notions to shame. Just like a summer day on the Island, students here *look* like the Toronto that Toronto, in theory, wants to be: multicultural, mixing together, and possessing great potential.

Situated along the Humber River, the college grounds are also spectacular. The college has its very own arboretum – an outdoor museum of trees, both native and exotic. Owls, foxes, and deer are seen regularly on the grounds, which extend into the river valley. A paved cycling and walking trail meanders south by southeast from here, running nearly twenty kilometres to Lake Ontario, a car-free superhighway. Ffolkes has spots of stunning beauty, unique amenities, and a cultural mix that Toronto should be proud of, and yet the potholes still trigger deep resentments and resistance to grand city-building plans.

"How do you get residents invested in the Finch LRT?" was one of the questions Burale asked herself, in a neighbourhood that could use a quick way in and out but is reluctant to get behind the light rail transit plans. "I told them it would take them half the time it does now to travel west. That matters. I had to get around the Ford message."

The proposed Finch Light Rail Transit line would run from Finch West Station on Keele Street, along the extension of the University-Spadina subway line, to a terminus at Humber College. But as much as this kind of rapid transit would benefit residents, giving them a quick and reliable connection to the rest of the city in a right of way that could bypass all other traffic, the scheme is hard to sell as an ephemeral thing: yet another transit plan to be scrapped, changed, or delayed in a city that seems to produce a new one yearly, or even monthly.

Burale found people in Etobicoke North, like many people in Toronto, skeptical to begin, with. But add to that nearly five years of the Ford brothers ranting against LRT transportation – mischaracterizing it as streetcars or even "trolleys" that would roll with mixed traffic rather than on a separated line – and LRT became a dirty word for many. Another bad plan from the top that wouldn't benefit them. It takes a lot of talking to get people onside an idea like this, and talking takes a lot of time.

As we explored the area, Burale revealed a place she thinks needs both big ideas and everyday attention to succeed. Her day job is at the MaRS Discovery District in downtown Toronto. MaRS is an innovation centre located among the University of Toronto, the Ontario Legislature, and the cluster of hospitals along University Avenue. Although the acronym originally stood for "Medical and Related Sciences," MaRS attracts people working on all sorts of social, communication, and technological innovations. Burale had been a MaRS fellow just before her run for office and had been researching ways civic engagement can be improved, especially in a place like Etobicoke North.

"I got tired of complaining about TOpoli," she says, when asked why she decided to run, using the short-form Twitter hashtag for local municipal politics. We were walking the area, to get a sense of its geography and neighbourhoods, but the ward is so big and spread out, with such great distances between the centres where people live, that we used a car to go from section to section, lest we spend the entire day getting to our destination.

This sprawl is a key difference between some of the wards in the inner suburbs and those in the older parts of the city, which, depending on the neighbourhood, one can sometimes travel in as few as fifteen minutes. The neighbourhoods in Ward 1 are spread across geography that often has physical barriers between where the people are located, and is a challenge political candidates here at all levels of government face that their more central counterparts don't. Retail politics, especially with a low budget, get incrementally harder as geography spreads out. Ward 1 itself is located between two branches of the Humber River, lush green ribbons of meandering parkland, serving as its southern and eastern borders, with the straight lines of the Mississauga and Vaughan borders providing the western and northern edges, respectively. It's a vast territory.

AFTER LEAVING Ffolkes we drove to our next stop, the Toronto Community Housing Corporation (TCHC) project along Orpington Crescent by Finch Avenue and Martin Grove Road, the neighbourhood where Burale grew up after emigrating to Canada from Somalia in the 1980s when she was six. "This is an original mixed community," she said, pointing to the TCHC townhomes across from single-family homes.

Orpington resembles many of the low-rise public housing built in the 1960s and 1970s in Canada: two-storey interconnected townhomes, sometimes with funky modern flourishes such as rooms that stretch over outdoor passages, with some units having their own fenced-in yards, some with laundry drying in the July heat. The designs drip with postwar optimism, a sunny version of the British council estates they were modelled on. But the details have left utopia an unfulfilled dream here.

"There are no front porches. It's a failure of design. There's nowhere to hang out so there is nobody around," said Burale.

Indeed, on the sunny afternoon we walked through the passageways of Orpington, few people could be seen, despite the courtyards that theoretically could be used as common spaces.

TCHC is Toronto's biggest landlord and is sometimes referred to as "Toronto's biggest slumlord" – a reference to the massive backlog of repairs this chronically underfunded agency is known for. Aesthetic features are rare. "What if we planted flowers in front of people's homes and instilled pride of place?" she said. "Why aren't there more benches to create community spots? Maybe that could help stop gun violence."

Burale isn't naive about gun crime but she says the current approaches of using more police and randomly carding youths aren't solving the issues, as she's seen during her work in various community organizations, including Positive Change TO, a "group of concerned citizens who have united to tackle youth violence in the Somali-Canadian community." Police carding, or police profiling, where people of colour can expect to be randomly stopped and asked to show identification as they make their way around their own neighbourhoods, is as controversial in Toronto as stop-and-frisk policies are in New York City. Despite the obvious inequity of carding, the issue had only been brought up by grassroots candidates like Burale during the 2014 election, or by Olivia Chow in the mayoral contest.

For instance, when John Tory was asked during his campaign for mayor if he would denounce carding, he said only that police have a difficult job and need all the tools available to "get the job done." As mayor, he was again reluctant to engage with the issue, defaulting to the police. It wasn't until the Black Lives Matter movement staged a two-week-long sit-in at Toronto police headquarters that he agreed to meet with and hear what activists had to say about carding and police violence. Although Yasir Naqvi, then provincial Minister of Community

Safety and Correctional Services, announced that carding in Ontario would stop in the fall of 2015, it continues to be a problem in practice.

Rarely do the political conversations delve into design issues that might contribute to higher crime levels in neighbourhoods like Orpington, but design is what Burale was most interested in talking about as we explored. "A sense of isolation is like a cancer," she said of this neglected housing project, which is about as far from city hall as it is from Regent Park, Toronto's most famous public housing project. The closer of the two to downtown, Regent Park is the public housing project that gets the most attention, in both media reports and in reinvestment, as it is undergoing a fifteen-year one-billion-dollar regeneration that has torn down apartment blocks built in the late 1940s and '50s and replaced them with a blend of market and subsidized housing. The plan is to do away with the isolated, single-use design of the area, instead incorporating shops and restaurants and reinstating the street grid across what had been a warren of cul-de-sacs and buildings with no street presence.

Alongside the urban design plans, the Regent Park project includes the creation of a social development plan, a kind of blueprint that supports social inclusion and cohesion through local employment initiatives, community economic development, and resident participation in deciding how their community is run. In short, the regeneration plan is attempting to bring Regent Park back into the city physically, as well as into its civil society and prosperity.

The revitalization was largely paid for by allowing developers to sell condos there at market rate, thus tapping into Toronto's seemingly insatiable appetite for real estate. It's a massive project and not without its critics, but the model could spread to other TCHC projects. However, for now, many of the

TCHC projects languish, breeding a familiar Toronto feeling of being forgotten far from downtown.

Although public housing conditions are much worse than the potholes on Ffolkes, Burale explained that resentment can fester on streets lined with single-family, owner-occupied homes, and in TCHC communities as well. "There's a new park here, but there are no benches for people to sit on," she said, referring to Jane Jacobs's "eyes on the street" theory, which holds that if there are people around, crime won't happen as much because there's always somebody watching. Good design has the potential to transform these places, a "build it and they will come" kind of design, with the hopes people will go there and share neighbourhood information, the way it happens on front porches elsewhere. These are all ideas, though. As simple as they might be to understand, getting people onside, just like with the LRT, takes much talking and effort.

Further north on Kipling we visited Panorama Court, where a collection of large apartment towers line the Humber Valley and Rowntree Mills Park. This is the old border between Etobicoke and North York and is one of Toronto's many clusters of apartment towers that create a big-city skyline far from downtown. There's density here, but the area was designed for cars, and each tower has a conspicuously big door that leads into the underground parking garage, a kind of gaping maw that dominates the landscape. You can imagine the architectural renderings of this when it was in the planning stages – a vision of cars whisking in and out, carrying people to work or do errands. But many people who live here today don't have cars and, because there are no amenities close by, must walk through this unappealing landscape to get to them. It's quite a hike on busy Kipling to the nearest shops at the Albion Centre over a kilometre to the south.

"Why not shipping container shops here?" said Burale, referring to pop-up stores that are often created in spaces where traditional stores haven't been established, and gesturing to the vast spaces in between the towers where parking lots and empty lawns are now.

Shipping container pop-up shops tend to only show up in trendy neighbourhoods right now, but it's here that the idea might have much greater utility – if Toronto's by-laws were loosened to allow for such things. There's no place here to get a coffee, even; imagine a container that is a makeshift café, as there is on the southeast corner of Bathurst and Dundas Streets downtown. People gather by those, and they would in Panorama Court too, if given the chance – turning a place to pass through quickly into a place to linger.

BACK IN the car, we headed to Jamestown. It's not far from Panorama, as the crow flies, but the circuitous streets make it seem much farther. There are no straight lines on the map here, save for the major arterial roads that are an extension of Toronto's famous grid layout, itself a vestige of Ontario's British concession system. Inside those mega blocks are a tangle of streets, courts, and crescents, demanding the kind of directional sense navigating medieval European cities requires. Jamestown is another TCHC neighbourhood that has experienced gun violence and it too, lacks porches and attractive community spaces. It's sometimes confused with the St. James Town neighbourhood downtown.

Unlike that James Town, with its cluster of thirty-storey towers, Etobicoke's Jamestown is a low-rise, tucked away, all but invisible from the major roads. We parked on John Garland Boulevard and walked through Jamestown's passages, not unlike

Orpington's, although built in a somewhat less mod style. Burale pointed out that in many parts of Jamestown there's one drive-way into each parking lot, and the dead-end nature of the arrangement increases isolation. She said that even here, one of the poorest parts of Toronto, she found support for Rob Ford when he was running for a second term. He looked marginal-ized, and bullied, explained Burale, and seemed to struggle "just like people here." That he was a millionaire didn't register, she said. Doug Ford, running for Rob's Ward 2 council seat in 2010 and then for mayor in 2014, never looked bullied or marginal-ized, but was able to embody some of Rob's everyman quality. The Fords had and have the gift every politician wants.

Ford support in unexpected places is a case study in how class connections can often be divorced from income and finances. Even when the Fords spoke of the family's properties in Florida or their Muskoka cottage, the emotional connection that poor people had with them remained strong. Rob was their guy, and when Rob and Doug (to an extent) were the ones speaking directly to them, telling them point blank they'd been left out, they listened. It didn't matter if either Rob or Doug's voting record suggest they felt otherwise either, as the many cuts to services they supported actually hurt these neighbourhoods.

Writing after the 2014 election in *Spacing* magazine in a piece titled "Ford Nation is not dead," Burale noted, "As the demographic data shows, people who voted for Doug Ford are overwhelmingly marginalized. They tend to live in parts of this city where the income divide is most evident. As a result of living in designated 'priority neighbourhoods,' they experience disparity in terms of access to quality city services."

Burale also wrote about why the big ideas don't often resonate: "Many of the people I met are working poor. They would rather vote for the candidate promising to lower their taxes (i.e. allowing them to keep more of their money) rather than the challenger who would increase taxes in order to strengthen the social safety net that would catch them should they lose their job."

She also found that many conservative immigrant parents voted for Ford "solely as a defense against a 'gay agenda,'" and that many were even union members. "The people who voted for Ford are as diverse as the city itself," she wrote, countering the notion that there is one kind of archetypal Ford voter.

It comes back to potholes. Service delivery is everything, something long associated with well-off suburban voters who enjoy things like sidewalk snow clearing and mechanical leaf collection, where leaves that have been raked or blown into piles at the edge of the road are collected by a truck. None of this happens downtown, where people must bag their own leaves, a vestige of the old Metro system, where some parts of the city received different services.

Fat cats who can't pick up their own leaves – that's the comfortable Ford Nation stereotype people who opposed Rob or Doug could easily understand, not this other, hidden population that seems to be opposed to the kind of collective city building that urbanists focus on – and that, arguably, Ford Nation residents would directly benefit from – such as the LRT or better designed public spaces in housing estates. A fundamentally different world view is behind this, as Burale explained in *Spacing*: people are "alienated from the progressive ideals of 'togetherness,' opting instead for the conservative notion of "self-reliance.'" When the neighbourhood has been broken and neglected for so long, why should residents be expected to put their faith in more ideas and institutions?

BURALE AND I cross over to the south side of John Garland Boulevard, where a sign reads "West Humber Park – Metro Parks and Property Department." It's the only indication that the river might be nearby, although the old weathered sign refers to a municipality that hasn't existed since the 1990s. The presence of Metro-era signs is often an indication of how little renewal and care a neighbourhood gets.

Burale led me along a steep, overgrown pathway descending into the deep Humber Valley. Pearson's airport flight path is directly overhead and the incoming planes above us were flying so low that we could easily read the branding on the fuselage – "FLY EMIRATES." As we walked through a scrubby meadow, the volume of the sounds around us alternated between a bucolic quiet and a roar so loud we couldn't hear each other speak. As with living next to elevated subways and rail lines, I could imagine even this could become white noise when it was heard every day.

This path is supposedly Jamestown's grand entrance into the ravine network, but the asphalt is old and rough, and we have to push back overgrown branches at times. There's nothing here that says to residents "Welcome to your river valley." Living near a ravine is a coveted thing in Toronto but there is so little regard for the public realm in Jamestown that this path doesn't matter.

Eventually the path narrows, dwindling to a thicket of brush rather than connecting to the busy, well-kept main trail on the other side of the river that leads to the arboretum and points elsewhere. No bridge; ancient signage; rough asphalt; dead-end paths – it's as if the city is saying, "You're on your own, good luck." Self-reliance will get you back up and out.

Ultimately, 46 per cent of those who voted in Ward 1 in 2014 opted to return incumbent councillor Vincent Crisanti to office, a position he's held since 2010. As for the mayoral election, an impressive 72 per cent voted for Doug Ford, with just 15 per cent for John Tory and 10 per cent for Olivia Chow. Ward 1 decided not to change much, but Idil Burale's city building days have just begun. Though she didn't win a seat she hopes that by running she will have inspired others like her to get involved.

Burale also sees "opportunity" as one of the Ford legacies. "Ultimately, Rob Ford's crass rhetoric and Ford Nation's rise to political significance revealed a deep division within this city that cannot be whitewashed with [John] Tory's 'One City' rhetoric," she wrote in *Spacing*. "The Fords gave Toronto an opportunity to better engage the disenfranchised communities spread across the amalgamated city. I wonder if the heightened interest in municipal issues sparked by the Fords could serve as a platform for this city, a wake-up call to the reality that there are large parts of Etobicoke, North York, and Scarborough that *have* been neglected. Maybe then, something can be done to confront the divisions."

CHAPTER FOUR

OUT BY THE AIRPORT, RUNNING AGAINST GIANTS

THE TORONTO Transit Commission 52A Lawrence West bus rumbles into the two active terminals at Pearson International Airport to pick up people waiting with their bags by the TTC stops, but most travellers taking public transit into the city don't get on it. They opt instead for the 192 Airport Rocket that goes directly to Kipling Subway Station and the rest of the city. The 52A is the local bus. It eventually gets to a subway station but takes a long route overland, rolling through the neighbourhoods peripheral to the airport. There will be some people with suitcases on it to be sure, travellers who live along the way, and others who mistook it for the express bus or wisely subscribe to the Toronto rule "Get on the bus you see, not the bus you're waiting for, because it might not come." Toronto is a bird-in-the-hand kind of transit city.

On the way into the airport the bus stops at Jetliner Road, a place not as jet-set as its name might suggest, more freeway on-ramp than Pan Am cool, but there will be a few more people here waiting, and they won't have suitcases. This local bus is also the worker bus for those employed in and around the airport, a place where thousands come everyday with no intention of flying, and the Jetliner stop is where airport employees often catch their ride. The airport is a formidable engine driving Toronto's economy, and these are the people who make it work. Modern airports have become cities unto themselves, with their own social and economic ecosystems, and the neighbourhoods nearby both service them and act as landing pads, places where new immigrants to the country first settle down, just as the neighbourhoods near old sea ports were often the first places where new arrivals lived and found work. If a motion picture studio were to shoot *On the Waterfront* today, they could move it from Hoboken to Toronto, out here rather than by the lake. And a modern-day Brando might ride a streetcar named Lawrence. But few have tried to cinematically romanticize this kind of working class life as of yet.

The first residential neighbourhood the bus reaches after a desolate series of hotels, chain restaurants and convention halls is a collection of apartment buildings along Dixon Road. Usually a few people will get off when the bus reaches Kipling Street or Islington Road, heading for the buildings or the single-family homes around it. Before Rob Ford made it part of the Toronto noir vernacular, Dixon was a road most people likely never gave much thought to, and although it still might take them a few minutes to find it on the map, it's a place the city has come to know.

"The airport is a blessing and a curse," says Munira Abukar as we walk between the apartment buildings that are also near the flight path of the airport, the roar of the jet engines echoing around the towers on a sunny September afternoon. Abukar says the airport hires locally and many people in the area work there, but theirs are service jobs, usually not the best paying or offering much upward mobility.

Although the industry their work supports drives the economy, these people often live precarious lives. Abukar recounts meeting a mom in the neighbourhood whose sons worked nights at the airport and went to York University by day. Abukar says the woman broke down in tears when she described the exhausting routine of driving them to work and school at all hours everyday. Abukar, a recent Ryerson graduate, was born in Toronto and grew up in the neighbourhood so she knows it well, and got an even more intimate take on it while running for the Ward 2 city council seat here in 2014.

ABUKAR'S PARENTS fled the Somali civil war and came to Canada, settling here in this landing pad neighbourhood. "Proximity to the airport is the reason the Somali community moved here," she says. The near-constant roar of jets as they pass overhead and the faint whiffs of jet fuel are regular reminders that the airport is nearby.

Toronto has had a decade's worth of debate over the Island Airport downtown and its effect on the waterfront and its residents, but rarely if ever is thought given to the people who live near the bigger and busier airport far from the city centre. To be sure, these mid-century neighbourhoods were built after the airport was a major hub. Then again, the island airport was established when Toronto's waterfront was a working one, filled with train yards and industry, so the evolution to residential is not so different there than here.

Lives are lived underneath the traffic of commercial aircraft that feed people and goods into Pearson, a place that contributes to making parts of this city very rich. But this place, in the view every day of thousands of passengers peering from their window seats as they take off and land, hasn't shared in the riches.

Like Ward 1 next door, Ward 2 is a sprawling territory in the northwestern corner of the city, bordered by the meandering

Humber River, Highway 427, and Mississauga. To the south the ward border follows Highway 401 and Dixon Road itself, with a small panhandle reaching down Scarlett and Royal York Roads into the wealthier neighbourhoods of central Etobicoke, where the Ford family compound is located. Vast parts of this area are industrial, divided by railway spur lines and street after street of warehouse-style buildings.

The street names here sound at once industrious and curious: Meteor Drive, Enterprise Road, Vulcan Street, Iron Street, Disco Road, Precision Road. It might be Toronto's most aspirationally named pocket. Most of the residential streets with single-family homes are clustered along the Humber River and its impressive expanse of parkland, a world away from the industrial lands. Highways, Woodbine Racetrack, and golf courses divide and occupy the rest of the area. As in many of Toronto's inner suburbs, there are clusters of residential high-rises too.

"What's frustrating here is we have all this open space but no community centre," said Abukar as we stood among six high-rise condominium towers on Dixon. In Dixon Park, between some of the towers, she pointed out a basketball court opened by Vince Carter in 2003 when he was the star Toronto Raptor, his stylized "VC" logo faded on the backboards. "Some of the young men will play here in the bitter winter because they have no other place to play." In a city the size of Toronto, having nothing to do seems impossible, but much of the city's public excitement is concentrated in a few places, and for youth – that period between being a little kid and a full-fledged adult that often seems lost in recreational planning – the options are even more limited, in the way that job prospects are limited in areas of Toronto like this. Ward 2 is, however, where Rob Ford began his political career.

FORD WAS councillor in Ward 2 Etobicoke North from 2000 until he ran for mayor in 2010. Encompassing parts of the Rexdale neighbourhood, this is Ford Nation's political heartland, where the family dynasty continued when brother Doug Ford took Rob's place as councillor in 2010, and where nephew Michael Ford won in a July 2016 by-election after Rob's death.

In 2014 Abukar expected to be running against Michael, the third generation of the Ford dynasty, because Doug had indicated he was ready to retire from city politics. But Rob's diagnosis of cancer in September led to some last-minute dramatic developments, including a mad dash to city hall before the final deadline to file candidate papers, six weeks before the election itself. Only minutes before the deadline to set the 2014 ballot, the Ford family had pulled a switcheroo, with Doug Ford now running for mayor, Rob running for his old council seat in Ward 2 and young Michael sent off to try for the local school board trustee seat.

Opponents of the Fords saw it as a cynical move and one that condescended to the constituents. It was also a sign of the supreme confidence the family had in their base – Ward 2 was their Camelot. But not all was well in the kingdom, as Rob Ford would make famous during the latter half of his mayoralty.

THE TOWERS Abukar showed me were the site of a Toronto police raid in 2013, part of "Project Traveller," a massive investigation into gang activity that eventually resulted in the seizure of a mobile phone that contained the Rob Ford crack video, an infamous digital file that even brought a New York reporter from the media news and gossip site Gawker up to Toronto for a clandestine viewing. This video was to Toronto's celebrity politics what the Pamela Anderson-Tommy Lee sex tape was to Southern California celebrity gossip of the mid-1990s.

Did the video exist? Who has seen the video? What happened exactly? After the raids, the then chief of police, Bill Blair, confirmed that the video did, in fact, exist, but gave no other details. Ford and city hall watchers lived for breaking news stories with the hope that the video would be embedded in one of them, and international news outlets continued to cover the story. Eventually a Rashomon scenario was cobbled together from a handful of reporters who had seen the video. Their scenario painted a picture of the mayor doing some heavy partying in the Dixon Towers area, a place that became synonymous with his ongoing scandal. While Ford was never charged with anything, the neighbourhood's reputation suffered a kind of geographic collateral damage, inflicted by Ford.

That drama seemed far away on the sunny day when Abukar and I took our walkabout. I followed Abukar into one, where she stopped to say hello to the women working in the ground-floor beauty parlour and ask about a friend they shared. It was the kind of main-street interaction people who live in twee downtown neighbourhoods experience daily, or so goes the mythology.

We went up the elevator to a random floor because Abukar wanted to show me the condition of the hallways. They were immaculate and looked like those of any nice condo tower or well-maintained apartment building in any part of the city. Dixon Road is a tale of six towers, three in good condition and up to normal Toronto middle-class standards, and three others that have been left to deteriorate around their residents.

Abukar also took me up to her aunt's apartment in one of the three buildings that aren't so well kept. The walls of the communal halls are scraped and marked with years of wear and tear, and their carpets thin and dirty. Down one hall, on a lower floor, her aunt runs a small day care in her apartment, one small piece of Toronto's hidden vertical economy that is tucked into high-rise towers across the city.

These older apartments, built before the latest condo boom shrunk unit sizes to a scale more in line with other global cities, are generously proportioned, and there was ample room for four or five cribs in the living room. Toys were scattered on the floor and it seemed like a happy place. The apartment is in good condition, with new hardwood floors and a new kitchen, but Abukar pointed out that the condo owner told her aunt to fix the broken balcony door herself, paying out of pocket. In buildings like this where people rent from individual owners – each unit is a separately owned condominium unit rather than a rental building with one manager or owner – their connection to how the building is run becomes arm's length at best and individual units can be haphazardly maintained. Other buildings across Toronto simply have bad landlords, despite the collective management.

The slumlord is an old urban story but one that keeps popping up in places just off the political radar. The City of Toronto has a promising plan to fix these high-rises, "Tower Renewal," which would repair and update the 1,200-plus rental towers in Toronto, home to more than half a million people.

The Tower Renewal project began as the thesis for University of Toronto architecture student Graeme Stewart, a fan of mid-century modern design who travelled Europe studying how older council blocks in the United Kingdom, Scandinavia, Russia, and other former Soviet republics dealt with their aging stock of buildings. The project was later taken up by former mayor David Miller as a way to address some of the inequality in the standard of living of many Torontonians.

These buildings are forty to sixty years old now, an age when they need major renovations and updates to environmental systems. Equally important is adapting their socio-economic aspects, so that they meet the needs of residents today. So many of the homes in these apartment buildings contain an incredible amount of economic capacity but many people, unlike Abukar's aunt, who was able to start a day care in her apartment, have constraints on what they can do in their apartments.

In older downtown immigrant neighbourhoods, people with skills and entrepreneurial chutzpah would turn their houses into stores or shops, building an addition out front that met the sidewalk, urbanizing the neighbourhoods along the way. Many of Toronto's downtown streets were once residential, and if you look closely you can see an old house peeking up behind many shops on Queen, College, Dundas, Bloor, and other streets, a phenomenon common in other cities too.

Such spatial expansion isn't possible in tower buildings, of course, but many are surrounded by underused and neglected green spaces, and Tower Renewal looks at ways these areas could be used to unleash some of the economic and social capital pent up in the towers or as places for urban agriculture. The economic benefit to the city could be massive, and as these open, unused spaces were filled in, there might be an urbanizing affect on areas such as Dixon Road. Predictably, the Fords were not fans of Tower Renewal, even though it could help the people they represented.

The architect of Rob Ford's 2010 mayoral win, campaign strategist Nick Kouvalis, took aim at Tower Renewal soon after that election, when he was briefly Mayor Ford's chief of staff. "I was getting briefed yesterday," Kouvalis said, as reported by the *Toronto Star*. "I was like . . . the Tower Renewal Program – what is that? We're subsidizing (installation of low-flow) toilets . . . Guys, you know that stuff's gotta stop. The priority is the taxpayer, to stop the gravy train, and that's what we're going to do." While there are towers downtown that the program would benefit, the majority are in Toronto's inner suburbs. Tower Renewal managed to survive the Ford years, becoming a permanent City of Toronto program, even though both of the Ford brothers routinely voted against programs such as this that could benefit communities like Dixon. It is a big idea, but it was all just part of the gravy train to the Fords.

"That's the biggest reason why I ran," said Abukar. "The taxpayer rhetoric is garbage. My aunt and her husband here are honest, decent, hardworking people. They just want somebody who listens to their needs." During our walk Abukar demonstrated a nuanced approach to that last sentiment. This part of Toronto has real needs, but it's also filled with the kind of decent people that other, wealthier parts of the city are assumed to be full of, although that reality runs contrary to how the area was portrayed during the Project Traveller raids and throughout the Ford saga.

Despite the design deficiencies of the area, especially apparent in winter, there is still much life around the towers, and people were everywhere on our walk. "You can stand at the bus stop and start talking to five people," she said. "It's close-knit here."

THAT CLOSE-KNIT feeling was evident again at Dixon and Kipling, where bus stops on each of the four corners often have crowds gathered, waiting. It's busy like a downtown subway station during morning and afternoon rushes, but here people are out in the open, exposed to the elements, and the buses are certainly not as frequent as the subways.

As if planted by Abukar to prove her point, a man started to chat with us before she even mentioned she was running for council, breaking the long-held Toronto rule of not talking to strangers in public. He lived in one of the well-maintained apartment buildings, but complained of construction noise and of bus waits, the same things Abukar was telling me about.

Out here, people talk about the same problems they do downtown, but they just articulate them differently, owing to differences in landscape. The common struggles they experience, just like the common values they share with other parts of the city, are overlooked, because a focus in Toronto has been placed on the urban and suburban divide that, by design, looks for differences rather than similarities. People here, like the fellow we met on the corner, complain about the Kipling bus the way that people in Liberty Village downtown lament the too-full and too-infrequent 504 King streetcar. These could become common causes and something to rally people around, but they are connections that get lost because it isn't in some politicians' interests to unite the city.

AS WE wander north up the narrow sidewalks busy with traffic along Kipling, Abukar explained her frustration with the obsessive and never-ending transit debates over the Scarborough subway. "Once rush hour is here you have to wait for the fourth or fifth bus to go by," she says. "We need an Etobicoke Relief Line" – a reference to the Downtown Relief Line, a long-proposed additional subway line to run from the near-east side around Pape Avenue into downtown, thereby relieving pressure on the overloaded Yonge subway line.

Although Rob and Doug Ford represented this ward, the Scarborough subway they pinned their mayoral hopes on would do nothing for the area, yielding debatable utility but siphoning money away from projects that could serve more people. Transit is intricately linked to quality of life, especially in neighbourhoods like this one where many lower-income residents must travel across the city for work, often an hours-long commute each way. Abukar mentioned an idea she and her siblings came up with called "Tots Trans" – buses reserved for moms with strollers, an issue that oddly became a scapegoat for a day or two in the news cycle when a few transit riders complained publicly about how much space strollers take up. When people turn on the moms, it's a sign the transit frustration is high in Toronto.

As we walked to the top of the Kipling overpass, a passing driver honked and gave the finger to another car, a road rage tableau seemingly staged just for us. Aggression is part of the Toronto transportation experience now. The rage is built in. At the top of the overpass, where Islington crosses more than ten lanes of Highway 401, there's a view of the vast industrial lands to the west and north. The overpass also affords a panorama of the historic geography of Rob Ford. There should be a scenic lookout here, and perhaps a sign directing sightseers to the points of interest, like those found on mountains in national parks or atop skyscrapers. This is where Toronto's high municipal drama played out.

The closest Ford landmark that can be seen here is just across the highway. Deco Labels and Tags, the Ford family company, is located on a dead-end street in the wedge of land framed by Highway 409 and the 401. These buildings are the source of Ford wealth and the seat of their empire, all conspicuously facing what is said to be the busiest freeway in North America. A FORD NATION flag flies along side a Canadian one for all passersby to see. Before Rob Ford became mayor, only the closest watchers of city hall and the machinations behind it would have noticed these buildings, as they look like any other light industrial concern found along Southern Ontario highways. They're reminders of the province's mighty manufacturing past, but now it seems somehow by design that the flamboyant Fords had some real estate easily visible to thousands of commuters a day, often snarled in heavy traffic.

When viewed from the panoramic overpass the south side of the highway is a big-sky landscape, with the towers on Dixon just to the south and the CN Tower and cluster of downtown skyscrapers in the hazy distance behind them. In between the Dixon Towers and Deco Labels and Tags is neighbourhood of low-rises and single-family dwellings – bungalows, split-levels, and the occasional out-of-scale monster home rebuild. It's typical inner suburban Toronto topography: the high-rises on the arterial roads with traditional suburban landscape in between.

On the eastern edge of this particular neighbourhood is Don Bosco Catholic Secondary School, a fortress of a building on Islington Avenue. It was here that Rob Ford pursued his true love and calling: coaching high school football. Rob Ford skipped out of city council meetings and missed votes in order to coach games during football season. He looked happiest when he was wearing the green-and-yellow Don Bosco varsity jacket and said this vocation was his way of giving back to Toronto, implying at times that these kids would have succumbed to ne'er-do-well elements had he not been driving them down the straight and narrow on the football field, a characterization many in the community objected to.

But even doing something he loved and did fairly well was not simple for Rob Ford. After one game at rival Father Henry Carr Catholic Secondary School in 2012 – this chapter of the Ford saga reads like a who's who of historic Catholic luminaries – an altercation between coaches and referees resulted in police officers being called to the scene. The cops eventually ordered a TTC bus to come and take the Don Bosco students back to their school. In a move that was against procedure, the bus was diverted from an operational route, leaving riders stranded on the sidewalk in the damp wet November afternoon, so some wondered if the mayor being the coach is what led to what one student called their "personal TTC bus." Nothing stinks like special treatment. Even when doing something that should have been apolitical, a storm cloud of controversy seemed to follow Rob Ford wherever he went.

In May of 2013, after the crack-smoking scandal had gone fully public, the Toronto Catholic District School Board announced they had fired Ford from his coaching position at Don Bosco, although the firing was purportedly not related to "current allegations."

Ford was the kind of guy who wore a Toronto Argonauts jersey to city council meeting and whose mayoral office shelves were lined with football paraphernalia not books. This firing had to hurt, especially since the bad news struck Ford at the heart of his home base.

Despite his talent for enraging and offending, Rob Ford also was remarkably able in attracting empathy from even his most ardent detractors, and as word spread of his firing there was a moment when it felt like everybody just felt bad for the guy. Rob Ford could make anybody relate to him, even his opponents – who hasn't lost something they really wanted, something that kept them going? It's a connection to people that most politicians will never know.

An event a month later that engendered much less sympathy was an undated photograph that surfaced of Ford standing in the driveway of a house at 15 Windsor Drive, a few blocks west of the Don Bosco football field and just north of the Dixon

Towers, in the middle of the low-rise neighbourhood. In it, a smiling Ford in a hoodie with what appear to be stains on the front is posing with three young men. One of them was Anthony Smith, later shot dead on King Street in downtown Toronto on a busy weekend night in March 2013.

The house in the photo became a notorious address in the geography of Ford. It had seen a lot of action: 15 Windsor had been called a crack house; police had been called to it numerous times; and once a "pipe wielding thug" had stormed into it, assaulting the residents there. This was a house where Ford reportedly partied during his drug and alcohol binges, and that digital image, as overexposed and blown out as an old Polaroid, and this house itself, serve as records of some of the darkest moments of the Ford saga.

The man accused of Anthony Smith's murder pleaded guilty. The two others in the photo besides Anthony were charged in the Project Traveller raids. Rob's behaviour was creating more collateral damage, this time human, as lives were irrevocably changed. The mayor seemed to be careening out of control but nobody, not even the police, could stop it, and while everyone around him, most of them people of colour, were charged with various offences, the mayor was not. After the Smith murder, Toronto's Ford saga could no longer be seen as an amusing political story. It was now a very dark and sinister tale that ran contrary to all that Torontonians believed their city to be.

This side of Toronto had always existed, but it had been easily ignored because it seemed remote or unrelated to the political class. Ford forced the city to look at this dark side, as he had for many other aspects of city life. Reckoning with it is a continuing challenge.

RUNNING AGAINST the Ford family was challenge enough, especially at the relatively tender age of twenty-two, but Abukar faced another challenge: repeated racist attacks on her campaign, which revealed yet another view of Toronto's disturbing reality.

Many of her campaign signs disappeared, and others were vandalized with words like "Bitch" and "Go Back Home" (never mind that she was born right here in Etobicoke). And strangely, after the election, 154 of her signs that had gone missing – stolen from the spots they'd been staked – were put back out around the neighbourhood. After an election, candidates must quickly remove their signs or incur a fine. Abukar received an invoice for $4,000 because of the reappearing signs, a penalty she fought.

During our walk she talked about other kinds of racism that had bothered her during the campaign. "My biggest frustration was Doug Ford saying Cynthia Mulligan was a Jihadist," she said. "We don't need this kind of BS in politics; it shows such disrespect to the people there." Abukar was referring to comments Ford made to Mulligan, a CityNews reporter, in which he characterized her line of questioning as a "jihadist attack."

It wasn't the first time he used this loaded word. In the spring of the 2014 election he was the subject of an integrity complaint after saying a home for autistic teens in the area he represented had "ruined the community." One of the teen's fathers launched the complaint, to which Ford responded, via the *Toronto Sun*, "He can go to hell, I don't even care" and "it is a full out jihad against us now." The Fords, as physically dominating and rich as they are, have always been quick to play the victim.

In addition to the Ford family, Abukar was up against a slate of candidates that included Andray Domise, the candidate in Ward 2 with the second-highest profile. Domise received endorsements from other councillors and media organizations such as the *Toronto Star* and became something of a Toronto Twitter sensation through the support of many people from outside of the area who wanted to get behind whoever was the front runner against Ford. Like Abukar, Domise did not hesitate to talk about how race factored into both Toronto politics and life in the city.

On July 2, 2014, Domise posted a piece called "Some Questions for Toronto's African Canadian Voters – an open letter to those who have given up on change" on his blog. The piece grew out of an encounter Domise had had with Ford at a Canada Day Ribfest at Etobicoke Centennial Park. Domise wrote that he had asked the mayor if he would apologize for "referring to African Canadians as 'niggers,'" as he had been surreptitiously recorded doing, and for characterizing "community grant programs as 'hug-a-thug' programs."

In the piece, Domise sketched out how Ford receives the support of a community whose members would not be afforded the same treatment if they did the same things. Recall the photograph: Ford remained free while one man was dead and the two others arrested. Domise was also talking to a community that, for all its support for the Fords, didn't get much out of the relationship.

"I've said before that Rob Ford's ongoing support is not just due to stubborn holdouts, unable to let go of their populist grudges," wrote Domise. "The reality is worse; these supporters – of which many of us can count ourselves – are people who legitimately feel utterly let down by their government. Their support of our disgraced mayor is an upraised middle finger directed at a political class that, from their point of view, could not care less about their quiet struggle."

DESPITE HIS being a millionaire, despite the racial slurs, and despite all the votes against programs that might possibly help the community, Ford continued to enjoy strong support. Thanks to the double helix of this part of Etobicoke missing out on Toronto's prosperity – so that citizens' trust in government and government-based solutions degraded, after being let down too many times – and the unique ability of Rob Ford to appear like a victim of the media and elites and foster "little guy" solidarity.

This support confounded people outside of Ford Nation: it just didn't seem rational. How could the Fords maintain such high levels of support despite all the scandals? The emotional connection this family, especially Rob, had with their voters, is the kind of political gold that politicos dream about. Rob Ford was like a swearing, drunk, out-of-control version of Bill Clinton who could "feel the pain," or at least channel it, of people whose lot in life was far worse than the wealthy one he inherited.

Rather than try to understand why Ford had support in places like this and around the Dixon Road towers, it's been easy to fall back on the so-called downtown-suburban divide, the idea that somehow these neighbourhoods are just inherently different, with foreign values. The complexity of the actual situation is overlooked with this lazy kind of analysis, because a substantial amount of Ford support came from downtown neighbourhoods, and many parts of the city thought to be bedrock "Ford Nation" in fact had large numbers who didn't vote Ford.

Abukar, for her part, was confounded by its continued existance, a divide perpetuated not just by the very mayor she ran against because it worked to his advantage, but by other folks who should know better. During and after the Ford years there were many calls to de-amalgamate the city, to return to the old Metro system of six municipalities, which existed prior to 1998. Calls to jettison the suburbs from the city came fast and furious when times were tough, doing little for social cohesion in Toronto.

"Sometimes when I tell people I'm from Etobicoke they look at me like 'what? you're normal,'" said Abukar. "We recycle, we compost too, like downtown." She would like to see Toronto, in her words, "moving forward together," and even found herself challenging her friends at Ryerson University downtown, where she had recently finished a degree in criminology.

"Calling for de-amalgamation is giving up on part of the city and discriminating against people," she says. "I'd like to challenge downtowners and ask them what they are doing to bring the city together. They don't understand how intersected we are." It's a hopeful note that the city needs to hear more of. All the same, voters in Ward 2 resoundingly decided to put Rob Ford back in his old council seat with 60 per cent of the vote, and gave Doug Ford nearly 68 per cent in his run for mayor.

Domise, despite his high profile and support from other parts of the city, came in third, with 1,600 votes, behind relatively unknown Luke LaRocque, who pulled in 2,100 votes. Abukar came in fourth with 1,200 votes, a good showing for running an independent campaign without much money against better known candidates.

Like Idil Burale in the adjacent ward, Abukar approached the campaign with some perspective, telling herself and the people she was talking to in the neighbourhood she grew up in, "I'm not just running a campaign to win, but an education campaign too. I'm not here for your vote, I want to show you we can change this place."

Change comes slow, but with her infectious energy for this city, it's unlikely Toronto has seen the last of Abukar.

CHAPTER FIVE

BARE-CHESTED POLITICS

"THIS PLACE is the heart of the community," said Keegan Henry-Mathieu as we took a summer walk through the sunny parking lot of North York Sheridan Mall at Jane Street and Wilson Avenue. "There's not much other public space around here where people can gather like this. It's an informal community centre."

We were exploring the southeast corner of Ward 7 in the former city of North York. "It would be nice to see some food trucks set up here," he said, looking at the expanse of parking lot filled not just with cars but people heading to the mall on foot, the pavement's vastness like an asphalt-and-steel moat they have to cross. Sheridan Mall is deep in Toronto car territory, but a lot of people who live here don't own vehicles and walk to the mall instead, bringing to mind the urban design mantra, "Cars aren't your customers, people are."

Sheridan Mall itself is not a glamorous mall, and unless you're from the community you've probably never heard of it. Like a lot of smaller community shopping centres around the GTA most of its tenants are independent retailers, save for chains like Walmart and Tim Hortons, and there are makeshift stalls outside selling CDs, flags, and bracelets in the parking lot.

The day we visited, a sound system was booming reggae music across the parking lot, giving the place a vibe that was more market than mall.

Even in this unpromising asphalt setting, culture and economy sprout like trees through the smallest pavement cracks. Malls like this are yesterday's idea, as there has been a return to either urban "main street" retailing or, at the other end of the spectrum, oversized power centres malls on steroids, yet these tired old malls have proven to be good at adapting to and serving their communities as they changed around them. Seniors come here and linger in the food courts, chatting or reading, sometimes walking laps in the morning. In the winter its corridors are some of the few big quasi-public indoor spaces in a city that seemingly forgets below-zero months. After school, these spaces fill with kids hanging out before heading home, sometimes dodging security guards who are always on the lookout for teenagers doing teenage things.

Often these kinds of old-school malls are disdained by the same people who fret about gentrification on main streets, wishing these eyesores would be redeveloped or gussied up. Could there be any places in the city less gentrified than these off-the-radar shopping malls and plazas in neighbourhoods like this one, with their affordable retail rents that come via market forces rather than policy? The great conundrum of gentrification, of course, is that *beautiful* often means *expensive*, while the humdrum remains within the reach of people and businesses with a lower income. And thus the value of places like Sheridan Mall get overlooked. And besides the value, there *is* beauty to be found here too, if you look for it.

"THIS IS the Toronto melting pot," said Henry-Mathieu of the area around the mall. "Immigrants have always come here. It's a mix of middle and lower incomes. The strip malls show all the variety and you can get everything you need done without leaving the area."

Henry-Mathieu was also excited about the potential of those nearby strip malls, suggesting tax incentives for owners could beautify and create better public areas around them and that the new rules around food trucks the city had recently brought in could make the mall parking lot even more of a meeting spot. Essentially, these ideas could add a little urbanity to places conceived as suburban place but operating today by urban rules.

Although he was running for city council here in Ward 7 while in his mid-twenties, Henry-Mathieu had been going to city hall since he was sixteen, for a time as chair of the Toronto Youth Cabinet, the City's official youth advisory panel. In 2014 he was undertaking his council run while still maintaining a day job in the financial industry.

Running in Ward 7 is a challenge of geography. The ward sprawls over considerable territory, with a number of barriers dividing it. Looking south across Wilson from the mall, Highway 401, the ward's southern border, can be seen in between buildings, the hum and transport-truck downshifting audible from the parking lot. Just west of the mall, Highway 400, the road to cottage country for Toronto's middle and upper classes, cuts one-third of the ward away from the rest; with only three places to cross the highway in the entire ward, connections in the ward are made difficult. Beyond the highway, the meandering Humber River is Ward 7's rather whimsical western border, with Jane and the 400 alternately serving as the eastern border.

Conjuring up a sense of ward identity is difficult enough in closer-knit neighbourhoods downtown, but here the bisecting CPR railway corridor further limits ward connections. There are also vast industrial zones with rather generic corporate facades, separating residential neighbourhoods and contributing to a dislocated sense of place. Yet, still, there's beauty.

"This corner of the ward is like a concrete jungle of busy roads, apartment buildings, malls and parking lots, bordered by a jungle of greenspace," Henry-Mathieu said, explaining why he wanted to start our walk at the mall. "Even though the space isn't really set up to promote the many cultures that make up the neighbourhood, people are making it happen anyways."

He also wanted to meet at Sheridan Mall because it's adjacent to Chalkfarm Park, where a series of four sentinel-like towers dominate the skyline and house around 4,000 people. "I was told to stay away from Chalkfarm because voter turnout is so low," he says. "Don't waste your time, they told me." Henry-Mathieu feels it's that attitude that has led to people feeling so disenfranchised and left out that, if you mention city hall, residents will "laugh in your face."

We made our way around the mall parking lot to the park with dozens of other people coming and going, crossing Black Creek to get to Chalkfarm. The creek wiggles its way through Ward 7, sometimes "channelized" in concrete, other times in a more natural state. It's one of the more elusive of Toronto's creeks and rivers, appearing in unexpected places despite being treated so poorly by the modern city. Here Black Creek separates the mall and residential areas, but a busy footbridge connects the two, with ducks underneath, resting on the banks or looking up expectedly for the scraps of bread their human neighbours sometimes feed them.

ONCE ACROSS we came to a pool outside the community centre filled with the noise of swimming children. The towers have been notorious for crime in the past, but they have been on the rebound of late, with revitalization efforts that include garbage clean-up and even community gardens. However, Henry-Mathieu says many of the apartments inside are often in deplorable condition, with "garbage coming out of the ceilings and rotted kitchen counters" – something he wanted to change, although there's cynicism around building repair in Chalkfarm and other low-income residential tower neighbourhoods.

"Lots of residents aren't keen on revitalization," he says. "They tried to get away from the stigma by renaming it The Oakes." Unfortunately, neighbourhoods and buildings are like kids in high school: once they get a reputation, unfair or otherwise, it is hard to shake. People remember bad experiences and bad moments (particularly the very bad, like a murder or a shooting), and these obscure the 99.9 per cent of the time when the places are in their everyday good and normal state. Even downtown Toronto intersections such as Bloor and Lansdowne or Queen and Sherbourne remain thought of as "bad neighbourhoods" long after the neighbourhoods have changed for the better (assuming they were even truly "bad" to begin with).

North of the towers are a half dozen streets of single-family homes, a high- and low-rise mix typical of postwar Toronto. Walking across a second bridge that leads from the park west to another residential neighbourhood, Henry-Mathieu said that "Black Creek could be our High Park if done right," but park projects here haven't the same political momentum as they might have downtown, and the local councillor here hasn't been known as a champion of these kinds of spaces, especially in the last few years. The incumbent Henry-Mathieu was challenging is Giorgio Mammoliti, who had been going through a major fundraising scandal at the time of our walk.

In May 2014, just as the various races were beginning to heat up, Mammoliti supporters held a $500-a-plate fundraiser in Woodbridge, northwest of his ward, outside the City of Toronto itself. Two hundred people attended and afterward Mammoliti accepted a cheque for $80,000 from event organizers, violating the city's code of conduct that prohibits such "gifts" to fund election campaigns. The *Toronto Star* reported that Mammoliti claimed the event was to celebrate his recovery from brain surgery the previous year, but he was rebuked by the city's integrity commissioner, Janet Leiper, city council voted to dock his pay for ninety days, and the Toronto Police began an investigation to see if any financial crimes had been committed. All this occurred after a 2013 audit that revealed Mammoliti's campaign overspent on the 2010 election by $12,065, so trouble with numbers and money appeared to be a pattern rather than a one-time mistake.

Alone, such malfeasance might topple any reasonable campaign or political career in Canada, a country where a senate expense scandal in the high five-digits seemed like a threat to Stephen Harper near the end of his run as prime minister. But the game is murkier in local politics.

The legendary Chicago Democratic Machine, officially known as the Cook County Democratic Party, is perhaps the most famous example of the dark arts of municipal politics.

Higher levels of government get all the attention and scrutiny and even the smallest transgressions can snowball into major scandals, but city politics run closer to the ground where all the dirt and mud is. With many dozens of races in a few dozen wards, all with their own dynamics, money trails, and connections, a lot can happen in the shadows where there isn't enough media to cover every move, a situation made worse by a shrinking industry. Among many voters and people engaged in local politics there's almost an understanding, an assumption, that things might not be totally square, even if it is. It's a built-in cynicism that is both corrosive and not altogether incorrect.

In Chicago those darker arts played out dramatically with Mayor Richard J. Daley's mid-century stranglehold on politics in that city, but in a place like Toronto ward politics can be like a melodramatic soap opera with bad writing and unbelievable plot lines.

Mammoliti's malfeasance during and preceding the 2014 election came as no surprise to those who paid attention to Toronto city hall. He's been a known entertainer for years, variously described as colourful or flamboyant, two of the kinder euphemisms.

Everybody has a first-time-they-heard-about-Mammoliti moment. For some it was in 1999, when he tore his jacket, shirt and tie off during a city council meeting, outraged that Hanlan's Point on the western edge of the Toronto Island park was about to become a city-sanctioned clothing-optional beach. "Today, it's a secluded beach, tomorrow it will be the beachfront and then it will be the streets," he declared, hands on his hips, wearing only a gold chain and crucifix above the waist.

Twelve years later he suggested the island become a red-light district – apparently letting go of his earlier defence of the park's honour – a place where all of Toronto's vice and prostitution could be put in a regulated, paid-sex zone, as if such activities would gravitate there from far-off Scarborough or Etobicoke or even the downtown. Sex and drugs are not the sort of things people are usually prepared to take a ferry ride to obtain.

"I'm not sure how wholesome it is with the whole nude beach," he said, as justification of why the island should be the location. "If you look hard enough, you'll find somebody without pants on."

Another time he proposed a giant flagpole in his ward that would be a beacon to people entering the city from the north along Highway 400. "It's going to change everything, everything, in this community. It is going to make the livelihood in this community be a lot better, it's going to provide jobs for our kids in our high schools, the work that is going to come out, the restaurants, the boutiques, the coffee shops," he promised. "With that flagpole, that 50-storey flagpole, we'll attract every tourist into a community that has rarely seen a tourist." Why tired cottage-goers would get excited about a flagpole after being stuck in rural traffic for hours as they made their way back into the city was left out of his vision.

On another occasion in 2009 Mammoliti was one of three councillors photographed leaving the House of Lancaster, a strip joint on the Queensway in south Etobicoke. All claimed they were inspecting the premises at the invitation of the Adult Entertainment Association of Canada, a story the *Toronto Star* had a considerable amount of deadpan fun with. City politics can read like a story from the satirical newspaper *The Onion*.

Mammoliti isn't all topless entertainment, though: in 2014 he led a campaign to ban electronic dance music at the city-owned Canadian National Exhibition on whose board he sat. When Gord Perks, a city councillor from the downtown neighbourhood of Parkdale, and others were able to overturn the ban, Mammoliti called Parkdale a "paedophile district" and asked who Perks was really representing, throwing innuendo around like soggy dynamite.

Mammoliti's puritannical interests got downright prurient at times, for example, when a rather menacing version of himself showed up with a video camera at the 2011 Dyke March, the

Saturday women's parade that is part of the weekend Pride cel-
ebrations that take over the Church-Wellesley Village each year,
one of the biggest such festivals in the world. The run-up to that
year's parade, as in other recent years, had been marked by controversy over a group called Queers Against Israeli Apartheid
(QuAIA), which advocated for Palestinians living in the occupied
territories.

Never say that Toronto or its city hall are inward-looking,
because hot-button international issues can become debated
fiercely in a place that usually deals with much more routine
matters. Councillors ended up discussing Israeli policy in public
meetings because Pride is partially a city-funded event, to the
tune in 2011 of $130,000. Some councillors, and even John
Tory, while running for mayor in 2014, felt the "apartheid"
component of QuAIA's name constituted hate speech.

Mammoliti was one of the most vocal opponents of QuAIA
and advocated, with others, to defund Pride. Provocative to be
sure, the group's decision in 2011 was to not march in the larger
Sunday Pride parade, as they had the previous year, and instead
join the smaller Dyke March on Saturday. It was a move meant
to placate some of their critics, but not Mammoliti and a few
other councillors, or some of those in the media who were sympathetic to their cause.

What was heretofore a relatively obscure fringe group became
the centre of a recurring debate at city hall, putting QuAIA and
their message in the news often. They were famous, thanks to
the fuss Mammoliti and others made. It's a classic example of
"Streisand Effect," a phenomenon named after Barbra Streisand
who tried to have aerial photos of her Malibu home taken off a
website belonging to an advocacy group that had photographed
the entire California coastline, but in doing so inadvertently
brought international attention to the pictures of her estate.

Although QuAIA didn't achieve the same level of fame as Streisand's house, the Middle East is one of the political issues that has powerful currency in all levels of Canadian politics, even at the municipal level. Although the Toronto city manager had said the group did not, in fact, violate city policy, Mammoliti still showed up on the Saturday afternoon, lurking around with his video camera in the linear chain of parks on the east side of Yonge Street where the Dyke March was staging.

While walking my dog that day in our neighbourhood I saw Mammoliti standing in the street, his camera trained on a group of women a couple dozen metres away who were preparing for the march. Another councillor in attendance even shouted "Come on, Giorgio," exasperated with the scene he was making.

Pride, all of it, is intended to be a safe place and space for marginalized groups who often face harassment and even violence elsewhere, so the attentions of a man like Mammoliti take on malevolent overtones, especially when the guy behind the camera has said rather unkind things about the LGBT community in the past.

Mammoliti began his career as a member of Bob Rae's left-of-centre provincial government between 1990 and 1995, and it was during this time that he voted against his own government on Bill 167 in 1994, a proposed act that would have provided same-sex couples with the same rights as other common-law couples, ultimately sanctioning what would later come to be known as civil unions. In the provincial legislature Mammoliti said gays were unfit for parenting and prone to AIDS. Although in 2013 he apologized for those remarks, telling *Toronto Sun* reporter Don Peat he had "had the church literally write up my speech," a sting like that resonates a long time in the LGBT community. Not good, especially when the same man is now surveilling women in that community with a video camera.

DESPITE ALL this, Mammoliti has been in one elected office or another for twenty-five years. After he was defeated in the 1995 provincial election, he was elected as a member of the former North York city council, a position he held onto after North York was amalgamated with the rest of Toronto in 1998. Although his antics are too numerous and tedious to mention in full, they're set against a lifetime of political switcheroos and back-and-forth allegiances that are dizzying to follow. Once free of the NDP he began to embody the persona of a populist conservative while serving on city council, gravitating toward wherever there was political power or where he could find a powerful opposition perch, an attraction that explains his on-again, off-again relationship with his best political frenemy, Rob Ford.

In 2002, while both were city councillors under then mayor Mel Lastman, Rob Ford called Mammoliti a "Gino boy" during a council meeting, along with the words "goon," "idiot," and "scammer." Ford also once called Gloria Lindsay Luby, a rival councillor, a "waste of skin" during a 2005 council meeting. The drama may be on the level of *West Wing*, but the writing sure isn't.

After Ford's insult-slinging, Mammoliti admitted there was no love lost between the two of them when the *Star* reported on why he filed a complaint with the human rights office over Ford's words: "It's no secret we don't like each other . . . and we don't like each other's politics," he said. "But to attack my culture, to attack the Italian community and to be discriminatory that way was inappropriate."

No matter – that same year, journalist John Barber and Rob Ford were in an argumentative scrum in city council chambers that was caught on camera during the filming of a documentary called *Hogtown: The Politics of Policing*. In it Barber is heard saying, "Answer the question, you fat fuck," to Ford, who appeared to get considerable amusement from the slip. As Ford was pestering Barber, asking him to repeat what he said, Mammoliti joined in, asking, "Why did you do it?" with a rabid tone that suggests he didn't feel the honour of a friend was at stake, but that a media controversy was brewing and he wanted to be a part of it. Eventually Barber left the chamber, exiting onto the roof of the city hall podium building, the only apparent way to de-escalate the situation.

Later in the decade the pretence of that temporary friendship would again be dropped. Mammoliti made an erstwhile bid for the 2010 mayoralty, in opposition to what became the Ford steamroller. It was a challenge that was quickly forgotten after Mammoliti withdrew from the mayoral race in July, running again for his council seat and going so far as to endorse Ford for mayor. After they both won that election, Mammoliti returned to his seat in council chambers positioned conveniently next to newly elected Mayor Ford, a proximity that reflected the newfound bond between the two. They developed an in-council connection that in terms of loyalty was second only to that shared between Rob and his brother Doug.

Famously, when a motion at council went to the vote, Mammoliti played an enforcer roll that involved his thumb. If the Fords approved of an item, Mammoliti would hold his thumb up, signalling to loyalists on council that they should vote in favour of it. If his thumb was down, they were to vote against it. It was a kind of whipped vote in a place where this kind of thing is usually done behind the scenes or off to the side in private in one-on-one conversations between councillors and the mayor. The thumb became a thing, for a while anyway.

After Rob Ford's funeral, Mammoliti issued a statement titled "Dirty Half Dozen" that laid into a handful of councillors who, apart from being long-time opponents of Ford, had attended the funeral. "If I die tomorrow, these six people need not attend the funeral," read the letter, noting the day City Council turned its back on Ford while he gave a speech at the height of his tumultuous mayoralty. "Even God was squirming in his own house with their presence" and "vermin that dwell in the underbelly of Toronto" were some of the phrases Mammoliti used in his letter, apparently even more steadfastly loyal to Ford now that he was dead.

WHILE MAMMOLITI is an intense presence on the floor of council and at city hall, his relationship with his own ward can be top-down and heavy-handed, with real consequences on the ground. In the summer of 2013 I was tipped off to a situation in a Ward 7 park that was described to me as "Toronto's saddest park," so I went for a long bike ride up the Humber River to see for myself.

At first glance, Rowntree Mills Park seems like yet another fantastic green space in the Humber River Valley, part of the area's unsung beauty and a continuation of a chain of parks and trails that connects neighbourhoods together, all the way down to Lake Ontario itself seventeen kilometres south. Rowntree is between Kipling and Islington Avenues in the northwest corner of the ward, just south of the Vaughan-Toronto border. The paved trail that meanders all the way up from the lake ends at Steeles, as Vaughan and much of the 905 region don't have the extensive trail system Toronto does, although work is slowly being done to improve that. There were even cottages here once, when this was still a rural landscape, until they were swept away by Hurricane Hazel in 1954. Rowntree is part of the flood plain that was protected from development after that cataclysmic event, a gift bestowed by accident that the city enjoys today.

Rowntree should have been an active place, filled with weekend picnickers like the rest of the ravine system is in the summer, but in 2009 Mammoliti had the park gates closed to cars due to reports of criminal activity and loud, rowdy parties where people would leave a wake of trash in the park.

Although it may go against the logic that suggests cars shouldn't be in parks, his decree turned what was once a busy, well-used park into a nearly deserted expanse of grass and forests. People needed cars to bring in their picnic supplies and to transport older family members. Empty parking lots meant an empty park.

When travelling the long ravine and valley trails like the Humber's one feels a rhythm to them, a pattern alternating between sections of dense forest and narrow trails, where there might only be one or two other people on a weekday, and between places that feel quite wild and others that resemble more formal parks found in Toronto neighbourhoods – wide open, with parking lots, washrooms, and easy access from the surrounding city.

Rowntree was one of those great parks, but when I arrived on a beautiful day in July the empty parking lots and unused picnic tables were downright spooky, giving the scene a too-quiet feeling that felt reminiscent of the Australian gothic horror film *Picnic at Hanging Rock* (where a class of Victorian schoolgirls visits a rock formation on a hot day but, mysteriously, a few of them disappear – creating a daylight terror that plays out as the cicadas buzz and breeze blows). There was nothing immediately menacing in Rowntree, but the emptiness was disconcerting.

"It's more dangerous now because nobody is there," Sana Hefez told me. She was a program worker at the nearby Delta Family Resource Centre and she had arranged for me to meet with a group of kids from the SWAG (Students Working Together as a Group) environment club run out of the centre who were hoping that the closed-gate policy in the park would change. Sana's sense – that despite the ban on cars, crime still exists in the park – again echoes urban theorist Jane Jacobs's famous "eyes on the street" concept, which says that generally the more people are out and about, the safer the community is, a sentiment Idil Burale shared across the Humber River in Ward 1. Since the ban and the decrease in human activity in the park, there had been a dramatic increase in wildlife. On a solo bike ride there I came within a few dozen metres of a grazing deer that seemed only mildly interested in my presence. Posted signs also alert passersby to a coyote presence.

"Bambi's family lives down here," said Aman Nahan, a then sixteen-year-old member of SWAG on the walk we took through the park, alluding to the wildlife that has moved in due to the absence of people. Nahan and his fellow club members had lived by the park most of their young lives and had recently organized a cleanup, because illegal dumping had become a problem.

The students, while acknowledging the park's previous troubles, thought a better solution could be found than simply closing the park to cars, and were suggesting more police patrols, paid parking with monitoring, or even security cameras. But with few people using the park, they too kept away from it.

Closing it and forgetting about it wasn't an option for them. "It could really be a 'city in a park,' like the Toronto signs say," said Eileen Santos, another teenaged club member. "But I wouldn't come here alone now." Henry-Mathieu complained of Mammoliti's other similarly heavy-handed approaches to perceived trouble in parks, saying that he had taken down basketball nets in the Chalkfarm neighbourhood.

As we walked along one of Rowntree's paths on the west side of the Humber, the kids from SWAG and I ran into a City of Toronto employee doing some work on the trail. Amicable but not willing to go on the record, he did mention that since the closure he too had seen a dramatic increase in the amount of wildlife that has made its way into this part of the park, absent of so many people.

He was ambivalent about the closure but clearly had a great affection for the place. Although he said it was a shame more people couldn't use it, he also lamented the way some park users treated it, leaving garbage behind. On the other hand, the increased wildlife was rather spectacular.

Rowntree was never completely closed. It could still be reached on foot or bicycle, but to bring a car now required a special permit – a level of bureaucratic hassle that prevented the easy picnics enjoyed elsewhere. Toronto is still a car city in many ways, especially here, where distances to neighbourhood destinations are much greater than downtown.

Cars facilitate the hundreds of weekend summer picnics that happen in parks across the city. Rowntree is a big park, and lugging barbecue supplies and coolers for a day's fun can be an ordeal. At heart this problem is about design. The postwar city makes it difficult to get by without a car. And it's ironic that Mammoliti, a councillor whose record is firmly pro-car, would ban cars at Rowntree.

ROWNTREE ISN'T a nature preserve like Algonquin Park. While it may be the edge of Toronto's municipal boundary, it's in the middle of a metropolitan area and should play a more critical role in the overall urban health of the surrounding neighbourhoods. On Rowntree's eastern side is a large neighbourhood of postwar single-family homes, some attached, others not. Many have incredibly lush vegetable gardens – evidence of the large

Italian population here – with zucchinis creeping under and fruit trees frothing over the backyard fences. The streets are well treed, the lawns are manicured and nourished, and the driveways are often hosed clean.

Known as Humber Summit, this neighbourhood also has a large South Asian population, with many shops and restaurants along Islington. Although somewhat spread out and car-oriented, it's also rather urban in terms of the variety and streetscape along Islington.

The west side of the river is much different, with high-rise apartments and condo buildings found in a north-south strip of land between Kipling Avenue and the edge of the Humber ravine. The towers across the river, including Panorama Court (where Idil Burale wanted to activate the dead space around the buildings), all line Rowntree Park like the towers do along Central Park in New York, rising above the tree canopy. On the ground, though, these buildings lack easy connections to the park and so heading down into the ravine is somewhat daunting. Only a few forested and ill-maintained paths slope down to the bridges that cross the Humber, which one must do to get to the park proper.

There are fences between many of the towers too, typical of these kinds of segregated developments that prevent residents from moving as freely as they should. The National Film Board's ground-breaking interactive documentary *High Rise* featured residents of these Kipling Avenue towers, some of whom spoke of the disconnect between their homes and the nearby ravine; despite the beautiful view they have of the Humber Valley and city beyond, it felt out of reach. Some *High Rise* participants thought of the park as a frightening place, even though it's so close to their home. The park closure by Mammoliti has only made this disconnect worse, and has discouraged the enjoyment of what could be one of Toronto's great urban parks. For a population without backyards of their own nearby, Rowntree could be like Morningside Park in Scarborough. Morningside is something to see when it's in full swing on a summer day, and an example of what Rowntree could be if made more of through better leadership.

When you are approaching Morningside Park, following a chain of parks and ravine trails much like Humber's, you will first hear the bass coming through the trees, then smell the food. As the Highland Creek trail leads into the park's vast expanse of lawn, the people finally come into view, sometimes hundreds of them on a peak summertime weekend. They'll be scattered over a few dozen picnics. Some will be playing games, soccer or badminton, and one or two will have a generator powering a big sound system playing hip hop, reggae, Motown.

People dance, on the grass, and in the sun. Kids play and yell. Couples linger under a tree or wander away slowly from the bigger group, trying not to be too obvious, perhaps disappearing into the forest for a spell to do the various things two people alone do. It's Toronto, so you might catch a whiff of weed competing with the smell of charcoal briquette smoke. This is the most comfortable the city gets. Even when you are passing through alone on a bike ride or hike as an interloper, the happiness is infectious.

The draw of cottage country and the backyard pools removes a large proportion of the city's middle class from city parks in the summertime, but Toronto's waterfront and the interconnected ravine system remain a summertime party for those left in the city. Variations of the scene at Morningside are repeated all around the city in places like E. T. Seton Park adjacent to Thorncliffe Park's apartment tower cluster, along Sunnyside

Beach or at Bluffers Park, and by the mouth of the Rouge River on the Pickering border.

There are yet more picnickers still in Earl Bales Park in North York, or Thomson Memorial Park in Scarborough, and in the upper reaches of the east and west branches of the Humber River as it snakes through the north of Etobicoke and Rexdale. These parks, like the Toronto Islands, are cottage country for the uncottaged, and embraced and cherished by the communities that use them.

A summer bike ride through the ravine system is an endless tour of these picnics. If you didn't know better it might seem like an organized festival called "Ravine Day" but it's mostly ad hoc, organized individually by families and small groups. Even on the hottest day there will be those who dress formally: men in slacks and dress shirts, women in flowing saris, the evolution of the great Edwardian photos that can be found in the archives of Toronto, where old Toronto WASPs dressed in their Sunday best while playing baseball or croquet in one of the ravines near Rosedale. Today it's a Toronto sartorial tradition kept alive mostly by New Canadians in so many parks, a kind of formality of leisure dress that seems lost in an era of board shorts and untucked T-shirts.

It's counterintuitive, but just as Parks Canada is having trouble getting a new generation of Canadians to embrace the national park system, an attraction to natural spaces happens easily in the country's biggest and densest urban centre. Rouge Park is set, despite some political and bureaucratic delays, to become Canada's first urban national park in a city where people are already in the parks. Now is an ideal time to exploit how Canadians in the city use their natural spaces and update the clichéd image of Canadians travelling far from cities to embrace nature.

Getting more people into the ravines won't happen entirely naturally, though: the city will need new ways of transporting people into the ravines, especially to parks in suburban areas like Ward 7. They may be in the city, part of its landscape, but access is an issue. These places are sometimes too hard to get to without a car and too often lack essential amenities such as public washrooms.

As more people move to Toronto, the ravine and park system we have will become increasingly critical to the quality of life here. The City of Toronto has put together a "ravine strategy" that addresses these and other issues, with plans for improvement. The ravines give people living in urban landscapes, whether downtown or suburban, a connection to Canada's founding myth of wilderness and rural landscapes. They also connect the city's neighbourhoods, despite the indifference of Mammoliti and others.

The ravines have seen elections and politicians come and go; they've been clear-cut and reforested, industrialized and cleaned up. The ravines were here long before the street grid was laid defiantly over their natural contours, crossed with bridges that make no gesture toward what's below, effectively pushing the ravines out of our collective imagination. Sometimes we even buried them. The ravines go back the entire 12,000 years of history here, well past the brief colonial episode we're more frequently reminded of in the city's history. They were used extensively by First Nations communities, yet the historic and geographic connections these features provided to this city have largely been forgotten – as have the many other ways the city is interconnected when the focus has been on what divides it, in Rowntree or in the middle of the city. That's why these ravines are so critical to Toronto, a city that rapidly changes.

The ravines are the city's memory, as author and Toronto's current Poet Laureate Anne Michaels has written, the constants that are unconcerned about arbitrary political boundaries and political divides between suburb and downtown. If Toronto ever needs a symbol to rally around, perhaps it should be a ravine because they connect all of it. The ravines, and the raccoons in them, should be the city's mascots. Not all of them are treated as shabbily as Rowntree.

BLYTHWOOD RAVINE runs through the middle of the Lawrence Park neighbourhood in North Toronto. It's a pleasant ravine in a wealthy neighbourhood. Sometimes Burke Brook is visible, other times it's buried, playing peek-a-boo along the way. The ravine arrives from the northwest, crossing Yonge Street, eventually running alongside Sunnybrook Hospital, eventually flowing into the Don River. It's a minor ravine and creek relative to the scale of some others, but it offers an off-the-grid link that connects Midtown with the Don Valley and everything in between.

Bythwood is just a few blocks south of the geographic centre of Toronto found on Wanless Crescent. There should be a marker of some kind here, perhaps an obelisk, that indicates this is the centre of a massive city of nearly three million people, a small connection to something greater.

Cities are the sum of their parts and the ravines are the city's local connections to the rest of the city. Imagine if a place as critical and as well used by local residents as Blythwood Ravine in North Toronto had its access curtailed. It wouldn't stand, and the residents there, all with ample agency, wealth, and political and social capital, would do something about it.

Yet Rowntree remained locked for a few years before enough momentum led to some change, led in no small part by the kids from SWAG who created their own political capital. When I contacted Mammoliti's office at the time I was promised a response but none was forthcoming. Later Mammoliti said public consultations about the future of the park would be held, and in spring 2014 the park was reopened on a trial basis in time for Victoria Day – the first time in four years.

In July 2014, after Mammoliti had wound down his mayoral campaign and returned to his council run against Henry-Mathieu and others, I received an email from a nearby resident who told me that at one of those meetings regarding the future of the park, only those living directly beside the park on the eastern, Humber Summit side, were allowed in, and that a security guard barred access to others. Members of Parks People, a non-profit advocacy organization for Toronto parks, were also prevented from entering that meeting.

"Residents only" and the like are phrases that come up from time to time during some contentious community meetings. Although these restrictions are ostensibly to allow residents to have a free and open discussion, there's often a whiff about them of keeping out "outside agitators" from other parts of the city, concerned members of civil society, or the media. However, a subsequent Rowntree meeting was open to all after the increased community pressure and Mammoliti moved forward with a plan to open one of the parking lots on the weekends. But what an effort and extended period of time it took.

It's never a surprise when politicians become more attentive during an election year, but Mammoliti's manic and unpredictable approach to populist politics continues to have many people in Toronto, regardless of their political stripe, wondering how he has been elected and re-elected so many times, keeping him in office for over twenty years despite changes in his party affiliation and the factions he's loyal to.

In May and August of 2014, before and after he dropped out of the mayoral race and re-entered the council one, the *Toronto Star*'s Daniel Dale conducted interviews with dozens of area residents to answer the question "Who votes for Giorgio Mammoliti?" Dale's conclusion was that there wasn't much difference between those who do and those who don't vote for him.

Dale's interviews revealed that most voters aren't aware of his history but are mainly concerned about local issues, just as Idil Burale found on the other side of the Humber River – suggesting a Toronto spin on Bill Clinton's 1992 campaign slogan "It's the economy, stupid" could be "It's the potholes, stupid."

WHAT HAPPENS at city hall simply doesn't matter to many voters in Toronto, a truth Henry-Mathieu discovered when people laughed at him when he spoke seriously about bigger issues at city hall. A senior from Italy who had lived in the area for over forty years told Dale she voted for Mammoliti because problems with snow removal were taken care of when his office was called. Another resident said he made the intersection of Sheppard Avenue and Weston Road nice with flower baskets, and that was enough. Yet another man said he didn't vote for him because a requested lightpost wasn't installed.

Other stories were similar; people were swayed for or against him based on small issues that could usually be seen from the individual's front lawn. The bigger issues just aren't part of the equation, even if a change there would directly benefit things that can be seen from those lawns. Although Toronto is entrenched in ideology and behind-the-scenes party politics, many voters are free of such bonds and will vote for the candidate that has either solved their problems or connected with them emotionally, telling them they matter.

The variables of retail politics and charisma result in the most unlikely of dovetails: there were many voters in Toronto who were as moved by Jack Layton when he was leader of the federal NDP as they were by Rob Ford, and many voted for them both, in various elections. Ford himself had admired Layton, saying that when Layton was a city councillor before his jump to federal politics, Layton was the only one who was nice to him and respected him around city hall.

While Mammoliti certainly lacks either Ford's or Layton's particular brand of charisma, Henri-Mathieu saw that he shared one characteristic with the Fords – the ability to appear as the underdog despite his millionaire status.

"The perception that the media is 'out to get' the Fords or Councillor Mammoliti was very widespread and some people were just unwilling to hear anything else," he said after the election was finished. "I found myself having to take breaks from canvassing every now and then just to get composed and to remind myself why I was doing this."

The underdog factor, his skill at retail politics, and the momentum of incumbency were enough to return Mammoliti to his council seat in October 2014, winning with a little over 6,800 votes. It was no runaway victory, as his closest competitor, Nick Di Nizio, ran a formidable campaign and was able to garner nearly 5,300 votes, suggesting that Mammoliti's twenty-year-run here is vulnerable. Despite his efforts in the towers and on the streets to court people who have been left out of the political spotlight in Ward 7 and Toronto, Henry-Mathieu came in sixth with just 471 votes, with no other challengers breaking 1,000 votes.

"Knowing what I know now about elections, I could probably write a trilogy of books on what I will need to do differently next time," said Keegan Henry-Mathieu, after the results were in. "I think the most important lesson for me was that I'll need to be more of a politician and less of an activist." Henry-Mathieu was getting at the challenge many idealistic people face when running for office: in order to get elected, a successful candidate usually has to make some compromises.

Those unwilling to budge might call it "selling out," an easy accusation to make from the sidelines, but Henry-Mathieu says a respect for the science and mechanics of winning election campaigns is something he learned on the fly.

"Often times I'd find myself slipping back into activist-mode, rejecting the limited conventional election wisdom we could get from other more experienced campaigns that opened their doors to us for advice." His thoughts were echoed in spring of 2016 by President Barack Obama, when he delivered a commencement speech at Howard University, telling graduates that getting a seat at the table can bring about change more effectively than yelling from the outside.

"I'm sure the fact that I was the eldest on my campaign, at twenty-six years old, didn't help matters, because no one ever really challenged my resistance to conventional wisdom. We were all a bunch of young policy wonks with zero electoral experience," he says. "I'm extremely proud of the outcome of my campaign. People now know what I stand for. We were noticed; that's really all I could ever hope for going into my first campaign. People now know I'm a young activist, who works as a banker on Bay Street with some pretty progressive ideas on how to build a better city."

With turnout as low as it is, there aren't many active voters to sway, and new ones remain reluctant to engage in a system they see as irrelevant, so new voices like Henry-Mathieu have a tough time breaking into city council.

"Residents across the ward feel like they've seen and heard

it all from politicians, and that no one is strong enough to make the transformational changes we need," he says. "Running for council definitely confirmed my worries that people are starting to give up the fight for a better Toronto and accept the status quo. Hope is just a little hard to find in York West right now."

It's the continued inequality in the city that worries Henry-Mathieu, and keeps him thinking about a 2018 run for city council. "I'm still convinced that if we continue on the path that we are on as a city, we will continue to see inequalities in our city grow to epic proportions. Toronto is still the child poverty capital of Canada. You know things are bad when our Walmart stores start keeping baby formula under lock and key. For the first time in a long time, the current generation of young people might just end up being poorer and worse off than their parents' and grandparents' generations. It's a scary prospect. York West is the microcosm of those realities."

CHAPTER SIX

HOW THE RULES CHANGED DURING THE SEASON OF HATE

THE YORK Civic Centre sits perched above the Black Creek River, just north of where Eglinton descends into the river valley west of Keele Street. The view from the centre is impressive, commanding – suitable for what was once the City of York's city hall. Inside the centre is a small museum with artefacts from York, and out front is perhaps the saddest time capsule around. Such buried memorials usually mark optimistic moments, looking forward, meant to remind prosperous civic descendants of what came before them. The City of York's is more of a tombstone, though; a memorial inscribed with the words "This Time Capsule to be opened in 2193 was buried in 1997 as a Farewell to the City of York." The year 2193 will mark the 400th anniversary of the incorporation of the Township of York in 1793 and a quadricentennial celebration that will never happen.

Cities aren't founded with an endgame in mind or a plan to dismantle them. Instead, great effort goes into building up a civic mythology, a sense of place and identity, for the residents who live there. The memorial on Eglinton reveals the melancholy York experienced in the late 1990s, a place still waiting to return to some of its former, optimistic glory.

"The thing that bothers me is the transience," said Lekan Olawoye of the empty and half-occupied storefronts on Eglinton Avenue further up the slope east of Keele. "I don't know what it is, the people here work hard, but nearby residents don't shop here. The local BIA [Business Improvement Area] doesn't have a lot of resources."

Olawoye was running for the Ward 12 York-South Weston council seat and we were standing in an area known as Eglinton Hill, a busy commercial strip that struggles the way many main streets do in Toronto, off the radar of trendy, prosperous Torontonians and competing with regional malls that draw their customer base away. This is the other side of gentrification, where retail strips struggle to make a go of it, while local residents wish there was something more to attract them to their main strip. The City of York and the former borough of East York were the two poorest of the six municipalities of Metropolitan Toronto, lacking the varied tax base other wards enjoyed.

Olawoye said the ward is roughly 40 per cent buildings of one kind or another, and 60 per cent single-family homes, with those houses ranging from an eclectic assortment of working-class homes to million-dollar ones in some northern neighbourhoods of what was once North York. Bounded at the north by Highway 401, Ward 12 is somewhat wedge-shaped and looks like the state of Nevada. It is bounded on the west by Jane Street and the rail corridor that carries both the GO Train and the Union-Pearson (UP) Express to the airport, and on the east by the CNR rail line. It tapers to an end around Rogers Road in the south. The name Eglinton Hill is no false boast; the area north and south of the strip is quite hilly.

The view west to Etobicoke, across the Humber River Valley and beyond, is unexpectedly panoramic, with clusters of high-rises poking up through the lush green canopy into the distance. The two-storey shops along Eglinton line the street like a giant staircase stepping down and have a pre- and post-war low-rise nobility to them, some with their original Vitrolite facades intact, the same elegant opaque glass tiling that was used on the interior of the original subway stations along Yonge Street.

The adjacent neighbourhood is Toronto's secret San Francisco, with steep streets, staircases, and unusual views of houses built in one of the hilliest parts of a city that is often thought to be flat, complete with California-style urbanism rolling across minor valleys, houses climbing up either side. It's some of the most unsung topography in Toronto and not part of the city's idea of itself in the way that Los Angeles embraces the Hollywood Hills, but it should be. Apart from the hills, the area is laced with ravine greenbelts, some the result of buried tributaries that flow into nearby Black Creek.

A hidden gem near the 401 is North Park, located east of Keele and north of Lawrence Avenue. Surrounded by homes, North Park's ravine is deep and its forest unusually thick and the sound of rushing water echoes up through utility covers at the bottom of the ravine. It's a fairytale landscape surrounded by culs-de-sac, and a secret to everyone but the locals. It's typical of Toronto's mix of urban and wild, a hybrid landscape where these buried creeks also contain some of the simmering problems of the city.

"There's a lot of basement flooding problems here," said Olawoye. "People feel like they've been neglected." There has been an increase in "severe weather events" that overwhelm the city's infrastructure, which is long overdue for renewal and reinvestment. The water also arrives faster and at greater volume, because much of the city is covered with impermeable surfaces now, which prevents the water from being absorbed where it falls. As a result it starts to run, and run fast. Down-spouts attached to drains contribute to the problem of over-whelmed sewers.

I saw this myself in the summer of 2013. I was on a bike ride through the lower part of the area near Rogers Road when I was caught in an intense downpour. Standing under a tree in the rain only works for about a minute before it trickles through the leaves, so I took shelter under the awning of a house that was divided into a few apartments, feeling a bit transgressive standing on private property, but the rain was fierce. After twenty minutes of intense rain, a river of water was rushing out from behind the house into the swollen street gutters, eventually filling the entire street. When the rain subsided I ventured out, the water still rushing on the ground.

In low-lying streets the water was a foot or more deep, pouring into basements through windows and doors. A man tried to unblock a storm sewer with a metal pole, in the process losing one of the Crocs he was wearing. He pursued his clog, splashing through the wake created by drivers who insisted on driving the flooded streets, even as the water immersed half their engine and they couldn't see obstacles like open sewers. This street had been dry just a half-hour before, and the speed of the flooding seemed like something out of the American West, where dry riverbeds flood quickly.

Yet, it's commonplace in Toronto now, with dramatic reports of cars stuck on the Don Valley Parkway, Highway 427, or downtown rail underpasses, sitting up to their windows in water. Here in hill country it seems counterintuitive that it should flood, yet it does.

Around the corner from where I had seen the man and his Crocs, water was cascading down the GO Train embankment onto Rogers Road, carrying debris and muck into the road. I followed the water as it poured downhill, toward the west and Black Creek along the route of the buried Lavender Creek.

THE GREATER Toronto Area has many creeks and rivers. Some, like the Credit, Humber, and Don rivers, are open-air, but others are buried or put into concrete channels, like much of Black Creek, Toronto's smaller version of the Los Angeles River. Garrison Creek is the most well known of the buried lot, but there are dozens across the GTA, and every dip in the landscape could be hiding one. Some have names, others don't, and they can be difficult to follow as the modern city is built overtop them.

"It's like a syncopation, back and forth between the street grid and the meandering creek," said Helen Mills, one of the people behind Lost Rivers, a project by the Toronto Green Community that has been mapping and advocating for buried creeks since the mid-1990s. "It's a kind of music, but you can lose the beat and forget which creek you're on."

I had asked Mills to go for a walk with me to trace Lavender's course through the area, which was in part an effort to understand where all the water goes and why places like this can flood. Lavender's headwaters are found around Fairbank Park on Dufferin Street, a few blocks south of Eglinton, where it's buried among the houses.

"These are all drumlins," said Mills – rolling hills created by glaciers. Long after the glaciers receded, working-class folks built their own houses in these hills, developing a kind of feral suburb in the early twentieth century. An unplanned neighbourhood, the homes here have a magnificent variety of look and style as they climb the ridges of what were Lavender's ravine walls.

The name *Lavender* suggests it could be Toronto's most beautiful creek, but modernity hasn't been kind to it. The creek might for a spell have flowed by these homes when they were new. Mills says it's likely that the creek then became quite foul with sewage and other matter, so that the municipality decided to bury it in a sewer pipe as they did with so many other watercourses.

During our walk tracing the creek we came to Charles Caccia Park. It sits at the bottom of a residential valley, where a massive basement-flooding protection-program project was underway, with a skyscraper-sized hole dug and a giant crane lowering materials deep into it. The new sewer overflow tank being installed here is meant to relieve both surface and basement flooding during storms and to reduce the amount of untreated water that discharges into Lake Ontario. The flooding here has been Lavender's revenge, what we've reaped by bulldozing and paving natural systems that once took care of the water and moved it to where it belonged.

West of the park and construction, the creek crosses Prospect Cemetery, still buried underground as it was as unsightly for the dead as it was for the living, with bodies now buried in the fill above it, a kind of urban layering that seems like something out of the first *Poltergeist* film. At Bert Robinson Park a long corrugated-steel pedestrian tunnel allows passage underneath an embankment carrying the Barrie GO Train rails, after which the creek continues in a southwest direction, crossing under the Rogers and Old Weston Roads intersection, and flowing under Hillary Avenue.

Here, according to Ian Wheal of the Lost Rivers project, when the houses here were first built, they had plank bridges crossing the then exposed creek to reach their front doors. In 2015 the street was completely torn up to lay new sewer pipes, because flooding has been a problem here too. Around the corner, past a Beer Store built atop the creek on the corner of Lavender Road and a dead-end segment of Keele Street, is a chain-link fence at the exact southern edge of Olawoye's ward. And just behind that lies the first exposed part of the creek, ingloriously oozing out of a sewer grate through trash.

On one of her maps, Mills pointed out that a brickworks had once been here adjacent to the creek – now there's a massive junkyard instead, its fence seemingly heaving out from the weight of all the cars piled behind it. Lavender trickles through this ugly-looking place, beautiful-sounding if you close your eyes and listen to the birds chirp, then disappears again under the old Grand Trunk Railway embankment, eventually empty-ing into Black Creek a kilometre or so to the west.

Infrastructure investment is hardly a sexy big-ticket item, but as Olawoye heard from residents when he was canvassing, a flooded basement gets people's attention quickly. Projects the size and cost of the one in Charles Caccia Park can just seem to happen, without the opposition that projects usually receive. Homeowners, when under threat, make politicians listen to them.

"When I go door to door, people complain about neglect," said Olawoye, pointing out potholed streets and some derelict houses in the area that haven't been dealt with. "We work hard, just pay attention to us, they tell me." It's the same sentiment heard across many of Toronto's outer wards. "We don't have representatives that understand the new, post-amalgamation Toronto," said Olawoye. "People here don't take an us versus them position, but there is a feeling here of being left out. 'We know we're entitled to stuff' is something we hear a lot at the door." Entitlement to stuff created the Scarborough Subway, but here there's something more useful coming: the Eglinton Crosstown LRT.

BACK ON Eglinton, Olawoye pointed out places that are busy along the strip by his campaign office, such as a Jamaican Bakery and a Portuguese barbecue restaurant that draw people in from other neighbourhoods and are robust businesses despite the general decline of area retail. Change is coming soon, though. We walked by Eglinton Crosstown construction, part of a nineteen-kilometre-long project that will see trains run from Black Creek Drive and the Mount Dennis neighbourhood in the west to Kennedy Station in Scarborough to the east. It will essentially function as a subway would (except with smaller cars), travelling underground from Keele to Laird stations.

Where this kind of transit investment occurs, development is sure to follow. "I know some business owners have already had visits from developers asking to buy them out," said Olawoye. "How do we keep diversity on the street and maintain the York-South vibe?" He'd like to see the local Business Improvement Area strengthened, to keep local businesses intact and provide the kind of services the neighbourhood needs. As development pressure increases along the new transit line, retail rents are sure to go up, because there are no commercial rent controls in Toronto as there are for some residential buildings.

When he was a community activist, he was also involved in trying to keep the TD Bank branch at the corner of Eglinton and Keele from closing. Although it eventually moved north to Lawrence, he said the bank compromised by leaving ATMs in the area so seniors wouldn't have to travel to another neighbourhood to get their banking done. Full-service neighbourhoods are something we take for granted when we have them. "TD was there for sixty years," he said. "My frustration was also that the cheque-cashing places start to come in when they leave."

Those cheque-cashing outlets, with the promise of quick and easy money, are neighbourhood vultures, in the long term sucking out wealth like a casino but without the thrill of a possible jackpot. Spotting them on retail strips is a quick way to gauge the general economic health of any neighbourhood.

Keeping the neighbourhood a place all people can afford to live now and after the LRT is finished is a continuing challenge, illustrated when I followed Olawoye into the Syme Woolner Neighbourhood and Family Centre on Eglinton near what will be Caledonia Station. Around noon on the day we visited, the drop-in centre was crowded.

"We have an affordable-food shortage here," says Olawoye. "This ward has one of the highest child impoverishment rates in the city." The centre has food and clothing banks, meal programs, employment services, harm reduction and other programs. It's one thing to look at poverty statistics in the city, but being inside one of the many centres like Syme Woolner across the city puts faces to the numbers. The busyness of these places drives home the need in Toronto and a sense of just how many people have been left out of the city's prosperous story. Like London and Paris, Toronto follows a European pattern in which communities in the inner city are wealthier, and poverty, and its attendant problems, orbit around the inner city, often out of sight.

While Toronto has not suffered the kind of civil unrest that the inner suburbs of Paris and London have experienced, the same potential for trouble exists here, when youth face diminishing prospects in their lives.

Olawoye led me down the Eglinton Hill to the busy Keele intersection where there are constant lines waiting for one of the buses going by, evidence of the need for the higher order of transit that is coming. We went into a barber shop on the northwest corner. It's a time-honoured tradition for politicians to wander into these kinds of places: getting a haircut is a chatty experience, and a captive one too. You have to talk, or listen, whether you want to or not.

The man in the seat didn't say much, because the barber, "Captain" – or Kirk Stephens as he's otherwise known – chatted with Olawoye about the neighbourhood. "This area needs representation for the youth," said Captain, with warm concern. "There's nothing for them to do here, they just stand around like fungus. It's hard enough for parents to just put food on the table. Nobody represents the youth."

Captain's place is directly across Eglinton from York Memorial Collegiate Institute, a public high school, so there are youth hanging around the front of his shop at lunch, when we were there, and after school. Barbers, when not cutting hair, do a lot of looking out the window, and they're some of the keenest observers of neighbourhood life. And like bartenders, they're some of the best listeners too, amassing a kind of institutional knowledge of the local area. Captain watched the construction of the Keele LRT station in front of his shop. "I know it's going to change here, but we need it to change with the people," he said. "It's not about poor or rich, the potential is here. We need somebody fuelling the community though."

ONE OF the many mayoral debates during the 2014 campaign took place across the street from Captain's place, in York Memorial's auditorium. Unlike elections for higher levels of government, where just one debate in each language can be the norm, the mayoral candidates schlep all over town from one debate to another – events sponsored by various media organizations, community groups, and institutions – sometimes attending more than one in a day.

York Memorial was also the site of the public debate debut of Doug Ford. It was September 2014, and Doug had recently replaced brother Rob on the mayoral ticket. He was facing off against John Tory and Olivia Chow, the only remaining big name candidates running that late in the race. Even before the debate began, the scene was raucous, as chants of "We Want Doug" were heard throughout the audience. Just after the debate began, one heckler was removed after refusing to sit down or be quiet, all to the screams and shouts of other spectators, a sign of things to come.

During the debate, a man named Earl Cowan, who identified himself as a Ford supporter, shouted, "Go home, Olivia! Back to China!" Another in the crowd then shouted, "She's Chinese! She's not Canadian!" *National Post* writer Christie Blatchford reported that when she went to speak to Cowan after the debate, he was proud of what he called his "racism."

After the debate Doug Ford distanced himself from the comments, saying, "We have tens and thousands of supporters out there, I want to make it very, very clear I don't condone that."

The wild, nasty, and explosive energy in the auditorium had been building for some time. The lid on Toronto's nasty side – a side that has always been there but just out of view of people who weren't on the direct receiving end of its abuses – had blown off during the Ford years. It was around the time of this debate that Kristyn Wong-Tam, a gay member of council representing the downtown ward, home to the Gay Village, received a piece of mail that said, "I hope you get AIDS and die in public office," signed by somebody who said they were a supporter of Ford Nation.

"Toronto the Good" isn't supposed to operate like this, but Toronto the Good is long dead. Although Doug Ford often tried to rein in their more vigorous supporters, Rob had unleashed the public expression of what used to simmer under the surface by making it, by example, okay to say awful things – revealing perhaps a more honest, if uglier, portrait of this city. It was a season of hate with many low points. The rules that were once abided by in Toronto seemed not to matter anymore.

A couple of months before the infamous York Memorial debate, on the evening of July 25, to be precise, I stood at dusk in Thompson Memorial Park in Scarborough, listening to a cover band play rock and pop hits on a stage at the bottom of a gentle slope that formed a natural amphitheatre. I was there with thousands of people, many wearing FORD NATION T-shirts. Members of the Ford family moved around the scene doing media scrums, as their fans crowded around the bright TV lights, chanting, "Ford More Years." One supporter even wore a shirt with "Doug Ford for Prime Minister" emblazoned across it.

As I stood observing the scene in the fading light – including the line-up for free hamburgers, hundreds of metres long, snaking through the park, next to the equally long line of people waiting to see Rob Ford himself, holding court "like a sultan in his tent," as Toronto writer Jonathan Goldsbie described the scene – it seemed like a bizarre version of Woodstock and reminded me again of a tent revival. But it most certainly wasn't a political event.

It wasn't a political event, because political events cannot be held in public spaces, and Thompson Park is a public space, so even if this event looked exactly like one, it wasn't. "Ford Fest," as the event was billed by the Ford family, is something they had held here at Thompson Park before, and at Etobicoke's Centennial Park earlier in the year. Previously these gatherings had been held at the Ford family compound – like the rally back in 2010 I attended, with all the friendly strangers – where political speeches were made and enemies of the Fords denounced.

The Fords said the event got too big for their mom's backyard, so it moved to the parks, meaning it was the same political event.

A week earlier, a city spokesperson said the Ford rally didn't break the rules, because the Fords hadn't described it as a political event on their permit application but instead as a "special event open to the public." Toronto is a city famous for its rule-abiding officiousness – with a by-law for everything, and another by-law dictating how *that* by-law will be obeyed – yet here was another example of what kept happening during the Ford years: over and over, whenever a blind eye was turned to bent or broken rules or antics that heretofore would scarcely have been tolerated, it was when the Fords were behind the misbehaviour.

None of that makes sense in Toronto where "No ball or hockey playing" signs greet children on neighbourhood streets and by-law officers fanatically patrol parks looking for off-leash dogs. People on the Island beaches enjoying a reasonable drink can receive fines for having open bottles of Niagara white, although the escarpment where the grapes are grown is visible just across the lake. The rules are simply followed in Toronto, or so we're led to believe living here, but the Fords changed that the way Trump changed what normal is during the American presidential campaign of 2016.

The non-political event in Scarborough back in 2014 saw the presence of LGBT activists who came to question the mayor about his observed tradition of not attending the Pride parade and the homophobic remarks he had made in the past. Certainly they were entering the lion's den by going to a Ford Fest to protest a Ford, but this was Toronto, where there's an assumption of safety: there might be some chanting and yelling, but that's it. Standing with their signs in the crowd on the side of the hill they were indeed shouted at, and then, after some violent pushing and shoving, had their signs ripped from their hands and trampled on the ground.

During the attack, a man in a Canadian military uniform put himself between the protestors and those threatening them – a hero from Ford Nation itself. Before and after the skirmish he was handing out handmade, photocopied flyers of newspaper clippings of Rob Ford posing with residents of Danzig Street, the sight of a horrific shooting in 2012, along with a photo of what appears to be Ford sleeping in the mayor's chair at council. Around these images are hand-written slogans: "THE MAN OF THE PEOPLE, WHO NEVER RETALLIATES [sic], HE LOVES HIS ENEMIES. HE IS HERE, HE IS THERE, HE IS EVERYWHERE IF THERE IS A PROBLEM" and "FORD ISN'T STOOPID [sic], HE WON'T MAKE GAY-YOUTH A TARGET LIKE THE BATHHOUSE RAIDS." The latter is a reference to the 1981 police raids of gay bathhouses in Toronto that was, until the time of the G20 Summit in 2010, the largest mass arrest in Canadian history. Those raids became a galvanizing Stonewall moment for Toronto's gay community.

At Ford Fests, no contradiction was surprising. On this occasion, although the vast majority of people attending the event were not engaging in any homophobic activity whatsoever, and the Fords did ultimately condemn the incident, the bizarre ugliness of these moments and the event's dubious legality itself, seemed, again, utterly unTorontonian, as if Toronto has gone through a few looking glasses and arrived at a point where wrong is right and where things that should not be are.

ATTENDING FORD events was exhausting. A festive but tense atmosphere, cognitive dissonance keeping those who came to observe on edge, everyone waiting for something to happen, for the next bit of spectacle to occur. Public political events always offer some fringe excitement, but the Fords attracted their own exaggerated brand of it. Attendance brought a deeper kind of exhaustion too, of hearing things that were simply untrue, over and over. It seems a kind of maze that is impossible to escape, a Kafkaesque world where the fact-checkers have endless work but few are paying attention. (Reporters covering the 2015/16 Trump US presidential campaign have also spoken of this feeling, daunted by the onslaught of lies and the futile fight to counter them.)

Equally exhausting is the fact that Ford Fests were full of really nice people, aside from the worst yellers and sign-grabbers. I had ridden my bike out along the Scarborough hydro corridor to Ford Fest that summer evening to meet Ivor Tossell, who was writing about Toronto politics for the *Globe and Mail* (a repeat of our outing four years earlier at one of the first events at the family compound). Toward the end of the evening, around 9:30 p.m., we had stepped away from the crowd and rested near the washrooms to take a mental breather from the action, when Patti walked by, looking a little confused.

"Can you help me find my car?" she asked. There were numerous parking areas at Ford Fest and large expanses of the park's lawn were taken over by vehicles. After we figured out where her car was, we told her we were both there reporting on the event, and the three of us started chatting about why she was there. Patti, eighty-five years old "and proud of it," had been in the park since 4 p.m., a marathon of a day for anyone. "I've been watching politics for forty years, and it's only once in a long while a sincere politician comes along who really cares about the people," she told us. "I'm for him because he's sincere and honest."

Like most people who voted for Ford, Patti did not resemble the troglodyte stereotypes often associated with Ford Nation. Thoughtful, articulate, hers was no rant, just a steadfast belief in what she saw as right. And yet hearing it was exhausting, because the facts she presented didn't often match reality. "Since Rob Ford got in three years ago, almost four, he's saved, and this has been verified, he's saved the people over one billion dollars." The Ford billion-dollar claim had been fact-checked as false numerous times, but it didn't matter, and no amount of explaining could dissuade Ford supporters like Patti from believing those claims, because, ultimately, the number amount didn't matter. What did matter was the unbreakable bond Ford had created with his supporters. He spoke directly to them and made them feel like they, "the people," mattered, whether they lived in Rexdale or the genteel culs-de-sac of Bendale around Thompson Park, where Patti lived.

Ford's cancelling of the vehicle registration tax was one reason that Patti admired him, and she applauded his (failed) efforts to remove the land transfer tax, a revenue source bolstered by Toronto's hot real estate market that has to put millions of dollars into a city budget that struggles to raise capital. Patti also shared a general cynicism about councillors and their perceived malfeasance, especially regarding money issues. "Some of these councillors, they're in it for what they want. They're in it for big raises. There's abuse of expense allowances."

When money doesn't seem to go as far as it used to, such feelings resonate with the voters. Their cynicism is a formidable wall to penetrate with reason, or the argument that not all politicians are on the take, all the time. When we asked Patti, seemingly as upright a citizen as Toronto the Good ever produced, what she thought about Ford's lying and crack problems, she was forgiving, to the tune of we all have personal foibles and we all make mistakes.

"You know what, have you ever lied? Have I ever lied?" she asked us. She recalled a debate in which Olivia Chow accused

Ford of lying even when he was "clean and sober" – a comment that got boos from the audience and was downright "mean," Patti said. Ford as a victim yet again.

The most surprising thing Patti told us is that she had been an NDP supporter in her younger years. "I thought they were for the people," she said. "When I was young and didn't know a lot about politics I was canvassing for Stephen Lewis and there was a coffee party and I was sitting there and he came over and said, 'You know what, the Conservatives, we don't think the same, but we respect them because they set out what they believe and they stick to it.'"

This is another glimpse of how the Ford and the NDP camps can dovetail when either side has a charismatic leader that makes people feel like they matter. The ideas, the big thinking, is not necessarily absent, but it doesn't forge the connection between voters and politicians. Patti, and countless upstanding people like her, maintained support for Rob Ford, and to a lesser extent for Doug, even as the rules and facts could not keep up with them.

TORONTO'S INTEGRITY commissioner, Janet Leiper, was the hardest-working person in the city for a while, so inundated was she with Ford-related requests to investigate. In July 2014, Democracy Watch filed a complaint that the Fords violated city council's code of conduct when they lobbied on behalf of a customer of their company, Deco Labels and Tags. Other times, she has been called to look into the behaviour of councillors such as Georgio Mammoliti.

Outside of city hall, Ford's antics even brought him to trial in a conflict-of-interest case involving his Rob Ford Football Foundation. The court agreed there was a conflict of interest but, owing to a trial error, Ford was ultimately not punished, even though removal from office was one of the judge's options, a fantasy his detractors salivated over.

Extra-political indiscretions and scandals involved drugs, booze, and a string of racist, misogynistic, and homophobic comments, but these got no traction in Ford Nation, although they inflamed outside observers and were indiscretions that would sink any other political career.

That there were even rumours of a sex tape (something that would certainly, finally, put an end to the Ford regime – or so observers thought) seemed not to faze his diehard constituency. It was one more sign of how far through that looking glass Toronto had gone: reality kept shifting, the bar kept lowering, and the speculations about what the next Ford bombshell would be got even wilder.

NOT SO long ago, Toronto politicians' transgressions had actual consequences: the computer-leasing scandal during the Mel Lastman era resulted in a months-long inquiry that led to changes in how the city does business. Recall, too, Lastman's racist faux pas during Toronto's ill-fated Olympic bid, where he worried that Africans might boil him in a pot. That comment was feasted upon by everyone for nearly a decade in a long frenzy of schadenfreude, after he famously said "sorry" in a press conference more than a dozen times. Lastman's transgressions stayed in public memory and haunted him enough that he chose to retire from politics and public life in 2003. The Toronto of his day would not stand for such behaviour, but times have changed.

Perhaps it was during the G20 Toronto summit – an event that occurred at the end of June 2010, four months before Ford took office – that rule-respecting Toronto truly died. During that event the public was lied to about secret laws by public officials such as the chief of police. All of them, and most of the police officers involved in what has been called the largest violation of civil rights in Canadian history, escaped censure or punishment. In the melee, police removed their badges, citizens were beaten and strip searched, and yet only one cop was charged – offered up as a lone sacrifice, paying homage to the corpse of Toronto the Good. For many Torontonians the G20 was a Watergate kind of moment, where something they believed in let them down, allowing cynicism to take root. Other people may have had that moment the first time they were carded by police while just walking down the street. For others, the moment might have been the bathhouse raids in 1981.

The city is slowly, awkwardly, and reluctantly lurching into nascent conversations about race and class in the space Rob Ford opened up. The end of Toronto the Good is a good thing because it was an illusion all along. Big cities have dirty corners and underbellies and long traditions of unseemly activity. Toronto's have been exposed, and they are something to deal with in order to keep the city moving forward. Can things go back to "normal," to when Toronto was "New York run by the Swiss?" Will the rules still matter?

Throughout the Ford years, the city's councillors and staff have kept on with their daily business, issuing tickets for dogs off leash in the wrong parks, and adding more rules to Toronto's ever-thickening big book of by-laws. Toronto has elasticity it didn't know it had: it's both officious and anarchic, as are some of the greatest cities. The rules still need to matter – they must – but perhaps there's now room to recognize the elements of city life that have always been here, even if we were wilfully oblivious to them, and to confront them. It will take time to do, and both activism and leadership to keep this self-examination going.

CHANGE IS slow back in Ward 12 too. Lekan Olawoye had registered to run on January 2, 2014, and had been campaigning for ten months while on leave from his role as an executive at a youth-focused non-profit organization. He said his team had raised funds almost to the allowable maximum, and he had 400 volunteers working in different capacities for the campaign. He was running against Frank Di Giorgio, a thirty-year incumbent who was a member of Ford's executive committee and at one point his budget chief, one of the most powerful council positions behind the mayor.

Late in election season, former MP John Nunziata made a surprise move by joining the race at the last possible minute on September 12 (though Olawoye smiled when recalling that, saying, "There are no surprises in politics").

"The vibe you get as you go door to door keeps you going," said Olawoye of the long election slog in Toronto, an experience that is a roller coaster of emotion and energy. Despite that vibe at the door, "Toronto is the screw face capital," he said, referring to the look strangers often give each other in this city; he wished people would "just say hi" more. Provincial and federal elections usually don't last more than five weeks, but municipal candidates have to keep at it for a long time, and the chances of that persistence paying off with a win can be slim. Olawoye said that this race was the first time Di Giorgio had been challenged with "an actual ground game," but despite the money Olawoye's team had raised, and the volunteers he had, Di Giorgio won with nearly 4,800 votes, followed closely by Nunziata, a candidate with high name recognition across the city, with 4,500.

Olawoye came in forth with 3,400 votes, behind third-place finisher Nick Dominelli with 3,700. "Eked out" is how the *Toronto Star* described Di Giorgio's win, and the relatively equal spread between the four candidates suggests Di Giorgio's long run as a councillor did not leave him invulnerable. In 2021, the behind-schedule LRT will have opened on Eglinton, and the changes it brings could bring new tracks politically too.

CHAPTER SEVEN

THE HEART OF A BIG CITY
THAT ALWAYS THINKS SMALL

"**THIS IS** the heart of Toronto," said Jean-Pierre Boutros, looking around Eglinton Park, a few blocks west of Yonge Street. "It's pretty much the geographic centre of the city." The park is similar to Christie Pits to the southwest, a sand excavation yard-turned-park on Bloor Street West. Eglinton Park was formerly the Pears Brickyard, established in 1885 and a going concern until the City of Toronto purchased it in 1926, converting it to parkland.

Early Toronto had quite a few brickyards in town feeding its growth, and a number of them were converted to parks like this one, the giveaway to its prior use being the sloped sides and square shape of the park, but otherwise you would never know there was a heavy industrial use here, especially in this long-established genteel neighbourhood. Today the concrete plants located on the periphery of areas of growth serve the same purpose, themselves often consumed by the city once their work is done. Beneath Eglinton Park is buried Mud Creek, crossing the landscape as it meanders southeast, defying the street grid, until making a brief appearance just before the Don Valley Brickworks and then emptying into the Don River.

In many ways the intersection of Yonge and Eglinton could be the spiritual heart of the city, a place connected to everywhere and everybody else, but the connections aren't always apparent, like Mud Creek flowing below ground. While the actual geographic centre of Toronto is a few kilometres northwest of here on Wanless Crescent, "Yonge and Egg," as it's known, has never been terribly trendy. But then the centre of things usually aren't, as they represent too many things to follow fashion.

"I see Yonge and Eglinton as the new Yonge and Bloor in twenty years," said Boutros, in reference to the tremendous growth that has occurred at and around the intersection. Unlike Bloor, often regarded as the main east-west street in Toronto, Eglinton reaches across just about the entire city, from the edge of Etobicoke south of the airport on the west side, and deep into Scarborough where it meets Kingston Road and Lake Ontario in the east (although there is still more Toronto before hitting the city limits there).

Yonge Street runs from top to bottom, of course, and is the spine of Toronto, so there's a sense standing at Yonge and Egg that the whole city is spreading out in each compass direction, if you use some imagination. It's high country too, with a subtle but commanding view over the southward-sloping city to the CN Tower. Walk up the street a few blocks and the North York City Centre skyline comes into view. Yonge and Eglinton has a big city feeling, not at all parochial. With the Crosstown light rail line coming, the intersection is set to become even more important as a crossroads and place of connection, like Yonge and Bloor is now. The cranes are already in the sky in anticipation.

Boutros refers to Eglinton Park, the biggest in this part of town, as the neighbourhood's commons, a place that produces more soccer and hockey players than building materials now. "In the winter it's the epicentre of the area because of the skating. I hate winter because I grew up in a Mediterranean home but we put my son in skates and he loves winter."

Boutros lives near the park and got to know the area well while running for the Ward 16 city council seat. He spent part of his youth in a Don Mills public housing complex, but with a Greek mother there were often trips to Greece. For many first- and second-generation working-class and middle-class immigrants to Canada, a trip "back home" is their version of going to the cottage, and a journey that was saved for the entire year, sometimes longer. Despite the cost of international air travel, it's still cheaper than maintaining a property in traditional cottage country. However, cottages are a destination this ward knows well too, as the people who live here are mostly middle or upper class.

Toronto writer John Barber once cheekily wrote in the *Globe and Mail* that this city has no ghettos except the North Toronto WASP ghetto, a reference to the old Toronto power base that still exists here, but the reality today is much more ethnically mixed. Ward 16 specifically is rectangular in shape, bounded by the 401 in the north, Bathurst to the west, with Yonge and Eglinton rounding out the east and southern sides. Avenue Road runs up through the middle.

A continuum of comfortable affluence, to be sure, but change happens here too and the area continues to see its share of monster home controversies, when older, smaller homes are torn down and new ones built as large as by-laws allow, often towering over neighbours who haven't yet upsized. The result is bizarre streetscapes with new homes that are a pastiche of classic styles, all with large garages for large cars.

On the periphery of these neighbourhoods larger multi-unit, mid- and high-rise residential buildings are being built – a more reasonable kind of upsizing because more people can move in – and more are expected, with the Crosstown line feeding the development speculation. "The area is going to go through lots of change," said Boutros. "Everyone who has moved here in the last ten years knows that. It's mostly single-family homes now, but that will change. It just has to be planned correctly."

Indeed, the intersection of Yonge and Eglinton has been under construction in various ways for years now, whether the work is related to the Crosstown itself or the one- and two-storey buildings that will give way to the kind of density fitting for an area on major transit lines. An advocate of mid-rise buildings, especially along Eglinton, Boutros says the neighbourhood needs more amenities to keep up with the growth. As we walked along Yonge Street after meandering the neighbourhood, he said he'd like to see more grocery stores too, as there's only one major store nearby. The city amenities and infrastructure haven't yet caught up with the changes, an outcome of fast growth that sometimes causes residents to worry that change is coming *too* fast.

AT MONTGOMERY Avenue and Yonge, the historic Postal Station K is becoming part of a new residential tower development, its facade with the rare royal cypher of King Edward VIII, as it was designed during his brief reign in 1936, preserved as part of it. As it's being built up, this southeast corner of the ward is becoming "like Leslieville" to Boutros, because nearby house lots are just fourteen or fifteen feet wide, a downtown kind of narrowness that contrasts with the dimensions of the larger, older lots in the rest of ward. Similarly, there are both long-time residents who have lived here forty or fifty years and new residents, young families coming in who can't afford the larger houses to the north and west. Cute streets with little homes, near big streets with big buildings that are getting bigger, it's a typical mix found all over Toronto, where tall and small is the norm.

With all those people moving in, more of that common, public space is something Boutros thinks the ward needs more of, like the green space around the Bannockburn School in the northwest part of the ward.

Like a number of schools in the city, Bannockburn was declared surplus by the Toronto District School Board, who wanted to sever the property and sell off the yard to developers. "We can't get it back once it's sold, it's absurd," says Boutros. With growth patterns as they are, the area will need all the green space it can preserve now, but when demographics make schools – for the time being – obsolete in an area, the money gained by selling off the land in a hot real estate market is hard to resist.

It wasn't too long ago that the intersection itself had a small-town feel, or more accurately, a small-city feel, to it, despite the tall buildings that were already here. Yonge north of Eglinton still has two-storey retail along some blocks, a main-street land-scape that would be at home in Timmins or Orangeville, not the main street in a city of nearly three million. All over Toronto there are main avenues with this kind of low density, even along subway lines operational for half a century.

It's a cityscape that can easily lull people into believing they live in a village, an appealing delusion. However, the "village" narrative has been taken to extremes across the city. Toronto has what might be called a village fetish, where neighbourhoods insist, despite all evidence to the contrary, that they are indeed a village. Take Yonge and Bloor: it's on the border between the Church-Wellesley Village and what is sometimes called the Village of Yorkville. Visitors here have their pick of villages, but also ready access to two subway lines, four major grocery stores, two skyscrapers with rooftop bars, and twenty-four-hour restaurants. If it's a village, it's on methamphetamines.

Toronto calls itself a "city of neighbourhoods" (what city isn't this?) and many of its neighbourhoods tack on the word "village" to their names. Some came by the designation honestly because, historically, they were once villages, which were consumed by the growing city – for example, the Village of Swansea – and the identity stuck through the generations, even as it grew beyond village proportions. Local business improvement and neighbourhood associations named other "villages" more deliberately, perhaps based on wishful thinking.

Yonge and Eglinton was originally settled as a farming community and called the Village of Eglinton in the early nineteenth century. The village moniker was lost long ago, although there is an "Upper Yonge Village Daycare" here that's giving the old village nomenclature a new run. However, all across the city there are fictitious villages everywhere. In the old City of Toronto there are the likes of Ossington Village, Bloorcourt Village, and Roncesvalles Village, all of them on either streetcar or subway lines, some with populations that would qualify them as large towns or small cities in their own right.

Then there's Liberty Village, with its cluster of high-rises that could *use* a subway stop of its own. Etobicoke has Mimico Village, Lakeshore Village, and Humber Valley Village. In North York, both Emery Village and Bayview Village will disappoint tourists looking for a village setting, and Scarborough even has a neighbourhood called Scarborough Village, to further confuse things. The only place that comes close to being an actual village around Toronto is Black Creek Pioneer Village by York University, a reconstituted historic village of buildings moved to the site from around the city.

The notion of villages within a city is quaint and mostly harmless, a great way to explain how the city evolved and celebrate cute houses, but village thinking is harmful in preventing the city from getting to where it needs to go. Calling a place like Toronto a village is a denial of its very urbanity. When one takes a moment to parse the idea of a city village, the notion is revealed as clearly absurd: if these city villages were actual villages they'd be totally dysfunctional. They aren't self-sustaining and they need the rest of the city for employment, services, and entertainment.

People in villages tend to make much less money too; it's doubtful that people in Bloor West Village or elsewhere would give up their big-city paycheques to stay true to their village vision.

In true village life everybody knows everybody, and their business. I don't know everybody in my particular city village, nor could I, nor do I want to. I don't know my neighbour. We say hi. She smiles at my dog. I hear occasional noises from her apartment that remind me she's alive. That's enough. Being a little anonymous is one of the great advantages of city life and a reason why people move here. Real villages are full of busybodies who eye new arrivals suspiciously and aren't always neighbourly. In some, people who may have been there for decades are still referred to as "from away" because their roots do not go deep enough. That's not what Toronto is presumably about, but in practice there's a strong resistance to newcomers in neighbourhoods across the city. Perhaps the word *village* should be banned in Toronto, a move that might deter people from kicking the ladder out from under them because they got there first.

Dropping the village hang-up doesn't mean Toronto's charming residential streets of single-family homes need be torn down, although they're increasingly a way of life in Toronto that only people who qualify for mortgages over a million dollars can afford. It simply means letting other people move in who can't buy those expensive houses, making room by filling in the gaps, building more densely, and replacing some older structures that have negligible heritage value. "Radical infill" is how one civic official termed what needs to happen here. Toronto is a living city, it has always been changing, never a morgue or a place frozen in amber. People who argue otherwise are ignoring history.

In early 2015 a man in Bloor West Village wrote a telling letter to the editor in the *Toronto Star*. The reader was responding to an article in the paper's "Divided City" series during the 2015 election that looked at contentious issues contributing to the notion that Toronto was a city irrevocably divided. Intensifying the "avenues" in Toronto – essentially, building apartments and condos on the main streets and arterial roads – was proving controversial in established, middle-class neighbourhoods. This particular man claimed his neighbourhood, billed as "a small village in a big city," was being inundated by "extreme mid-rise development pressure." Clinging to the village illusion, this poor man must not have noticed the three subway stops near his "village," and that it was on a major east-west street and near High Park, one of the best city parks in the country. *Of course* people want to live there, just as people want to live near Central Park or Hyde Park.

Similar tensions were playing out a few blocks northeast of Yonge and Eglinton on Keewatin Avenue; a manifestation of the concerns Boutros was hearing about regarding changes in the area and the rest of Toronto. A group calling themselves the Density Creep Neighbourhood Alliance sprung up in the spring of 2015 in opposition to a row of townhouses planned for the north side of the street.

Keewatin is the frontier between an older neighbourhood of single-family homes to the north and, beginning on the south side of the street, an apartment tower district that was developed in Toronto's expansive postwar era, a part of town as Upper East Side as Toronto gets.

Although in dwindling supply, these mostly mid-rise blocks around Yonge and Eglinton still have old, pre-war houses scattered here and there amid the buildings that replaced their neighbours and brought big-city density to the area fifty years ago. Those that remain are Toronto's version of Chinese "nail houses" – old homes in rapidly developing cities such as Shanghai that resist removal like a nail that can't be pulled from a board.

The planned townhomes along Keewatin replaced eight low-density, oversized homes on large lots, with eighty units of compact housing appropriate for a midtown neighbourhood. When they launched their campaign, the Density Creepers were somewhat careless with their language, and likely naive about how it would play out in the media, as a representative of the group said she was "really concerned" that property values in the area would go down, because the new houses were only worth $500,000.

In the same statement, a reference was made to the transient nature of the people who would live in this kind of penny-stock housing: people who can only afford 500K are naturally a shifty lot. Predictably, the good folks on Keewatin were savagely mocked on Toronto social media, but the online mob aside, the pushback at such overt NIMBYism here and elsewhere in Toronto is a sign that many recognize that the only way the city will remain remotely affordable is to build new housing of all kinds, including these far-from-budget townhouses.

In doing so the city might avoid the situation San Francisco has found itself in. However, for a local councillor the noise made by NIMBYs is louder than the pressing needs of everyone else trying to find their bit of Toronto to call home, and the fact that the whole city has to share in their accommodation. Local parochial politics doesn't work that way though as the view is narrow.

"Post-amalgamation, Toronto city council is an organization designed to cater to and balance the needs of almost three million people in disparate areas," said Boutros. "When you have councillors routinely choosing the interests of their distant ward, whether urban or suburban, lobbyists or themselves, over the city, you really can't city-build. Why employ expert city staff if you aren't going to rely on them, as happened with the LRTs and Gardiner East?"

The Gardiner East issue was debated in 2015 and centred on tearing down an underused section of the elevated Gardiner Expressway. Long the bête noire of Toronto urbanists, the elevated waterfront freeway was a 1950s transportation solution that, while still a crucial bit of infrastructure in some areas, needed a near-complete rebuild. Although both data and experts suggested that removing the stretch east of Jarvis to the Don River would not result in a traffic apocalypse but instead would unleash property value in the redeveloping East Bay Front neighbourhood, Mayor John Tory burnt an incredible amount of political capital in his fight to rebuild the Gardiner. Its near-billion-dollar price tag defied logic but was a political decision to appease a broad base of voters that see any reduction in automobile infrastructure as a volley in the culture war that is transportation planning.

The LRTs that Boutros was referring to were part of the light rail plan for Scarborough that was scrapped for the Scarborough Subway, a kerfuffle that has become a nearly Seven Years War for which he had a front-row seat. Boutros was transit advisor to Karen Stintz, Chair of the Toronto Transit Commission from 2010 to 2014 and councillor for Ward 16 since 2003. She and Boutros first met each other as parents waiting outside the school their kids attended, chatting politics and transportation, becoming friends. When Mayor Rob Ford appointed Stintz chair of the TTC she, according to Boutros, asked if he would be her transit advisor. Boutros is a walking case study in how traditional ideological assumptions don't always work at the municipal level, because he might seem an unlikely person to be an advocate of public transit and sound planning.

"I'm a Bill Davis Tory," he told me, referring to the former Conservative premier of Ontario who presided over an expansive time in the province's civic life. Although not formally a member of any political party, Boutros describes himself as a Red Tory, an adherent of the long-lost kind of conservatism that Davis most certainly embodied.

Despite his advocacy for public transit, Boutros is also passionate about Formula One auto racing, having travelled to Belgium to follow his "hero," driver Ayrton Senna, in 1990. Later he became a Formula One promoter and agent, dealing in memorabilia, a business profitable enough that he was able to go into public service even when the remuneration was initially low – the first year he worked for Stintz, he says, it was without a salary. Urbanists, then, can come from many background and points on the political spectrum.

STINTZ HERSELF was elected to city council on an early wave of local antipathy to the change the area was experiencing in the early years of the 2000s, ousting long-time councillor Anne Johnston, who had supported a double-tower condo development on the southwest side of the Yonge and Eglinton intersection, just outside the ward. Though Johnston had been a sitting councillor since 1972, only taking a break in the mid-1980s to run for mayor, local residents were so upset with her that they rallied to defeat her.

Stintz had answered a candidate recruitment ad placed by some of those disgruntled residents and immediately had their support: she was their anti-development candidate. The condos in question, called Quantum I and II, eventually were built, and the courtyard between them was named after Johnston. Councillor Stintz settled into the informal right-of-centre opposition to Mayor David Miller. When Ford was elected and appointed her chair of the TTC, the story gets complicated, a narrative of U-turns.

In 2012, city council voted to reject Mayor Ford's Scarborough Subway plan, a moment when Stintz broke ranks with the Fords and came out in favour of light rail in the suburbs. However, the following year Stintz came out with her own "OneCity" transit plan that included a revived Scarborough subway, a move many call her great flip-flop.

Boutros recalls writing a speech for her as late as March 2013 when she was invited to Calgary to speak about her support of the LRT plan to Mayor Naheed Nenshi and others. Keep in mind that at this time the LRT plan was fully funded and approved, with shovels set to hit the ground for the first higher order of transit construction in Scarborough since 1985. All that changed when Stintz and other councillors brought the subway scheme back to life. This is how Toronto transit planning works, with the best-laid and funded plans torn up. Back in the 1990s, tunnels already dug for a subway along Eglinton were even *filled in* when there was a change in government. Boutros stayed on as Stinz's advisor after the flip-flop, but looking back now he says he should have done things differently.

"[I should have] resigned on September 12, 2013, the day after the premier told her at Queen's Park that council's July 2013 conditions for the Scarborough subway weren't going to be met," he said in retrospect. Although it seemed like a defeat, Stintz pressed on with her plan, and in October of 2013, council voted 24 to 20 to proceed with the Scarborough Subway, an event that caused Boutros to speak out publicly against the plan his boss and friend supported.

"The 2013 LRT-subway flip-flop she triggered gave the city a new billion-dollar-property tax hike and reversed the province's many millions of dollars of transit cost uploading," Boutros said. "It also corrupted Stintz's political future, as she became a new embodiment of self-interested voter cynicism. Torontonians remain aghast at this betrayal, rightly, in my view. Their grandchildren will pay for it."

The opportunism Boutros alludes to was Stintz's eventual run for mayor in 2014, a move that in hindsight could explain her confounding flip-flop. Officially entering the race in February of that year, Stintz ran on a platform that included the establishment of a transportation "czar" to deal with traffic congestion and the possible selling of Toronto Hydro to fund transit construction. The sunflower logo her campaign used was more optimistic about her potential leadership than the voters were, and by August she had dropped out of the race and retired from politics.

IT'S NATURAL for a staff member of a city councillor who is either retiring from politics or moving on to run for another office to then run for that seat. It's also customary for the departing city councillor to endorse his or her former assistant. But as a sign of how much acrimony had developed between Boutros and

Stintz, she not only refrained from endorsing his candidacy, but endorsed one of his opponents, Christin Carmichael Greb, mere days before the election. Greb went on to beat Boutros and a ballot of sixteen candidates, winning with just 17 per cent of the cast votes.

"This was my first campaign," Boutros said. "Absolutely, I should have started earlier, as early as possible. I was reluctant to start door knocking, which felt hypocritical at first, because I hate when people knock on my door uninvited. Once I started, I worked very hard, day and night, and I found I loved having front-door conversations with people who were (or became) interested and engaged in municipal issues. For better or worse, Rob Ford made people aware of the city's issues."

Ultimately, that could be one of the legacies of Rob Ford; he made municipal politics exciting and something to pay attention to. During his mayoralty, national and provincial commentators oft fell over themselves with condescension, expressing feigned surprise at how interesting the city was. Municipal politics are close to the ground and decisions affect people's front and backyards. The personalities involved sometimes seem straight out of 1980s evening soap operas, complete with vendettas and petty vindictiveness.

There's an excitement to it all, and the council chamber can be the best political theatre in the country. "In my time at city hall I became saddened at how people allowed themselves to create and carry so many skeletons in their varied closets, and amazed that decisions were ultimately made based on them," says Boutros of the long political memories that exist inside the walls of city hall and fuel a drama that plays on, and on, and on.

CHAPTER EIGHT

WHERE DOWNTOWN AND SUBURBS MEET

"BRUCE COCKBURN lived up there," said Alejandra Bravo as we walked by 1160 St. Clair Avenue West near Dufferin Street, a Canadian celebrity landmark that, like many of its kind, hasn't a historic plaque. Toronto is a city of subtle landmarks like these, which is perhaps why it felt the need to build the CN Tower in the 1970s.

We were walking along St. Clair on our way to see what some people refer to as "Toronto's smallest house" on Day Avenue, a few blocks north and west of here and another quiet neighbourhood attraction. Everyone likes to point out local landmarks, the places that might not have a plaque but, for the people who live there, represent a bit of history that matters, personally or otherwise, and gives a place meaning.

"Over there was La Sem café, which had Toronto's first patio in 1963," she said a little further west, pointing across the street to where the now-closed Invictus Restaurant and Bar was until recently at the corner of St. Clarens Avenue. This is one place that should have a plaque, even though La Sem later moved to Mississauga. "The city didn't know how to receive the request and public health questioned why anybody would want to eat outside." Toronto's come a long way since then, but it was immigrant-heavy neighbourhoods like this that began to shake up the city's historically uptight ruling class who only ate indoors at tables with white linen.

After World War II Italian immigrants made this area, Earlscourt, one of their Toronto destinations, along with College Street to the south. "Corso Italia," as it became known, had what might be called its coming-out party in 1982, when Italy won the world cup and 500,000 people took to the street to celebrate. That occasion is sometimes said to have had – in that Toronto way of adding an anecdotal superlative to events and places here – the greatest number of Italians gathered together in one place outside of Italy itself, lining the streets in a days-long celebration, the kind that happens routinely in dozens of Toronto communities when the World Cup rolls around every four years.

As immigration from Italy began to slow down, people coming from other countries started to arrive, such as Bravo and her family, who came from Chile in the 1970s, and other patios opened and people continued to eat outdoors and live to talk to about it. The line for gelato a few doors down from Invictus at La Paloma routinely stretches past the threshold, even down the sidewalk on warm summer nights. City life is rich on St. Clair, and it's where Bravo's campaign office was located during her run for the Ward 17 city council seat in 2014.

This stretch of St. Clair and the surrounding streets, with its heterogeneous jumble of stores and houses – a defining characteristic of much of this part of Toronto – was also ground zero for the great St. Clair Disaster of 2005, perhaps the only disaster in the world to occur in range of a proper espresso while one watches a soccer game.

"Disaster" is how the Ford brothers referred to the street and its new streetcar-only right of way that runs down the middle. Construction began in 2005 and, through a series of delays, wasn't completed until 2010, when Rob Ford was running for mayor. He and brother Doug used the project as a blunt rhetorical instrument to rail against former mayor David Miller's Transit City plan, which would have brought surface light rail to large parts of the city suffering from inadequate transit and brought a higher order of transit to more of the city relatively cheaply.

Although there is a significant difference between the streetcars on St. Clair and the light rail transit scheme that was Transit City – light rail uses larger vehicles, and the right of ways that were proposed were generally outside of the denser parts of the city, where atrial roads have ample room to accommodate the rails – the St. Clair Disaster became one of the top Ford catchphrases, repeated by not only his supporters, who saw the street's redesign as part of the war on the car, but also by his detractors, who mocked the over-the-top disaster bombast.

A group called "Save our St. Clair" (sos) sprung up opposing the plan, their signs visible in merchant windows along the street. sos managed to stop construction for months through a court action that cost the city $2.7 million and caused a series of delayed tenders that required further rescheduling.

To be sure, the group had legitimate complaints around cost overruns, long delays, and design issues on St. Clair: cyclists weren't happy there was no bike lane, and the street remains an uncomfortable squeeze to ride on; pedestrian advocates were unhappy that the sidewalks were narrowed in places to accommodate turning lanes for cars; and the general fit and finish in some places along the street were not as great as they could be. Even the street trees died, but they're a perpetually endangered perennial wherever they're planted on Toronto's harsh streets, where concrete and nature have a fraught relationship.

In short, the St. Clair right of way was a perfect bureaucratic-transit-construction-money storm delivered into Ford's lap exactly when he needed it in 2010, and he and his brother continued to fan the flames of outrage for the next four years, ensuring it was still an issue in 2014.

FOR A time during Ford's mayoralty the two brothers hosted their own Sunday afternoon radio call-in show on CFRB 1010, whose studios were then at Yonge Street and St. Clair. On air they would often mention the difficulty they had getting there, due to the St. Clair "disaster" and its attendant gridlock. The disaster comment was meant to bolster their argument for below-grade public transit, namely the Scarborough Subway, and make above-grade light rail seem unappealing at the very least, although the situation on St. Clair was hardly a disaster.

The Fords could also use a streetcar to disparage light rail transit because it had never been branded properly; the short form LRT is professional jargon and a transit geek's word, not something that's part of the city's day-to-day parlance. Nobody writes songs about LRTs, but they do about streetcars (*clang clang clang goes the trolly*) and the subway (*take the A-train*), so the Fords had a lot of room to create fictions and fears about what a disaster LRT would be if it were to spread to other parts of the city. Battles over LRT are common in other cities too. Brampton, Hamilton, and Kitchener have all had skirmishes of various intensities as they debate their own LRT lines, as did European cities such as Edinburgh.

Business owners will always complain about construction as it can strangle their cash flow. But the street has bounced back – and even improved since the right of way was finished, because it included a complete reconstruction of the streetscape and burying of hydro wires, a common sight on Toronto streets that some considered shabby remnants of the city's rougher times.

My first Toronto apartment in 2000 was at Yonge and St. Clair, and whenever we headed west along St. Clair in the evening to find something to eat or drink it seemed that the restaurant and bar offerings were slim. Entire blocks might have had just one open establishment, and some had none. It felt dark and unlived in, even though the neighbourhoods around it were, and are, dense.

Now there is much more life, and even more patios, and the retail offerings are getting more diverse and interesting. The street is currently enjoying the elusive and ephemeral sweet spot between being down and out and gentrified, so that there are businesses catering to a wide economic swath. There are new condo towers on St. Clair today too, putting more people on the sidewalk and creating new retail where there wasn't much before. Apart from banks and a few other outlets, most businesses along St. Clair are not corporate chains either, ranging from older Italian and Portuguese cafés to an upscale dog boutique.

Farther west, past Caledonia Road and Earlscourt Park, auto body shops and other very light industrial operations join the mix. There are even some storefront churches. Reporting for the *Globe and Mail* in 2012, journalist and St. Clair neighbourhood denizen John Lorinc found there wasn't much evidence of a disaster at all, even then, writing that since the completion of the right of way, traffic volumes had dropped and transit ridership increased by 13 per cent. The *Star* also reported round-trip times on transit were down 14 per cent on average, with a midday Saturday trip reduced to 56 minutes from 70. These are real gains for the more than 30,000 people who use the line each day: more frequent streetcars, free from traffic delays, attract more people. At the same time, a sense of order was brought to driving the street, as collisions and personal injuries were down by one-third.

None of this mattered much to the Fords, for whom transit planning in Toronto was driven by politics rather than facts.

As Bravo and I walked along St. Clair, where there are still vacant storefronts, as there was before construction, she pointed out that landlords are a hidden issue here. "Many owners are sitting on property and not willing to rent space at market rate," she said. The inflated rents make it harder for mom-and-pop businesses, with narrow margins, to set up shop and continue the independent flavour along St. Clair, and rent increases often disrupt the stability of retail streets.

"The rent is too damn high," said one-time New York City mayoral candidate Jimmy McMillan in a memorable TV debate, and it applies here too. Routinely, businesses across the city that have been around for a long time, neighbourhood institutions, are forced to move or close up shop for good when landlords increase their rent to unaffordable levels. The landlords see dollar signs creeping up their streets as the surrounding area becomes more popular, and the corporate chains will always have deeper pockets than the indies. Toronto landlords also get a vacancy tax rebate from the city on unrented property, a built-in disincentive to actively keep businesses on their properties.

AS BRAVO and I walked along St. Clair, poking in and out of cafés, we arrived at the busy intersection of Old Weston Road. The Weston Road Flea Market is a block north. "It's a little bit of South America," says Bravo, noting that not everybody likes such a chaotic, do-it-yourself kind of place in the neighbourhood. "You can get furniture, cheap produce, get your nails done. I'd like to see more of this mix." She also mentioned that there are many artists living in the area, a fact that isn't well known as there aren't any arts hubs in the neighbourhood. Some neighbourhoods present their artful population on the street, with galleries, dive bars, cafés, and other places artist types like to frequent. The Junction neighbourhood, only a kilometre away, has evolved into the kind of place creatives and their followers find comfortable, but it's on the other side of a major rail corridor and feels farther away than it really is when you're on St. Clair.

Bravo and her team had difficulty finding a place in the area to hold their election night party, because no spaces were big enough. Although businesses like the flea market and the indie nature of the retail here suggest an urban messiness conducive to a burgeoning arts scene, this area was developed haphazardly as a streetcar suburb and tends to be on a smaller scale, save for some of the churches.

"This has always been a working-class area," says Bravo. "There are still many multigenerational families here and an above-average number of people working in skilled trades. Earlscourt even has the highest number of war widows in Toronto." To the south of St. Clair the ward trends more toward middle class. Bravo alluded to the aging population here, meaning demographic change will come, but said that there's also a sizable number of elderly people who don't exercise their vote, as well as many live-in caregivers who aren't yet citizens and can't vote, a kind of unrepresented population.

"I might only speak English three times during a canvass," she said of the diversity of languages she encountered, with Spanish, Portuguese, and Italian being the most frequent. During the campaign Bravo was on leave from the Maytree Foundation, a Toronto based non-profit that works to reduce poverty and inequality in Canada. She had worked on their campaign to get municipal voting rights extended to permanent residents. Myer Siemiatycki, a professor of politics and public administration at Ryerson University, has pointed out that, based on the 2006 census, about 380,000 people in Toronto (let alone the GTA), or 15 per cent of the population, cannot vote.

In neighbourhoods with large immigrant populations such as this one, the percentage is even higher. These residents haven't yet made it through the long process of becoming a citizen and are left out of municipal civic life, even though it's the level of government that affects their lives the most daily. All residents, citizens or not, pay property taxes, renters included, so in a sense it's local taxation without representation. Many opposed to extending municipal voting rights will say, "So what, become a Canadian citizen," but the rights and responsibilities federally versus locally are quite different. Cities provide basic day-to-day transactions and services; the national-level rights give us freedom of speech, assembly, mobility, and all the other things we ostensibly went to war to defend. But because cities don't have standing armies, we'll never be called up to defend Toronto the way we might Canada. The stakes at each level are radically different.

What does it mean to be a citizen of Toronto? Simply choosing to live in the city is a fairly strong statement of affinity for the place. What are our rights in Toronto? Garbage collection? Pothole maintenance? Who are we loyal to? The Leafs? (The latter tests even the most ardent Torontonian whose family has been here for generations.) Similarly, our city responsibilities are of a different nature and are based on civility, not citizenship: holding the door open for others, stooping and scooping, and letting traffic merge.

All of which boils down to large numbers of people left out of a political process in a city that celebrates its multicultural and immigrant population. With municipal voter turnout as low as it is, we should do everything we can to build it. Make a big deal about being a citizen of Toronto, throw street parties where recent arrivals get their citizenship, and make civics something exciting. It could lead to people applying for their Canadian citizenship sooner too.

The immigrant-friendly and working-class nature of the area can trace its roots to St. Clair's original streetcar right of way that made it easy for working-class folks to commute to the city core and industrial zones, areas where the jobs were. That original right of way was gradually removed in the 1920s and 1930s as an increase in car ownership required more road space for motorists. So, for seven decades, the streetcars here were at the mercy of traffic, as they are on most Toronto roads currently.

Many of the houses in the area, especially north of St. Clair in Earlscourt, were worker-built. That is, individuals built their own homes on plots of land they purchased, instead of developers building houses on an entire street or neighbourhood at once and then selling them individually. This process explains how quirks like Toronto's smallest house came about and why the neighbourhood is a delight to walk through – there's no such thing as monotony here. It's a counter-argument to overly regulated urban planning regimes that sometimes foist a sameness onto cityscapes.

Some of the most beloved neighbourhoods in cities everywhere seem almost feral, created before official plans made every detail of new builds conform to a shared standard. South of St. Clair the houses are more robust, larger, and have a certain respectable uniformity. The petite bourgeoisie have always had a desire to conform to one another and keep up with common fashions but it's here that great views of the city can be found along the ancient Lake Iroquois shoreline, an escarpment that marks the northern edge of the much larger ice-age version of Lake Ontario, along Davenport Road. The view is especially cinematic from back of the Regal Road Public School yard, where Toronto's low-rise central west end spreads south to the lake and downtown skyscrapers. In another city there would be signs here directing people to a grand belvedere or scenic look-off, but Toronto never thought the view was worth making a fuss about.

The ward Bravo was running in has seemingly arbitrary boundaries that zigzag through the area, making it difficult for most people to conceptualize Ward 17 and others like it in their mind's eye. People tend to identify with the neighbourhood first, and sometimes neighbourhoods with their already fuzzy, contested boundaries are divided between two wards. It makes for an additional challenge for council candidates who are trying to represent an area people may not have much familiarity with.

"Ward 17 looks like a tugboat," said Bravo of its shape on the map. Its borders follow roads and rails rather than any natural formations. The "boat" floats atop the CNR rail line that runs adjacent to Dupont Street and extends roughly between Old Weston Road in the west and Oakwood Avenue in the east, with a narrow "smokestack" extending north to Eglinton Avenue. Neighbourhoods overlap in each direction, but they do represent a transition from older to newer parts of the city.

"I see this part of the city as the edge," she said, referring to the way the ward bridges two areas of the city traditionally thought of as "downtown" and "suburb." "It's a gateway to other parts of the city." Indeed, the southern section of the ward is very much integral to what's offhandedly referred to as the "core" of the city. Although downtown hipsters joke they never go north of Bloor – there be suburban dragons and the like – the Dupont corridor, a former industrial street that is gentrifying in a westward direction, would never be considered part of

Ford Nation territory. Yet northern and western boundaries of Ward 17 do extend into areas some Ford nationals might claim as their own.

These are extremely blurry borders and who's laying claim to what is sometimes more interesting than the border itself. Undoubtedly Ward 17 is a transitional part of town – both pre-war and postwar, downtown and suburb – an imaginary border zone where a simmering political battle was being fought. Yet here on the edge, as Bravo put it, the differences between the two sides are hardly stark.

THROUGHOUT THE 2010 election, the Ford mayoralty, and the 2014 election, "the suburbs" were pitted against "downtown," but there were objections from people who lived in what is often called the suburbs, such as Scarborough and North York, to such characterizations. "We're not the suburbs, we're the city," is the sort of phrase I heard here and there when I made lazy, off-hand references to "the city" – meaning the old, pre-amalgamation City of Toronto.

"The city" is an easy kind of geographic shorthand, but as with the descriptors *downtown, midtown,* and *uptown,* Toronto has evolved past the old terminology. Yonge and Bloor was once considered midtown, but midtown most certainly is Yonge and Eglinton now, with North York City Centre serving as Toronto's uptown. *Uptown* is a Manhattanish way of referring to a city that is wider than it is tall, but it describes the Yonge Street spine well enough. The shift of "uptown" to North York corresponds with the rejection of the suburbs moniker and the slow assimilation of the six former municipalities into one entity.

For many people living here, the suburbs are generally the land beyond the City of Toronto's border in the 905 area code, separate municipalities such as Mississauga, Markham, Pickering, and so on. At the same time, formerly suburban places inside those borders – sometimes referred to as the inner suburbs – have become simply more of the city, even if their built-postwar form looks typically suburban.

In the nearly two decades since the dissolution of Metro Toronto, a municipal set-up that created an inherent old and new, downtown and suburb, civic dynamic by formalizing the old City of Toronto as a something separate from the surrounding newer municipalities, those interior Metro divisions are mattering less and less in terms of self-perception, even if politically the divide still has currency.

"We are the city." It's a sentiment that could be built on, but many choose instead to focus on the differences and run with them, as the Fords and others did and do. Yet when you look at how people actually live throughout Toronto it isn't so different, and Ward 17's in-betweenness, as Bravo pointed out, is a good place to think about what those terms mean in contemporary Toronto.

Think first of an archetypal image of a suburb and you might picture a single-family home on a crescent with yards in the front and back, a driveway, maybe some shrubs and trees. Picture then the city and an image of denser streets, some apartment buildings, and a high street lined with shops might appear in your mind's eye. One scene is more spread out, with daily life much more reliant on the car; the other, denser and, while still reliant on the car, with more options for getting around and walking the easiest of all, because most services are nearby.

Both of these places exist in Toronto in abundance but it's nearly impossible to draw a line between them. Try it if you can; where would you draw that line? There are more similarities than differences between the so-called downtown and the suburbs.

Certainly many people are happy with the term *suburb*, perhaps because they don't care about or give a thought to what the part of town they live in is called. Nonetheless, over the last few years these two parts of the city have been pitted against each other, as if a United Nations intervention and DMZ were needed. But as we've seen, there's so much overlap between the two that a peacekeeping force would not know where to go, especially in a place like Ward 17. Troops would wander around confused and retreat early to a café on St. Clair for a beer and the war would be declared over.

The exercise of defining *downtown* in Toronto is just as awkward. A few blocks from the skyscraper core there are neighbourhoods where houses have front yards, and some even have driveways of their own. There are residential streets between University Avenue and Spadina by Chinatown or in Corktown on the downtown east side that are an utterly suburban form at the heart of our city, if you take the "sub" in suburb to mean less urban.

Go to a city like Montreal and you will see many kilometres out of the city centre dense neighbourhoods of houses and apartments that are built right to the sidewalk, lending them a sense of old-world urbanity that Toronto lacks even in its downtown neighbourhoods. Montreal is downtown throughout, while in Toronto a sense of suburbanness prevails – although don't tell the people who tend to their postage-stamp front yards that they're anything but urban.

Then there are other parts of the Toronto city core that are actually streetcar suburbs, such as Leslieville and the Beach on Queen Street East, and Mimico in south Etobicoke to the west. Walk east out of the Beach along Kingston Road, past Victoria Park into Scarborough, and not much changes.

Downtown-seeming neighbourhoods extend far beyond the borders of the old City of Toronto too. Further west of Mimico in south Etobicoke at the corner of Islington and Lake Shore Boulevard, in the heart of the New Toronto neighbourhood, it would take quite a bit of imagination to see it as anything other than urban, with its solid blocks of retail along the sidewalk and surrounding neighbourhood streets often as dense-feeling as the Annex or Little Italy, with narrow Victorian homes of their own.

The former town of Weston along Weston Road at Lawrence is a neighbourhood as urban as any downtown, now with its own Union-Pearson (UP) Express rail stop that also serves as a GO Train station. If GO frequency increases to every fifteen minutes as planned, it will be as easy to get there from Union Station as is it to Yonge and Eglinton today.

As Toronto grew, it gobbled up villages like Weston, New Toronto, and other nodes around the city that retain their older urbanity. Even in areas where the culs-de-sac dominate there are often apartment towers on the peripheral arterials housing hundreds of thousands of people who live downtown, apartment-style lives far from the core, in neighbourhoods that are a patch-work of traditional urban and suburban landscapes.

The suburbs are often called "dull" or "monotonous." At the same time, people who don't like downtown condo towers call them "vertical suburbs," a kind of snobbish slur, part of a fusillade of slurs that are fired in every direction.

Toronto's suburbs are where much of the city's valued multiculturalism lives, and its strips malls often have more variety than downtown streets where you can see another Starbucks from the one you're in. The old categories don't work in Toronto. There is no downtown. There is no suburb. There is only Toronto, and Ward 17 is a hybrid of all of it.

APART FROM the Lake Iroquois escarpment, the defining characteristic of the area Bravo was running to represent is the hydro corridor that diagonally crosses it – beginning at Old Weston Road and heading southeast to Dupont Street, where it turns due east, until ending just north of the Annex neighbourhood near Poplar Plains and Davenport Roads, not far from Yonge Street. A grassroots design competition in 2013 established the idea of creating a "Green Line" system of linear parks, inspired somewhat by the High Line in New York, which took an unused elevated freight rail line and converted it to a grand promenade through Manhattan's meat-packing district.

The Green Line is less dramatic but no less connective, as hydro lines, here and otherwise, preserved open swaths of space through the city that would otherwise have been developed. They provide a tremendous opportunity for the city to create a linear park system with pedestrian and cycling bridges over the north-south streets along the Dupont corridor, where they dip below grade to slip under the railway.

Nearby, the West Toronto Rail Path is a precedent for giving new uses to old infrastructure corridors, but there are even more ambitious projects like the 606 in Chicago that Toronto can look to. Named after that city's area code, it's a 2.7-mile-long shared path connecting four different neighbourhoods built in an elevated concrete channel that once carried a freight rail line through north Chicago.

When I visited Chicago in June 2015, just a few weeks after it opened, cyclists and runners were already using it en masse and it seemed like a long-essential part of the city, even as the saplings planted alongside the path were just taking root. The Green Line has the same potential in Toronto. However, Chicago architect Daniel Burnham's most famous phrase, "Make no little plans; they have no magic to stir men's blood" might not fly in Toronto.

The 606's budget was US$95 million; a figure that could deter any public project in Toronto, but of late a Friends of the Green Line group has formed and is slowly getting people excited about the notion. Like Waterfront Toronto's long slog of community consultations years before much was built along the harbour, and the $1 billion Regent Park public housing revitalization project that began with community meetings in fluorescent-lit rooms around folding tables, this is how big ideas can happen in Toronto.

Toronto has a history of "Friends" groups that have supported various civic organizations. Supporting museums and individual parks and the like, the friends offer more ordered expressions of the strong civil society this city has always had, despite the comings and goings of bad mayors and councils with little vision. Some of these groups are formally organized, others more ad hoc, playing a quiet and methodical long game that has transformed parts of this city. One of the most successful friends groups has been the Friends of Dufferin Grove, which turned what was a derelict park across from a then-downmarket urban mall into a model for community parks, with a communal pizza oven, farmers market, and other elements that have become standard in park revitalizations. Yet they were never a formally organized group.

Here's how they describe their own history on their website: "The friends of Dufferin Grove Park no longer exist. They were never an organization. There was no executive, no annual meetings, no formal status. There was no written agreement anywhere between the friends and the city. But in times of trouble, there were impromptu park-user meetings, usually attended by 30 to 100 people depending on the issue."

It's a phenomenon that has been repeated across the city, where civil society rises up to advocate or protect something or, in some cases, to create something brand-new. The proposed Green Line could ultimately continue along the hydro corridor northwest of Earlscourt, beyond Old Weston Road, deeper into parts of Toronto that have been without these kinds of connecting, high-design projects.

People here are nervous about change, says Bravo, as in so many other parts of the city. Even something positive like the Green Line could bring increased house prices to the area, good for current residents, less so for those trying to get in. Despite the meteoric rise of housing prices here as elsewhere in Toronto, the area will stay somewhat mixed because of places like the Primrose Housing Co-Operative on Primrose Avenue along the Green Line, the kind of place that keeps some sense of stability in neighbourhoods in flux. Finding the balance between keeping neighbourhoods livable for the people already there, and accommodating new ones comfortably, remains one of Toronto's greatest challenges and a looming crisis, if not already one.

This neighbourhood was the first place Bravo said felt like home to her. Her parents moved with her from Chile to Canada after the 1973 coup that ousted Salvador Allende. The family eventually settled along St. Clair. "You could get leather kids' shoes and a *café con leche* with a little glass of mineral water," she says, adding that the 1982 soccer win for Italy made the place feel even less lonely. The 2014 election was her third run for city council; she'd run in Ward 17 in 2003 and 2006, losing both by margins well under 1,000 votes.

"The first time I ran I was thirty-two and they said I was too young," she says, recounting the difficulties women getting into politics face. "I think there's only a small window between ages forty-three and forty-seven when it's acceptable for a woman to run." Bravo also recalls being told by men to wear heels and get a makeover to look older, a kind of advice men themselves don't much get. (There are and have been young male councillors in their thirties but they're often referred to as being wunderkinds or, in the case of David Crombie – elected mayor when he was thirty-four – the "tiny perfect mayor.") Even after the 2014 election, she received threats most male candidates don't. The reputation Torontonians and Canadians have for being friendly does not hold up during election season.

"Four days after the election, the signs were collected and stored, the office was cleaned out, and I had one day off before returning to work," she said. "After sending my boys off to school, I listened to a message my campaign manager had forwarded, with instructions to immediately call the police. It contained a detailed threat of violent gang rape, which included my home address. My husband came home from work to help me receive the young police constable who would, horrified, hear the recording.

"An investigation found nothing. The call was made from a phone booth at the McDonald's at St. Clair and Keele. The security camera wasn't working at the time. The impact on my family was repeated visits by police, changed locks, new security protocols. As parents, we were relieved that our daughter would spend the following months during her gap year in South America. I am a neighbourhood person, however, so I felt secure as my neighbours enveloped me with their support and solidarity when we informed them of the circumstances. Can't keep us down."

Her challenger in Ward 17 was Cesar Palacio, a Ford loyalist who has been in office here since 2003, when he succeeded Betty Disero whom he had served as an executive assistant for a number of years. Executive assistants often run to succeed the retiring councillors they worked for, and Palacio, born in Ecuador, was the first Hispanic person to be elected to Toronto

City Council. Palacio's loyalty to the Fords is evidence of the split personality of the ward, and he appealed to both working-class and older immigrants in the neighbourhood, who also felt Rob Ford spoke to them.

Despite all the walking and talking, Bravo's message couldn't win in a ward where Ford populism still resonated, although she came within about 400 votes of Palacio's nearly 8,300 vote win. Placing third was newcomer Saeed Selvam, who captured 1,400 votes and took quite a bit of flak for ostensibly splitting the vote. Selvam, a policy wonk and involved in various community initiatives, also spoke the city-building language, so it's debatable if he did indeed split the vote, and on various occasions he publicly took umbrage that he was pressured to step aside to let Bravo win.

However Palacio's increasingly narrow victories and the demographic and income changes that are occurring in Ward 17 suggest the 2018 election results may be different. The close 2014 race got quite nasty as well.

"Palacio threatened to sue me twice, serving me with a notice of libel during and again in mid-November," says Bravo. "I'm still waiting for the lawsuit, which I suspect will not come because I was simply holding him to account for his public voting record. I still say bring it."

Bravo's campaign message tied Palacio to Rob Ford, a move she thinks was a mistake and may have caused her to lose the election. "By tying Palacio to Ford, we motivated people who supported Ford to vote for Palacio," she said. "It is possible that we might have tapped into voter volatility by simply saying, 'It is time for a change.'"

"The Fords were very much alive here," said Bravo, a fact that forced her to consider how a city builder like herself could confront Fort Nation populism, something that has stymied so many other people who felt they could not compete with the slogans and Willie Stark rage. "Ford embodied a rage that is out there among people who feel excluded: from the labour market which demands more skills for bad-paying insecure jobs; from the housing market, which isn't creating affordable, livable communities; from power and representation. Every time Rob Ford said something he put his finger on something palpable, but solutions are more complex."

Bravo continued: "We should be more sympathetic to people paying their bills and we shouldn't be afraid of being populist, but about the good stuff. Boil it down to what matters. Canvassing is the most powerful public education to confront the Tea Party identity politics that's come to Toronto."

As Toronto's prosperity grew in the last two decades, all the civic pride and booster messages before Ford's election didn't resonate with the people Bravo found on her canvasses of the neighbourhood, and often scapegoats were blamed. "There is a lot of work to do in this city," she said. "I heard many racist messages at the door, many against Muslims. I heard from people that social assistance should be eliminated, that refugees are the cause of economic woes working-class families face. Taking this on is a big challenge to the left."

CHAPTER NINE

CHASING TORONTO'S MYTHOLOGY ON THE SUBWAY TO NOWHERE

LIKE THE tree it's named after, Willowdale is as leafy as leafy neighbourhoods in Toronto get. In the former city of North York, the neighbourhood is home to some of the city's oldest postwar suburbs within Toronto and also to some of the newest, where the evolution of suburban design can be seen moving east from Yonge Street.

Close to the Yonge corridor there is a loose faithfulness to the traditional urban grid pattern that begins to break up east of Bayview, where streets begin to curve and meander across the landscape into a warren of culs-de-sac, courts, and crescents.

Although loyalty to the grid is ultimately lost, there's a comfortable, secure feeling deep in the jungle of homes, with mature trees and quiet streets, isolated from the rest of the city and the busy arterial roads that cross through the area. Dominating the landscape here is the Finch Hydro Corridor that runs across the top of the city, just north of Finch Avenue. Currently most of it is neither as manicured as an urban park nor as wild as the city's ravines, but it's a favourite place for kids to play and dogs to enjoy long walks. An incomplete cycling path runs through some of it and the corridor is at its most dramatic when it crosses the East Don River's valley, where the tall hydro towers climb the slopes in each direction.

I met Dan Fox in Bayview Village Park, two blocks north of the Bayview subway station on Sheppard Avenue. Bayview Village is there too, a mid-sized luxury mall, indicative of the wealth of nearby residents. The adjacent area is overwhelmingly middle class, with a few very wealthy enclaves, some tucked in along ravine tributaries of the East Don. Originally an open-air mall, Bayview Village was later enclosed and became an indoor version of Rodeo Drive over the last few decades, a designer redoubt for those who didn't want to make the trek down to the chic shops of Yorkville. In the park Fox and I walked past a ball diamond to where it narrows into a greenbelt, following a small brook running between spacious backyards. At Bayberry Crescent the brook disappears into an underground drain, eventually flowing into the Don just a kilometre east of here, so we took to the streets.

"Some people I canvassed didn't know that when you vote for mayor you get to vote for councillor too," said Fox. "I had to explain what a councillor does. People are more interested in the race for mayor than the ward races."

Such was life on the streets of Ward 24 Willowdale, where the mayoral campaign sucked up all the political oxygen, as it did all over the city, save for the few wards with high-profile city council candidates. The race Fox was running in flew under the radar to all but the close observers of city hall, a situation incumbents find favourable. Ward 24 is in the shape of a T, running along the top edge of the city between Steeles and Finch, with its western border at Yonge Street, the eastern border at Highway 404, and a panhandle that runs down to the 401 following the east branch of the Don River.

Many of the houses here are typical examples of mid-century ranch and bungalows designs sprawling across generous lots, built at a time when the car was king and there was still much open country around Toronto. When walking the streets there it's easy to forget this low-rise landscape is just a few minutes from a subway station. Although not as dense as neighbourhoods in the core of the city, it isn't terribly dissimilar to much of the Bloor-Danforth subway line, where single-family homes make up adjacent neighbourhoods to it along most of its length, a situation that seems absurd, but it's been like this since the subway was opened in the mid-1960s, as buses bring the passengers from farther afield.

When we emerged from the neighbourhood onto Sheppard Avenue, we were across from one of the most enigmatic subway stations of all: Bessarion. Lonely, forlorn Bessarion, the least-used station in the system. In 2013, Toronto comedian and writer Jeremy Woodcock made a wistful short film called *Finding Bessarion*, where he searched for the station "to prove that it exists."

Exploring the Sheppard Line, what Woodcock refers to as the "the purple line," the film is funny not just because of his comedic talent in discovering a place that has been open since 2002 – "it's beautiful . . . was this built on Friday?" – but because the Sheppard Line, or "Line 4" as it's officially known, is considered a folly by transit advocates. The pet subway of Mel Lastman, a dream that began when he was mayor of North York, the line is sometimes called Mel Lastman's Subway, and alternatively, the "Subway to Nowhere."

When the project was given a green light in 1986, the Sheppard Line was going to be one of a number of new subway lines, including one along Eglinton. However, all but this one were cancelled when Mike Harris's Progressive Conservative government came to power in 1995.

When the subway was planned, Sheppard was an arterial road through low-density neighbourhoods. Once built, it began at the Sheppard station on the Yonge subway line, but it didn't connect to any other major transit lines and terminated, as it does today, at Don Mills Road and Fairview Mall. Perhaps the epithet "nowhere" meant something thirty years ago, but it certainly does not apply today. The Sheppard Avenue corridor has changed dramatically since 2002; while there are still streets and neighbourhoods of single-family homes, there are clusters of mid- and high-rise towers. More are on the way too; some of those bungalows are shuttered and have development signs on them, an indication that towers are planned for the site.

Just east of Bayview are the "NY Towers" or "Chrysler Condominiums," a complex of towers and townhomes that opened the same year as the subway. Although the NY could suggest North York, the development is an homage to old-style New York skyscrapers, as two of the buildings are stubby pastiche versions of Manhattan's Chrysler building. Toronto's obsession with comparing itself to New York is often overstated, but it can't be denied that the condo logo still has an outline of the Statue of Liberty in between the NY letters, lest there be any doubt as to its inspiration. The NY Towers development gives way to a handful of streets with homes and low-rise apartment buildings, some of which hug the Highway 401 noise barrier, until Bessarion Road, a short street that runs south of Sheppard and dead-ending at the 401.

Along Bessarion itself, mid-century duplexes, some with tropical-looking carports, would be at home in a sleepy seaside community in Florida. That the station was named after this low-density street is perhaps too convenient an example for those who think building a subway here was a mistake. Yet as quiet as its namesake street is, Bessarion Station itself is going to get much busier in the coming years, as all the land east of here, once the site of the distribution centre of retail giant

Canadian Tire, is going to be entirely filled in by residential towers and townhomes.

A condo cluster has sprung up by the IKEA at Leslie Street, one kilometre east of Bessarion, and is already feeling quite lived in, open for a few years now. The IKEA and Canadian Tire store here are both big-box holdovers from another era that sprawl over their sites, but the rest of the area will be filled with thousands of people and Bessarion won't be lonely for long.

ELSEWHERE ALONG Sheppard the street continues to change as a result of the subway arriving. Old plazas where shops display phone numbers without an area code, always an indication of a vintage sign, still exist, although they've all certainly been speculated by developers and will redevelop eventually: the land is just too valuable. On our walk Fox even pointed to the location where a Mountain Equipment Co-op is being built across from Bessarion Station, so residents here won't have to travel downtown for their fleecy needs anymore.

Eventually the development at Bessarion and Leslie Stations will be continuous, a large cluster on the western edge of the vast Don River valley, where the view east to Don Mills Road and the terminus of the subway a few kilometres away is spectacular. There, another cluster of towers is multiplying by Fairview Mall, in the adjacent ward, also thanks to the subway, so these two nodes are like Emerald Cities on their respective hills. While the subway is no Yellow Brick Road, a new infill development at Don Mills is actually named Emerald City, adhering to the Toronto tradition of giving over-the-top names to ordinary buildings. Emerald City is made up of rental and condominium buildings that have been deftly woven into the existing apartment tower community of Parkway Forest.

"We were inspired by Ontario's Places to Grow Act," said architect Len Abelman of the provincial legislation that encourages density in strategic places such as this throughout the Greater Toronto Area. "So we came up with a master plan that intensifies and revitalizes the neighbourhood." Abelman's firm, WZMH Architects, was awarded the master plan contract a decade ago and began planning the large-scale infill project.

TORONTO IS full of neighbourhoods that look like Parkway Forest used to look: a cluster of late-mid-century apartment towers and townhouses, similar to dozens of others across the city. Most of them share the same tower-in-the-park design philosophy, whereby green space surrounds the apartment buildings.

Originally meant to be idyllic parkland, a front and backyard for residents, these places often became neglected and were given over to surface parking lots, becoming places where few wanted to spend much time. It was into that space that Abelman and his firm put the new developments, and he says they were able to do so without taking away much of the green space by building on the surface lots.

"The infill buildings are all also linked below ground with the old ones," said Abelman of a solution that meant they could share the same entrance and loading docks, so there are fewer ramps and utility areas now. "There was a lot of dead space around the buildings so we created street edges where there weren't any before, either as patios or retail space," he said. "There are no blank walls and there are now eyes on the street."

Although a number of townhouses were demolished, all rental housing was replaced as per city of Toronto rules, and Abelman says residents had assistance moving into the new buildings or were given funds to help them move elsewhere. Walking through the area today, a landscaped and pedestrian-friendly concourse runs southeast from the corner of Sheppard and Don Mills, curving through the tall buildings and lined with new townhomes and connecting to a neighbourhood park, school, and the brand-new Parkway Forest Community Centre designed by Toronto's Diamond Schmitt Architects.

Two things stand out along the way: the first is a series of public artworks by Douglas Coupland. Called "Four Seasons," the series consists of four colourful Laurentian pencil crayon–inspired columns sixty feet high and other decorative elements on buildings with the same theme. Coupland also did a number of pieces inside the public areas of the new condominiums. The other notable aspect is the number of kids coming and going from both the new and old buildings, a marked difference from some downtown condo neighbourhoods that seem devoid of children.

Abelman explained there are two- and three-bedroom units in the buildings, space for families, and that they were also able to fit a number of playgrounds in between the buildings. Although Abelman estimates it may be into the 2020s before the entire community is finished, it's one model of how more people are going to fit into Toronto in the coming decades, in complete communities with access to amenities and services. None of this would have likely happened without the subway to nowhere.

BACK IN the newly dense neighbourhoods along Sheppard, Fox was worried about how well rounded the not-yet-complete communities are. "What we need are more grocery stores and cafés," he said.

A councillor in this ward has to balance the concerns of the established neighbourhoods, which are wary of the speed of change and change itself, with the new, urban parts along the subway line, which are waiting for the city to catch up with population that's already here. Critics will rightfully point out that even with all the development that has already occurred, ridership on the Sheppard Line is very low, with fewer than 50,000 boarding during each weekday, much less than the 65,000 riders who board the jammed King Street 504 surface streetcar every day.

At the same time, although over a billion dollars in development has occurred along Sheppard, the city is left subsidizing an overbuilt line that not enough people use yet. Those who do ride it are fed onto the already overtaxed Yonge Line.

That ego-driven politics and the potential for real estate development might have been behind the Sheppard Line rather than good, evidence-based planning is comparable to the ongoing Scarborough subway controversy, where a subway that is expensive to build and operate is planned for a low-density part of the city. Ridership projections in Scarborough are incredibly low, and there's no indication that the Scarborough councillors who championed the subway in this city of legendary NIMBY battles will also support the increased density needed to make the new subway even approach being a rational planning decision.

Toronto is a place that has often succeeded despite (or to spite) its leadership and the decisions they make, and moments of grace from its past could and should be inspirations for future decisions. Keep in mind both the Scarborough and the Sheppard subway lines while considering the work of Roland Caldwell (R. C.) Harris. His name is familiar to Torontonians because of the water treatment plant named after him, but far fewer know the full story of his life, one that burns through some of the cynicism Torontonians have regarding their city's development and future prospects.

IT'S A Canadian thing not to tell our own stories enough. When we have, it's traditionally been a particular kind of story, usually involving the taming of something wild, like an ocean, a forest, a prairie, or a mountain range. Or the story is about some lonely person in one of those landscapes, making a go of it on their own. These are all fine stories to tell and they've had a lot of play in defining the Canadian identity, but what about epic tales of how our cities came to be, of how our urban infrastructure came to be, stories that might better relate to the reality of Canadian life today?

Most Canadians live in and around cities and unlike oceans, forests, prairies, and mountain ranges, natural forces didn't create those cities, people did, and they expanded greatly in the twentieth century as the country grew. The built monuments of this era are sometimes great, sometimes invisible. Vancouver has the Lions Gate Bridge, opened in 1938, allowing the British Pacific Properties land to the north to become a new part of Vancouver's metropolitan area. In 1955, Halifax and Dartmouth were connected by the Angus L. Macdonald Bridge, making the two small cities seem like one much bigger one, like San Francisco and Oakland joined together by the Bay Bridge, but on a Canadian scale. At Niagara Falls, Sir Adam Beck harnessed an entire river for hydro power, letting the province grow.

Across the country there are depression-era works projects that continue to carry cars and trains, and trunk sewers and sewage plants that we happily never see or hear from, content that they'll keep our cities running. These are epic stories and if Canadians knew more of them there might be a greater appreciation of their cities.

In the last two decades there has been a growing movement of Urban Explorers in cities worldwide, begun in part by Toronto's late Ninjalicious (a pseudonym) and his legendary zine *Infiltration*. These are people who venture into places that are generally off limits, like rooftops, abandoned factories, and non-public areas of public buildings. There's a subset of these folks called "Drainers," who, as their name implies, have a different relationship with utility covers than the rest of us. They explore and document the sewers and channelized creeks that run below the city, usually producing artfully lit photographs that they share on websites and in books. Since it is sometimes an unspeakably filthy adventure, most of us are happy not to take part, but their hobby reminds us of the herculean infrastructure that keeps the cities we live in running. While it might seem frivolous to take photos of concrete trunk sewers and quaint to tell stories about the people who built them, taken together they give us a sense of how the cities we live in came to be. The stories of what's below offer a layer of meaning to the idea of "home." That there can sometimes be drama to these stories suggests it's all something worth getting worked up over. Water pipes may seem boring, decidedly unsexy things, but one of the greatest films ever made about cities is a story about infrastructure: *Chinatown*.

Roman Polanski's fictionalized version of William Mulholland and the California Water Wars evokes the time when Los Angeles made bold decisions that allowed it to become a great city. The L.A. of Chinatown is pre-war craftsman bungalows, wooden telegraph poles, orange groves, and the dusty newness of a city pushing its way into the hills and around the vast oceanside basin it would eventually fill up and spill out of. The story famously has everything in it – adultery, politics, incest, money – but tying it altogether were characters who knew that the place where they lived was going to be important, a real contender even. So for good or evil or an ambiguous mix of both, the characters in Chinatown got in the game. They had vision. In Canada we've come closest to this kind of expansive infrastructure celebration in all the fussing the country does over the Canadian-Pacific Railway and the *Last Spike* story, although Pierre Berton's rendering of events had somewhat less incest and adultery. In this genre, arguably the best offering from Toronto is the story of R. C. Harris, the City of Toronto's public works commissioner between 1912 and 1945, a figure with vision who pushed back against parsimonious small-thinkers on Toronto's city council and prepared the city to be the great metropolis that it would become.

HARRIS DOES live on in the imaginations of Torontonians, and even other Canadians, thanks to Michael Ondaatje bringing Harris to life in his 1987 novel, *In the Skin of a Lion*. It's in those pages that people who weren't city wonks or infrastructure nerds heard about how Harris built the Prince Edward (or Bloor) Viaduct across the Don Valley, linking east and west Toronto, while anticipating the subway to be built decades later and designing it so trains could run underneath the roadway. Toronto is not known as a city of bridges but this viaduct and the half-dozen other ones Harris built across the city's ravines are Toronto's smaller versions of the Lions Gate or Macdonald bridges. Ondaatje's phrase, "The Palace of Purification," describing the art deco gem of a treatment plant Harris built in the Beach neighbourhood, has become the widely used nickname of the plant, something residents here are proud of and something nobody ever asks the cost of.

But imagination-capturing doesn't happen overnight. *Chinatown* was released back in 1974, and William Mulholland already had one of the most famous, fantastic, and sinister roads in the United States named after him: L.A.'s Mullholland Drive. Harris had his treatment plant named after him later, but people tend not to immediately connect workaday things, even grand ones, with the long-gone civic officials they're named after without writers and artists helping that mythology along.

Americans also simply tend to hold and tell their own stories more confidently, to revere both their heroes and their anti-heroes, without the reserve and deflection average Canadians employ. Others revisiting Harris's legacy have bolstered Ondaatje's evocation of the man, weaving him into a steampunkish and vital Toronto creation myth.

Toronto journalist John Lorinc covers both the minutia and grand narratives of city politics and has written extensively about Harris. In a piece in the winter 2006 edition of *Spacing* magazine called "The City Builder," Lorinc outlines Harris's life work and dedication to civic works but uncovered what might have been the driving force behind building the Palace of Purification and other clean-water initiatives: Harris's six-month-old son, Emerson, died of erysipelas and pneumonia in 1906.

As Lorinc explains, the baby's death was yet another statistic in the "public health catastrophe" that was afflicting Toronto in the early twentieth century. The bacteria causing erysipelas thrived in unhygienic conditions, like those found throughout Toronto due to open sewers that flowed directly into Lake Ontario, the source of the city's drinking water.

With this in mind, Lorinc draws comparisons with New York's vilified Robert Moses, who built similar infrastructure, but arguably destroyed parts of the city in doing so. Lorinc writes, "Harris embodied a more humane vision, a sense that a city's public works – no matter how monumental – are ulti-mately there to benefit its residents as they go through the workaday routines of daily life."

R. C. Harris is beginning to live in our imaginations, with one foot in Lorinc's historian camp, the other in Ondaatje's fictionalized version. This is how myths are created, with a bit of fact and a bit of creative liberty. A 2013 exhibit called "The Water Czar" at the city-run gallery in St. Lawrence Market traced Harris's thirty-three-year career, building on what is already known by mining the city archives for photos and ephemera. It revealed that Harris struggled with councillors then as some civil servants do now over their professional advice, and political cartoons of the day lampooned his extravagant materials and grand designs.

And yet, today these same things are the beloved bedrock of Toronto, the buildings and works people are proud of and identify with when they try to think of why Toronto is a great place, why they want to live here or even like living here. It is an odd thing to be a Torontonian: we are always longing for the city we don't allow ourselves to have.

Like the Los Angeles depicted in *Chinatown*, and Toronto today, Harris's city was growing fast; the black-and-white photos in the exhibit showed a new but rough city pushing north into Ontario farmland. To the south rubble was dumped into the lakefront, first by horse and cart and later by truck, allowing the growing city to expand. In some places, ravines in the way of neighbourhood expansion were filled in with the same material so the street grid could be continued.

In one photo a utility cover is at the top of what appears to be a concrete smokestack built in a ravine by High Park, but the caption reveals it's actually the top of a sewer outlet and the ravine was to be filled in and the Bloor roadway built overtop, eventually meeting the top of the stack at grade. It takes some mental wrangling to accept this fantastic scene as real, but it happened, in Toronto.

Monumental works and foresight are things we don't necessarily associate with Toronto today when transit planning is political and development sometimes seem haphazard. What would Harris think of the Scarborough subway, or the Sheppard Line, for that matter?

BACK IN Ward 24 the new neighbourhoods along Sheppard, and the subway itself, haven't received much mythological treatment yet, but a street called Esther Shiner Boulevard does get it for a few blocks west of Leslie Street, by the IKEA store. It's a bit of small-scale mythmaking, as its namesake was a North York city councillor who held office from 1973 until her death in 1987. In 2014 Dan Fox was running against her son, David Shiner, who had represented the area since 1991, first as a North York councillor and then as a Toronto one, post-amalgamation. With decades of name recognition in the area, Fox said he felt like he was "up against forty years of Shiners."

Toronto is a city of family dynasties from all sides of the political spectrum. The Ford family and their continued aspirations have been the most prominent, but the current council roster has a number of others. Mike Layton, councillor for Ward 19, Trinity-Spadina, is the son of the late Jack Layton, a former long-time councillor and federal NDP leader. His neighbour in Ward 20, the other Trinity-Spadina, is Joe Cressy, son of Gordon Cressy, a Toronto city councillor from 1978 to 1982. Josh Colle, councillor for Ward 15, Eglinton-Lawrence, is the son of Mike Colle, MPP for the area. Stephen Holyday of Ward 3, Etobicoke Centre, follows in the council footsteps of his father, Doug, who was the last mayor of Etobicoke prior to amalgamation, a Toronto city councillor, and, until 2014, an MPP.

Similarly, Christin Carmichael Greb, councillor for Ward 16, Eglinton-Lawrence, is daughter of former MPP John Carmichael. Michelle Holland of Ward 35, Scarborough Southwest, is spouse to yet another sitting MPP, Lorenzo Berardinetti. Egalitarianism may still be the Platonic ideal of Toronto electoral politics but the number of dynasties across the city means name recognition and familiarity are huge obstacles for new candidates to overcome. On election day in 2014 Fox garnered a respectable 5,649 votes but still didn't come close to Shiner's nearly 11,000.

AS WE headed back to Bayview Village mall from Bessarion, Fox led me through the pedestrian passages by St. Gabriel's Catholic Church on the north side of Sheppard. Lined with tall grass and trees, the passages are as lush as the nearby hydro corridor, but more cultivated. The church has new condo neighbours now, people living urban lives even here in postwar Toronto, an area evolving from a car-oriented one to a more urban, walkable place, waiting for those cafés and grocery stores to come in and animate the street life as they do downtown.

Mistake or not, the subway has turned a nowhere into somewhere, or rather, turned a place that was already somewhere into something bigger, where the story is just starting to be told.

CHAPTER TEN

FINDING A PLACE TO LIVE IN THE MILLION-DOLLAR CITY

THERE ARE trajectories one can take across Toronto that pass through areas of endless and immense wealth – street after street, neighbourhood after neighbourhood, one leading to another in a continuous pageant of wealth. It's best experienced on bike; cars are too fast and cocooned from the environment, and walking is too slow and doesn't cover enough territory.

In the space of one or two hours and a few dozen kilometres on a long ride one can pass through neighbourhoods where homes can't be had for less than a million dollars. Sometimes these neighbourhoods are even wealthier, sometimes a little less so, but their magnitude when considered together, the sum of all these connected parts, is remarkable when experienced physically. Where do all these people work? What do they do? Where does the money come from?

Most of the wealth isn't particularly conspicuous; other than the Bridle Path or certain streets in Forest Hill or Rosedale, Toronto's wealthy neighbourhoods are handsome but tend to be indistinguishable from one another. Even the monster homes that have been replacing more humble dwellings tend to look like each other, a steady march of stucco walls and Doric pillars. Toronto's monotony of money forms a kind of asymmetrical

"T" through the city: a wide trunk up through the centre of Toronto and extending east and west to neighbourhoods in the former municipality of North York and out to parts of central Etobicoke in the west.

Traversing these neighbourhoods on a long bike ride, the scale and expansiveness of wealthy Toronto can be felt, the spread-out equivalent of the downtown skyline with the towers that are the most conspicuous sign of wealth and power in this city, one that can be seen in a glance. This is where some of the money goes to rest after hours as it drains out of the office towers, to be safely tucked away in neighbourhoods like Graydon near Don Mills Road and Highway 401.

THE NEIGHBOURHOOD'S namesake is Graydon Hall, a twenty-nine-room Georgian manor in the middle of Graydon, built on a hilltop in 1936 and complete with a private nine-hole golf course, racetrack and stable. Although now used as an event space for weddings and the like, the estate was built by broker Rupert Bain, a kind of suburban analogue to Casa Loma, Toronto's downtown folly similarly built atop a hill. Graydon lore has it that Katharine Hepburn, Vivian Leigh, and Mary Pickford all stayed there at various times.

Like fellow financier Sir Henry Pellatt, the man who built Casa Loma for his wife but only got to live in his castle for ten years before financial troubles set in, Bain spent only a short time living on the estate he built. By 1950 he sold part of the land to E. P. Taylor, the developer who would soon begin constructing Canada's then-biggest planned suburb just to the south called Don Mills. A year later, Bain sold the house, and soon after was dead at the age of fifty-four, suffering a cerebral hemorrhage during a horse-riding accident, concluding a brief but magnesium-bright climb up Toronto's aspirational property ladder.

There was still money to be made in these hills, though, and in the 1960s, a portion of the estate was developed. Today Graydon Hall is surrounded by a public park that shares its name and single-family homes that all sell for well over a million dollars, sometimes two.

In the late 1930s, *Canadian Homes and Gardens* wrote of Graydon Hall's gentle placement within its landscape, its orientation to the sun and view of the gardens from the house, all things the new neighbourhood around the property pays little heed to: apart from the steep grade of some of the streets and the occasional narrow vista glimpsed between houses, the landscape has been steamrolled out of sight and mind, and these houses could be anywhere in the city.

There are exceptions to the sameness in Toronto, such as Don Mills itself, designed by Macklin Hancock who left the contours of the land intact, or Humber Valley Village in Etobicoke, designed by famed architect and planner Eugene Faludi, where the streets roll with the topography. Instead, the standard Toronto development method was followed: creeks are buried, trees are cut, and hills are flattened, resulting in a repetition of form that continues outside the city in the parts of the 905 that are still developing. Some older, beloved neighbourhoods downtown weren't so different, but they've had a century to get quirky.

One million dollars was a landmark number that became the average selling price for a detached home in Toronto in 2015, a figure that continues to rise. It's an incredible number, one that used to suggest an unattainable sum or a person of tycoon-level wealth, yet it's the new reality for people who want to buy a home in the city.

"FOR ME, there's either do more or sleep," said Mary Hynes, explaining why we were walking uphill along a residential street in Graydon on a hot summer day in the rain. I caught up with Hynes in 2014, when she was running for the Ward 34, Don Valley East, council seat, at the age of seventy-one. It's an age when many people think about a quiet retirement or ways to relax more and enjoy life, but instead she was showing me around the neighbourhood. It was quiet and few people were out and about in the heat and humidity of the day, Graydon experiencing the eerie stillness of Toronto neighbourhoods during the dog days of summer. The middle class have decamped to cottages, and without the front porch as an interface between public and private in single-family-home neighbourhoods like this one, the two spheres become separate solitudes, and the life inside is hidden.

It's much harder to get a read on a neighbourhood like this simply by walking around, and for an upstart candidate, it's a tough slog from house to house, wondering if anybody will answer the door.

Without the main shopping streets that the downtown areas have, it's difficult to find central places where people in the neighbourhood congregate. "There's no such thing as walking down the street talking to the merchants here," said Hynes.

Even if ward populations are generally the same, and spending limits are equal, the geography and built forms of individual wards provide both advantages and disadvantages for candidates. Like other wards outside the core, Ward 34 covers a big, sometimes disconnected territory bordered by the 401, Victoria Park Avenue, railway corridors, Don Mills Road, and the Don River itself.

It's a hard ward to pin down, geographically and conceptually. The Don Valley Parkway bisects it as well, a significant barrier that only has a few crossing points. The Don River and a few tributaries also separate area neighbourhoods, and although there are paths through some of the ravines and park-land, a large part of this lush landscape is inaccessible to the public due to Donalda Club, the private golf course that sprawls along the river. The distance to cross the ward from the 401 to its most southern reach is about 5.5 kilometres and would take at least an hour to walk, in contrast to the dense downtown wards that can be crossed in just ten or fifteen minutes.

When we had met up in midsummer, Hynes had been walking the sidewalks and knocking on doors for weeks, running a barebones campaign that consisted of her and a few volunteers. A fundraiser was planned for early September and she had tweeted out a need for more help canvassing, but hers was as small as legitimate campaigns get. Just like the geography of various wards, the scale of city council campaigns can vary wildly.

Discounting fringe candidates who appear only on the ballot and nowhere else, or those who show up at public events with little more than flamboyant antics and wild speeches, real campaigns that have boots on the ground can be as small as Hynes's and her nearly one-woman show, to campaigns that have storefront offices, thousands of lawn signs, fully maxed-out fundraising targets, and an army of volunteers.

Raising the money is one thing – council candidates are each allowed to raise $5,000 plus 85 cents per eligible elector living in their particular ward – but some have access to volunteers and voter information that others don't. It's these non-monetary items that create powerful campaigns; they come by way of associations with political parties and other groups such as unions that share information and rally troops.

When I met her during the campaign, Hynes carried around a folder with her campaign material that included an information sheet and bookmarks listing her platform planks. One woman and a folder and a lot of walking; it sounded daunting, but the resolve of candidates like Hynes is remarkable – trudging on, nearly alone, and well out of the spotlight that mayoral and some downtown ward races get. She estimated that about only 20 per cent of the doors she knocked on were opened, and then only some of those residents were willing to engage in a conversation about the election.

Campaigning is a bit like fishing, but instead of sitting in a chair on a dock it's an endless walk, and in Graydon that means up circuitous residential streets that twist and turn.

HYNES SPOKE often about kids, their lot in the city, and what can be done to improve it. She said there's a lack of public space for "older kids" in the area, the often left-out youth roughly between the ages of eight and their early twenties, when there's the greatest chance for boredom to turn into something more serious. Teenage years are inherently awkward, but a teenager in the city can be even more so: where can they just hang out without being either under suspicion or asked to move along?

This is especially acute when teenagers grow up in apartments without a basement to retreat to, private clubhouses that have long been the domain of postwar suburban youth, and as the city gets more dense, more kids will be growing up in apartments or condos and looking for public places to hang out in that have more amenities than a standard city park with just a basketball court and little else.

Hynes's interest in youth came naturally as she had been a school teacher since 1966, first in New York City, where she is from, and then later in various capacities in Toronto until retirement in 2001.

Like 40,000 other Americans, she and her husband moved to Canada in 1971 to escape the Vietnam War draft. Hynes had long been an activist as well, working on issues such as public education, food security, health, and the needs of Toronto's growing senior population.

She came to wider renown when her satirical deputation at Mayor Ford's "Core Service Review" in 2011 – twenty-two hours of non-stop deputations from Torontonians who voiced their opinion on impending budget cuts – became an Internet sensation as she urged him to close down the entire library system. Satire is difficult to pull off in activism and politics, but this one got a lot of mileage half a year into the Ford mayoralty, when his informal opposition on council was only beginning to coalesce and gain some traction after what seemed like a land-slide win and "supermajority" of supportive councillors the previous fall.

Neighbourhood livability was one of her concerns, so she took me to the corner of Don Mills Road and Graydon Hall Drive to show me a condo under construction across from her own building. She lamented that it wasn't being planned as a mixed-use building, but instead would be primarily a resi-dential one.

"It's 1.8 kilometres to the nearest grocery store from here," she said, a distance that ensures either a car trip is needed or a long slog with full bags along busy roads, a common sight in wide-open parts of Toronto like this. More often than not, those folks with the bags don't have a car at all, although they live in a neighbourhood built for wheels, without the proximity to retail services that some of us take for granted. It's these kinds of condos that get a low "walk score," a rating of how many walkable services and attractions a home is near. Walk scores have come to be seen as a quality-of-life indicator and are even listed on realtor websites, meaning good scores can translate into higher selling prices.

Although there is a nascent rental-building renaissance of sorts in Toronto, with a few new buildings around the city either being designed as rental from scratch or switched from condo to rental, the condominium has been the dominant form of residential construction throughout the city since the boom began nearly twenty years ago.

Apart from other concerns such as the size of units, general design, and their internal governance model – there's no political drama like that of a condo board – where the building meets the sidewalk is routinely an issue: repeating bank branches and Shoppers Drug Marts and other big chains create a boring city. Although they are useful, and the kind of stable tenants developers and condo boards like and who can afford rents in new places, such chains don't provide anything like the granular variety of urban streets that have developed organically and serve the varied needs of the surrounding community. Instead, they've contributed to an interchangeable sameness of urban retail strips in Toronto, with a few exceptions such as older condos where an evolution in main-floor tenants has occurred over time.

When retail isn't part of a development, the streetscape is only offered condo lobbies styled to the latest design-magazine standards, private spaces few people use and where Barcelona Chairs go to die. It's a most-useless built form where useful things are needed most. Hynes's desire for something better on the sidewalk is universal in Toronto and felt just as keenly in other parts of the city facing intense growth pressure.

Condos get a lot of flack in this city, blamed for a variety of urban woes, but they're essentially the new reality of starter homes for the middle and working classes who feel the compulsion to pursue the Canadian dream of home ownership. So, the ground-floor issue is still one the city needs to figure out, and as Hynes has pointed out, is key to making life easier for a lot of people.

Because of its spread-out geography, the area is dominated by single-family homes that take up much of that geography, but there are pockets of density like the one near the new condo building. Behind it is a cluster of five mid-century high-rise towers, all without much in the way of ground-level commercial amenities either, although these "towers in a park" are well kept and their green spaces are lush and welcoming, unlike those around many downmarket buildings in the city with less conscientious landlords. Although the wealth here seems continuous, it's only homogeneously wealthy at first glance, and there are pockets that aren't as well off. Not by any means slums, but places that working- and middle-class people can afford.

Hynes herself lives in one of these pockets on the west side of Don Mills Road, across from the new condo, in the Duncan Mills Housing Co-operative. She took me up to the roof where there are garden boxes that residents can use and an incredibly green panoramic view of Toronto. One of Toronto's taglines is "a city within a park" and it's the truth when seen from above at a place like this in the summertime: it looks like a forest spreading out below, with occasional buildings popping up through the canopy. In Toronto it's sometimes hard to see the trees for the forest.

"There's so much potential here," Hynes said, looking out over all the green. "We could have a school for the environment up here. There are lots of underused schools." She gestures to the west side of the building, overlooking the meandering Don River Valley. This eastern branch of the Don snakes its way up from the south of Don Mills, through the Donalda golf course,

under Don Mills Road and then northeast, where it slips underneath a particularly wide stretch of Highway 401.

There's a paved trail here that connects the parkland on the
north and south sides of the highway named after Betty
Sutherland, a former member of the North York's city council
from 1979 until 1985 and an advocate for the city's regional
parks system. The trail was dedicated to her contribution to
those parks in 1988 but unfortunately doesn't directly connect
to trails north and south of this section, blocked by the golf
course and the Sheppard and Leslie intersection.

Better connections here would make getting to the developments by the IKEA at Leslie and the "Emerald City" at Don
Mills, both along the Sheppard subway line, easier. For now,
they seem farther away than they are. If there were a trail
through the golf course, Hynes and her neighbours would have
a direct car-free connection south to the waterfront.

Hynes downplayed her role in it, but the community garden
on her building's roof, a project started in 2006, was her idea.
It's mainly for growing vegetables. She first explored if there
was interest among her neighbours, then secured a federal grant
to get it built. The co-op's board gave their permission with the
caveat that they would not be able to contribute any financial
resources. Lack of resources is a common theme in co-ops across
the city, and just one sign of a looming crisis for a form of
affordable housing that still provides many thousands of people
in Toronto with a place to live.

The majority of co-ops the city has today, some 17,000 units
throughout Toronto and York Region alone, were created
between 1973 and 1995 under federal and provincial funding
programs. "Canada's co-ops were recognized in the 1990s as a
'global best practice' by the United Nations because there are
no financial barriers to entry," said Michael Shapcott, director

of housing and innovation at the Wellesley Institute, a research and policy organization that looks at health, housing, and equality issues. Shapcott noted the irony that the recognition came just as we discontinued the programs.

Unlike standard apartment buildings or condos, co-ops are governed collectively, and offer a mix of subsidized and market rents. There are many varieties across the GTA that appeal to all sensibilities. The modern Hugh Garner co-op east of Parliament Street on the edge of Cabbagetown feels like a 1970s Swedish design dream, and at the foot of Bathurst Street the Windward, Harbour Channel, and Harbourside co-ops have a mix of apartment building and rowhouse styles designed with seaside flair. Some co-ops cater to artists, such as Beaver Hall or McCaul Street just north of Queen, and the Arcadia co-op, also at Bathurst Quay.

Many have emergency funds for tenants who find themselves unable to make rent. Co-op living isn't for everyone, as the anonymity that big cities afford decreases and there are expectations of a certain amount of participation in the social life of many co-ops, but as decent housing is increasingly out of reach for a rapidly growing number of people in the Toronto, co-ops might be a good idea in need of reviving.

THE PARALLELS between today and when co-ops were first established in Toronto are striking. Two of the earliest were located on the near east side of the city: Spruce Court in Cabbagetown and Bain in Riverdale, both of which celebrated their centennial anniversaries in 2013. "They were both established at a time when Toronto was straining under devastating income and health inequality," said Shapcott. "Many of the newcomers, Jewish and Irish, primarily, flooding into the city were being segregated into slums with terrible housing conditions and, as a result, the health outcomes were atrocious." High infant mortality rates and other public health concerns eventually led to slum clearance programs that began after World War II, resulting in neighbourhoods such as Regent Park, a massive housing project that began in the late 1940s.

"A century later, Toronto may look a lot different from the Toronto of 1913, but we are straining under a devastating burden of neighbourhood-based inequality," says Shapcott. "Good quality, affordable housing was a great innovation in the Toronto of the Georgian era, and it continues to be a much-needed solution to many of the most pressing social and health issues of the early twenty-first century."

Shapcott outlined for me what he called Canada's "proud history" of non-profit, non-equity co-ops, noting it really took off in 1973, when a national housing plan was launched during Trudeau's minority government period, funding a proliferation of new co-op builds, aided in Ontario by funding from the province, beginning in 1985.

Consisting of both subsidized and market-rate rental units, they proliferated in the city until the federal government stopped funding new construction in 1993, followed by the Harris government in Ontario doing the same in 1995. Only a handful have been built since, which explains why so many of the most recent co-ops built in Toronto have a conspicuously post-modern architectural style to them, built as they were in the last days of PoMo's fashionableness.

The various federal and provincial programs funded three things: development of the building; operating and reserve funds; and rent-geared-to-income (RGI) funding to help "cover the gap" between what low-income households could afford to pay and the money the co-op needed to stay solvent. The looming crisis is because under the Chrétien government in 1996, with Paul Martin as finance minister, a program began where they "stepped out" of their co-op housing commitments.

"Co-ops funded under federal programs from 1973 to 1993 typically received a thirty-five-year operating agreement that governed the flow of funding, most importantly, the RGI funding," said Shapcott. "As those agreements expire, and if you do the simple math, you'll see that the agreements have started to expire in the last decade and the number expiring will rise rapidly over the next twenty years. Then co-ops will be starved of funding, especially for low-income households, which means that they may have to bump the rents up to the market level and economically evict many low-income households who will no longer be able to afford the rent."

So just as the city's real estate market is pricing vast numbers of people out and talk of moving to cheaper cities such as Hamilton, Guelph, or Peterborough spreads virally in this city, those who are already in affordable housing may yet find their foundations are shaky as well.

SOLUTIONS TO Toronto's affordable housing crisis are complex and difficult to fit into campaign-sized bites. Hynes was running against Denzil Minnan-Wong, one of the more vocal and visible members of city council and a politician adept at finding positions on issues he can easily communicate. An ally of Rob Ford, Minnan-Wong didn't break rank and publicly denounce his antics until the mayor's personal troubles reached their zenith.

As a small-government fiscal conservative, Minnan-Wong voted against programs such as the city's environment days and the vehicle registration tax that Mayor David Miller's council put into effect. The latter was part of Toronto's so-called "war on the car" and Minnan-Wong was on the front lines of the car side, blowing a bugle, criticizing pedestrian scrambles at major downtown intersections, and voting to remove three bike lanes in the city, although he considered himself a supporter of bike infrastructure, advocating for separated lanes on certain streets.

Another political bee in his civic bonnet has been Waterfront Toronto – an arms-length partnership of the municipal, provincial, and federal levels of government created in 2001 – and its work redeveloping the former industrial shoreline along the city's inner harbour.

Transforming Toronto's post-industrial waterfront is a project that has been a dream for generations of Torontonians that has heretofore proceeded at a snail's pace, if at all, leading to much cynicism around waterfront redevelopment. However, change has been happening quickly in recent years, and large tracts of Queens Quay are unrecognizable from just a few years ago. New residential and commercial buildings have sprung up, including a new harbour-side campus for George Brown College, and new public spaces such as the Sherbourne Commons and Sugar Beach have opened. Unlike Toronto's parsimonious traditions, Waterfront Toronto doesn't do things on the cheap, instead building public spaces of a quality that would be at . home in any of the prosperous alpha cities around the world.

Minnan-Wong's populist ranting against Sugar Beach – which is located at the foot of a former industrial quay across from the still-industrial Redpath Sugar refinery – is an age-old kind of Toronto opposition to nice things. It's a cliché now, and a boring one at that, but Toronto has long struggled with being a "world-class" city, a dead-horse phrase that brings up insecurity as it induces cringing. It's a struggle that publicly plays out around developments like Sugar Beach, where materials and infrastructure are top-quality, ostensibly the kind of thing people want when they argue Toronto is ugly and shabby, an eternal complaint among the grumpy classes.

Equally eternal, though, is the unwillingness to pay for the things the city desires, such as subways to Scarborough or, as is the case here, beach furniture. Inevitably a picture of Minnan-Wong appeared in the *National Post* with his arms crossed and his face in a very sad frown as he looked at one of the thirty-six pink umbrellas that, along with the Muskoka chairs sitting beneath them, dotted the human-made sandy beach. It was a wholly Torontonian gesture: we've done this before.

Fifty years ago when the new city hall was set to open, the Minnan-Wongs of the day objected to the cost of *The Archer*, the Henry Moore sculpture destined for Nathan Phillips Square out front, which has become a beloved and inseparable part of the city's civic heart. When the cheap burghers of Toronto said no, private money was found and the sculpture was ultimately installed as planned and the controversy is less a historic anomaly than one in a long line of precedents.

Although Minnan-Wong's complaint had political currency in the usual circles, the waterfront also has its vigorous defenders. When the councillor went to nearby Sherbourne Common and, still frowning, held a cardboard sign with the price of building the public washroom behind him on it, he was mocked relentlessly on social media and his sign photoshopped with silly sayings.

A meme for a few days, the reaction was nevertheless part of a wave of genuine affection for Sugar Beach and the waterfront redevelopment plans that crested a few times when under attack, whether it was Doug Ford's idea for a giant Ferris wheel that would scrap plans years in the making or, most recently, when Mayor John Tory wanted to rebuild the crumbling

Gardiner Expressway and squander a once-in-a-century water-front opportunity.

It's important to note that the organic-seeming swell of defence for all things waterfront was not entirely ad hoc but rather cultivated through a decade's worth of public consultation undertaken by Waterfront Toronto that created a built-in constituency. These were plans that "civilians" put considerable effort into making, and people became invested in them and wanted them to succeed, a testament to the long-term benefit of public outreach done right, something that hasn't always happened in the city, but Waterfront Toronto has both the budget and the mandate to do it.

That thousands of people snap and share pictures from Sugar Beach with the skyline behind it, amounting to millions of dollars' worth of free international advertising for Toronto, and that the land around these public spaces has become incredibly valuable and will result in a bountiful harvest of tax revenue each year, is lost when the immediate focus is on umbrellas, chairs, and rocks costing just under one million dollars, in a park with a budget slightly over fourteen million, consistent with other multi-billion civic showpiece redevelopments around the world.

MINNAN-WONG IS the antithesis of what has become known as a "city builder," the kind of civic leader who has an overt approach to creating a city's public spaces, transportation network, art, quality of life, and so on. It's a qualitative approach as much as it is (necessarily) a quantitative one. Hynes's own political leanings decidedly fall on the left of the spectrum and she spoke the city-building language, but also with a nod to how much things cost.

"People need to know you give a darn about them," she said. "But you've got to tell them tax is finite. You can't have everything." Back in mid-summer 2014, with three more months of campaigning ahead, she was optimistic, ready to keep walking the hilly streets but under no illusions, as the long slog takes its toll. "Volunteers and donations are growing slowly," she told me. "I'm getting people at the door saying they're tired of Denzil or that they've voted for him in the past, but not this time. I think Denzil is beatable but some days I get down."

On October 27 of that year almost 12,000 voters in Ward 34 chose overwhelmingly to return Minnan-Wong to city hall as their representative, with Hynes coming in second in a field of six, with just under 4,000 votes. Although nowhere enough to win, it's a respectable amount of votes for a grassroots, tiny budget campaign like what Hynes was running against a high-profile, career politician who has represented the area as a councillor since 1994, first when it was part of North York and later after amalgamation in 1997.

For his part, Minnan-Wong was awarded one of the coveted deputy mayor seats by Tory soon after the election and has continued to be critical of urban initiatives well outside his ward, such as the long-awaited Bloor bike lanes and other initiatives that cost too much money. It's almost as if the only thing people will easily spend exorbitant amounts of money on in Toronto are houses. Those who can, that is.

CHAPTER ELEVEN

WHILE NERO TWEETED

"DON'T DISMISS us as a sleepy suburban community," said Manna Wong as we wandered up Birchmount Road in Scarborough. "You have to walk around and talk to people, taste their foods, and hear their stories." We met at Huntingwood Square, a plaza on Birchmount across from the city-owned Tam O'Shanter golf course. "The community is safe, the trees are abundant."

The trees are indeed abundant but so are the fences in this deepest part of deep Scarborough, north of the 401, an area that was developed toward the end of the mid-century boom, during the 1970s or later. The neighbourhoods here are some of the newest parts of Toronto, the ones that swallowed up the last swaths of Ontario farmland inside the old Metro city limits, save for a few patches that still exist in the northeastern corner of the city by Rouge Park and the Toronto Zoo.

Urban dystopia was in the air when this part of the city was built. On Birchmount, along with places in Markham, Mississauga, and Toronto, new housing subdivisions turned their backs on the big roads that run through the middle of their neighbourhoods. The experience of walking up a busy arterial like Birchmount is akin to walking along a very wide alleyway with four lanes of traffic, a sidewalk that hugs the road and a wee strip of grass next to a near-endless line of backyard fences, as if the entire neigh-bourhood is hiding from the very roads the people who live here travel to get to and from their homes.

It's the suburban manifestation of the anti-urban senti-ment that was prevalent at the time these were planned, a phe-nomenon expressed radically in a whole genre of films during the 1970s, where the city was seen as something scary, some-thing to hide from, falling apart and filled with perps and low-lifes. Think *The Taking of Pelham One Two Three*, *Death Wish*, or even *Midnight Cowboy*; cities became very bad things and people fled to the suburbs, where the urban design seemed almost fortified, with its back turned to the public realm, all hatches battened down.

This is not a reflection on the people who live there now or the community that they have created in the interim; the neigh-bourhood design is simply a product of the sensibility of its times, and people find their place in a city like Toronto guided by a whole bunch of variables – affordability, availability, work, family, serendipity – not simply by choice and aesthetic prefer-ence. Those latter things are a luxury in Toronto.

FOR AN outsider, neighbourhoods like this remain mysterious, the life within quite literally tucked away and hidden, down dead-end culs-de-sac, behind big garage doors, and obscured by all that fence, but as we walked Wong talks about this place in the same way people who love, and live in, more demonstra-tive parts of the city.

"This is my neighbourhood," she said in the parking lot of Huntington Square. "Try the Chris Jerk." She's referring to Chris Jerk Caribbean Bistro on one corner of the Huntingwood Square strip mall, a plaza she is quite fond of. "It's like a microcosm of

Toronto. The Vietnamese restaurant has award-winning dishes. There's Greek, Chinese, Mexican; my kids come here too."

Wong has lived nearby for over two decades and raised four children here. As we talked and walked she mentioned her own children often and her love for children in general. It's why she ran for the Toronto District School Board's Ward 20 Scarborough-Agincourt trustee position in 2014.

"The children" have sometimes seemed like an afterthought in a series of crises at the TDSB in recent years. It wasn't always like this; Toronto once had a model school board. An institution that was the backbone of the city, the TDSB was a kind of civic citizenship machine that took students from every background imaginable and turned them into Torontonians. Its stated mission, "to enable all students to reach high levels of achievement and to acquire the knowledge, skills, and values they need to become responsible members of a democratic society," put it squarely in the realm of "peace, order, and good government" – as inspirational and aspirational as Canadian statements go.

Apart from adapting to Toronto's rapidly changing demographics, the boards operated alternative schools for the gifted, for children with special needs, and even a series of arts-based high schools that, like the one in the 1980 movie *Fame*, managed to produce some of the city's most creative people, feeding the local arts and indie music scenes: the Etobicoke School of the Arts produced members of the Broken Social Scene band, and Earl Haig Secondary School in North York, with its Claude Watson Arts Program, gave us filmmaker Sarah Polley.

So rich is the talent coming out of these schools that if you didn't know better you might think they are as expensive and exclusive as Julliard in New York, but all a student has to do to get into these public institutions is pass an audition or provide an acceptable body of work. The arts schools are just one example of how elastic and all-encompassing the TDSB was and, to a degree, still is.

The TDSB was the bedrock that kept the city together, and it did so quietly in the background, with Torontonians confident it was doing its work just fine. However, the story began to change in the late 1990s, when the amalgamation of Toronto also created one single board, now the fourth-biggest school board in North America, with upward of 250,000 students. Previously there were six boards, one for each of the individual municipalities in the old Metro system, all of them functioning under one umbrella board that coordinated operations.

Funding changes by the provincial Mike Harris government at the time undermined the TDSB's financial stability as well, creating a decade and a half of slow-burning problems. The trouble wasn't evident at first, perhaps only noticed by people within the system or parents and kids who were negotiating it.

Historically, school boards could raise funds themselves through local taxes, thus the need for the role of the trustee, ensuring there would be taxation with representation. Harris removed that function of the board, so that trustees have been, essentially, casting about for a purpose. Most voters didn't pay them much heed, and there have been calls to do away with them altogether.

Many, if not most, trustees genuinely care about the state of the city's schools and see their role as analogous to that of members of corporate or charitable organizational boards: to guide and advise. Some embrace a wider community leadership role when serving as a trustee, growing into the role the way charismatic leaders often do, and of course it's a place where the politically ambitious begin their long runs for a city council seat or other higher level of office; the first rung of the ladder, as it were, albeit out of the spotlight.

Ontario Premier Kathleen Wynn herself was a TDSB trustee before she was elected as an MPP in 2003. Despite her rise to the highest office in the province, trustee candidates will tell stories of having to not only explain who they are during municipal elections, but also explain the existence of the board itself. In Ontario, voters are also faced with the choice between the public board and the publicly funded Catholic board (a historical anomaly that goes back to Confederation and is particular to Ontario).

Wong faced geographic issues too. We walked together for more than an hour but only covered a tiny part of the area. TDSB Ward 20 is made up of two Toronto city council wards, in this case 39 and 40. There are more challenges still: the ward numbers for the school board do not correspond with the city council ward numbers, so it's even more confusing.

"We have to establish a new identity," said Wong. "I sometimes have to tell people our election is on the same day as the mayor."

From a candidate's perspective there is also the added difficultly that people who donate to trustee campaigns don't receive a rebate from the city, although donations to council and mayoral races do. "Are schools less important?" asked Wong. "A rebate would be a real incentive for people who have a hard time giving otherwise."

Sometimes the line "the children are our future" is enough to get people interested in trustee politics, but other tactics are often necessary. "Neighbourhood well-being is closely linked to our children and school," says Wong. "One woman lit up when I said it connects to property values too." Real estate is always a reliable way into the hearts and minds of Torontonians.

THE TDSB (and its Catholic counterpart) are essentially like a parallel city council, complete with embarrassing antics and monetary scandals. In 2013 TDSB's director of education, Chris Spence, resigned from his position after he was caught plagiarizing an op ed he wrote for the *Toronto Star* and questions were raised about the integrity of other articles he wrote, including his 1996 Ed.D dissertation.

His successor, Donna Quan, was equally controversial: in 2014 her contract details revealed she had negotiated a salary $17,000 more than was legally allowed. When questioned, she obfuscated and actively tried to hide information. Throughout the year a series of other small spending scandals broke, reminiscent of the old stories of how much it cost the Pentagon to purchase a hammer: in the TDSB system, electrical outlets went for $3,000 a pop; a replacement green bin came in at $2,703; hanging a picture in an office cost $700; and, the item mentioned in most news stories, attaching a pencil sharpener to a wall, cost taxpayers $143. On top of all this, with the smell of mismanagement, mendacity, and malfeasance in the air, there was Trustee Sam.

Sam Sotiropoulos, or "@TrusteeSam" as he's known on Twitter, where he became locally famous for his outbursts, was the incumbent candidate in Ward 20 and the man Wong was running against in 2014. Unlike most trustees, he managed to become quite well known throughout the years for his curious and sustained prurient interest in a handful of issues, either speaking to the media about them or using his Twitter account to broadcast his uncensored thoughts that surprised many people, especially coming from a trustee who was endorsed by the progressive Toronto and York Region Labour Council in the 2010 election.

He first surfaced when he took issue with the very small contingent of people who attend the annual Toronto Pride parade naked among the hundreds of thousands of clothed people, railing against the "buck naked" men at the event, a phrase he borrowed from Doug Ford, as if they were an army of sexual outlaws keen on taking over the city. After sparring online with a few city councillors and other folks who pushed back on his attack, Sotiropoulos said he was being bullied and discriminated against by the LGBT community, claiming he was a victim of, in his words, their "homosexism."

When his quest to ban nudity in the parade was unsuccessful, he took to an AM radio call-in show to insinuate there were pedophiles in the crowd. "Can you definitely guarantee to me that there may not be a kiddy-diddler mixed up among them?" he asked, with classic fear-baiting rhetoric. In the summer he again took to Twitter to attack some of the most vulnerable young people within the school system, tweeting, "Until I see scientific proof that transgenderism [sic] exists and is not simply a mental illness, I reserve the right not to believe in it."

Writing in *Toronto Life*, Philip Preville reported that at one TDSB trustee meeting, Sotiropoulos arrived late and held open the doors, "annoying the trustees who asked him either to enter and close the doors, or leave. In response, he called St. Paul's trustee Shelly Laskin a 'fucking pig,' repeating it to her face: 'Pig, pig, pig, pig, pig.' He then called York Centre trustee Howard Kaplan a 'stupid, mindless son of a bitch.'"

While Toronto's city council can be the most juvenile of places, with councillor antics shockingly dim-witted and embarrassing, they've rarely, if ever, sunk as low as the TDSB did during this period. The more Sotiropoulos made the news, the more folks were asking how this guy managed to get as far as he did in politics, even securing that labour endorsement, and why did the good people of Ward 20 vote him in? The fringe was inside the gates, and yet another bit of Toronto the Good's veneer was peeled back. When I asked her about Sotiropoulos's comments while she was running, Wong didn't want to talk about him.

"I just want to do my thing," she said. "We have to put our students first, they can't be discriminated against, and they all need to feel like they belong. This is a public school system, we have to accommodate everyone."

Sotiropoulos wasn't the only one to become Twitter-famous in the area: Norm Kelly, the long-time councillor for Ward 40, became known to the city at large when, as deputy mayor, he took over as acting mayor when Mayor Ford's authority was stripped from him by council at the height of his erratic behaviour. However, it wasn't until Toronto's own pop super-star Drake called the avuncular seventy-something councillor the 6 Dad, "The 6" being the nickname he bestowed on Toronto, a strange and unexpected spotlight was directed at city politics from an unlikely source. In doing so, @norm, as he's known on Twitter, gained well over 200,000 followers and tweeted out a steady stream of, well, dad jokes, funny pictures, historic facts, selfies, and aphorisms, all to the delight of Drake fans. Kelly has expressed an interest in both hip hop culture and the youth who retweet him, but not without criticism.

In the *Globe and Mail*, columnist Denise Balkissoon blasted Kelly, writing that Twitter is not his job, but doing good for Toronto is. "The politician says his interest in hip hop is youth-centered," she wrote. "Well, great. Scarborough has 100,000 residents under 14 and the city's highest population of 15-to-19-year-olds. But in the past five years alone, Kelly has voted against letting young people use city pools for free and against using millions of provincial dollars to create badly needed child care. He's also made insanely glib comments about climate change, the world's most pressing issue and one that matters more the younger you are."

With a diminished role in John Tory's mayoralty, Kelly is no longer at the centre of political power, and remains another oddity in the city council constellation. Sotiropoulos, no longer a trustee, although continuing to use the same Twitter handle that suggests he is, continues to tweet a transphobic monologue into the ether.

BACK IN the corporeal world, Wong and I continued our Scarborough exploration, walking north from the Huntington Square area, deeper into Ward 20. A perfect rectangle on the map, it's bordered by Steeles Avenue at the top, Victoria Park Avenue on the west, a CNR rail corridor between Kennedy Road and Midland Avenue on the east, and Ellesmere Road at the bottom. The area is bisected by the Finch Hydro Corridor and Highway 401, but otherwise it's a collection of mega-block subdivisions that house around 110,000 people, a mid-sized city unto itself.

"The population here is so big it's not possible to reach everyone at the door," said Wong of the additional challenge of being a TDSB candidate with such a large electoral area.

At Finch Avenue Wong pointed across the street to some apartment buildings, mentioning they're part of Toronto Community Housing Corporation's stock of affordable housing. "It's really a mixed community here," she says. "The neighbourhood also has $1.5 million homes." When she was able to meet people at the door, they told her the cost of living in Toronto was an issue, one that affects students profoundly.

"There are issues here of affordable housing," said Wong. "I talked to a principal with students who came to school hungry in the morning and he paid for their breakfast out of his own pocket." Toronto is full of unsung people like this school leader who hold the city together in their own, unofficial ways, but individuals can't address the deeper systemic causes themselves, and schools remain on the front lines of food insecurity and one of the critical points where the domestic and civic realm intersect.

There's an abundance of food in Toronto, so it's a double tragedy that there are hungry kids here. Cities are all about food, and getting food into one as big as Toronto is a daily military-like operation. The Ontario Food Terminal in south Etobicoke is the largest wholesale fruit, vegetable, and flower market in Canada, and one of the five biggest produce markets in North America. Toronto's "food and beverage cluster" itself generates sales of $17 billion a year and is one of the biggest on the continent. Supermarkets are also a measure of when an urban neighbourhood has matured, as they are usually one of the last businesses to arrive. They need a critical mass of people to make them financially sustainable.

Nearly a decade ago a Sobeys opened in the Terminal Building on Queens Quay, a near-last addition to the central waterfront that meant people didn't have to leave the neighbourhood to shop. Similarly, when CityPlace got its Sobeys on Fort York Boulevard west of Spadina Avenue, the new neighbourhood started to feel complete.

The foodies will argue about which market or vendor has the best produce or frown at chain supermarket butchers they're not on a first-name basis with, but for many people being close to a supermarket or market is one of best things about living in a city, especially come summer when Ontario farms start producing truckloads of produce.

Not all of Toronto is like this, though, and those of us who live in neighbourhoods with grand food palaces, such as the Loblaws supermarket at the former Maple Leaf Gardens arena and cheaper alternatives nearby, maybe take it all for granted. The city and other organizations have found areas that are called "food deserts" and "food swamps." A desert is an area where access to good quality and affordable food within walking distance is limited, and swamps are where there is an over-abundance of unhealthy food.

In 2000, Toronto city council voted in the "Toronto Food Charter," placing food and access to "nutritious, affordable and culturally-appropriate food" at the centre of its social and economic mission. If a neighbourhood has a few choices nearby, it's doing pretty well, but across the city it remains an unequal harvest.

The latest *Vital Signs* report from the Toronto Community Foundation, a deeply researched and useful annual document on the state of Toronto, points to the widening gap between rich and poor, happening here at Finch and Birchmount in deep Scarborough, and elsewhere in the city. Toronto has the second-biggest income gap in Canada after Calgary. The numbers are jarring, especially considering how much some parts of this city have grown and prospered since the recession of the 1990s. In Manna Wong's part of town a casual walk or drive along the streets doesn't necessarily reveal who's rich and who's poor; the landscape isn't one of extremes that would indicate there's a problem.

But there is a problem, and it's potential disaster for the city. "The median family income of low-income families ($14,630 before taxes in 2012) doesn't come close to supporting a household," cautioned a recent *Vital Signs* report. Considering a one-bedroom apartment can cost upward of $1,000 a month for even a small and not particularly well-kept unit, there isn't much left over for anything else, and that includes a nutritious breakfast. The report states that income inequality is rising faster in

Canada than in any other OECD country other than the United States and "impacts everyone, as median incomes and income mobility stagnate, poor health outcomes among those with low incomes leads to lost productivity and higher health care costs, and income polarization creates a widening achievement gap in city schools."

Almost one in three children were living in poverty in Toronto in 2012, and in fourteen communities across Toronto that number went as high as 40 per cent: "Many of these children and their families live in unaffordable, overcrowded, and unsafe apartment high-rises in the inner suburbs, and are at some risk of housing vulnerability." The report also notes that this poverty is racialized, with residents of African, Asian, Middle Eastern, Caribbean, and Latin American background much more likely to be in the low-income bracket. It's also much more of a problem in the inner suburbs, where visits to food banks have skyrocketed since 2008, with a 38 per cent increase.

That Ford support closely matched the map produced by David Hulchanski's *Three Cities Within Toronto* report is telling, charting how Toronto's neighbourhoods fall into three groups based on income change during that period. Recall that "City 1" is the predominately high-income area in Toronto where incomes have risen "a great deal relative to the Toronto Census Metropolitan Area (CMA) since 1970 and are generally found in the central city and near the subway lines," reads the report. "City 3" was different, "a generally low-income area of Toronto, in which neighbourhood incomes have fallen substantially over the past few decades compared to the CMA average."

City 3 neighbourhoods are mostly located in the northwestern and northeastern parts of the city, including Manna Wong's Ward 20. In-between City 2 represented middle-income areas where income has remained relatively stable. These are important shifts in the Toronto reality that contrast with the egalitarian view of the city, which suggests that opportunity is equal, something embodied, ideally, by the TDSB's historic mission. With the middle-income areas of the city having shrunk dramatically between 1970 and 2005, and high-income area increasing slightly, it's been the low-income areas that have increased substantially, consuming more of the city.

The report and its corresponding map also showed that poverty has moved away from the centre of the city to the edges. When the poor lived in the central city, they at least had access to good transportation and other city services. However, the inner suburbs grew too fast, and there's meagre support infrastructure for people in need, so people like the principal Wong spoke of are taking up some of the slack. Living in Wong's neighbourhood, a job in another part of the city could take at least an hour on transit, time that eats into quality of life.

A 2016 study by McMaster University professor of labour studies Stephanie Premji and Access Alliance Multicultural Health and Community Services made a connection between precarious work and long commutes on poor transit systems designed for nine-to-five jobs. Participants in the study reported they spent between 10 and 20 per cent of their household income on commutes that could take between three and six hours a day.

The *Three Cities* report is careful to point out these are all long-term trends, not a recent phenomenon that surprised everyone, and that the segregation of the city by income is not inevitable or irreversible. Nonetheless, for those facing it today, there's little hope on the immediate horizon that it's going to get any easier.

Despite all this, and as Wong pointed out, these parts of the city remain desirable places to live. As we made our way north we passed by the Agincourt neighbourhood, named after the

Battle of Agincourt during the One Hundred Years War, part of Toronto's long tradition of naming parts of the city after British history and geography. Also in Toronto fashion, Agincourt has evolved away from its Anglo-Saxon roots and is today considered one of the city's three Chinatowns, adjacent to Markham's large Chinese population.

Wong also pointed out there's a large Tamil population here too, plus the mix of backgrounds typical of Toronto. Wong, an immigrant from Hong Kong herself thirty years ago, describes the work ethic of immigrant families who come here and struggle for a better way, a familiar trope, but on the corner of Finch and Birchmount a bulletin board on a bus shelter was entirely filled with tutoring notices for students.

"The people who came here sacrifice everyday for their kids," says Wong, referring to all the notes and the apartment tower behind them, and the drive to succeed. "It's why you see so many Saturday math classes."

Away from the wide arterials we walked into clusters of tightly knit streets with townhouses and more apartment buildings within these superblocks, a hidden density and urbanity that Toronto's inner suburbs don't get enough credit for. These interior streets curve gently and as it was an overcast day, without the sun to orient myself, I lost my bearings.

We also passed branches of Highland Creek with pleasant walking and cycling trails along the banks. Here, well north of the wild ravine and naturalized state of the creek in the southern part of Scarborough, the waterway is narrow and channelized in concrete, cutting across neighbourhoods in straight diagonal lines, and only allowed the freedom to meander naturally in a few places.

Like those fences along Birchmount indicated, the neighbourhood is from the same era when the natural landscape was something to be tamed by urban planning, concrete, and bull-dozers, which erased most traces of the natural topography and restrained the sinuous nature of the creeks.

It wasn't always like this, and not far from here Don Mills, "Canada's first planned community," followed the contours of the land it was built on in the 1950s. Still, the passageways created by Highland Creek are oblique routes through the neighbourhood, making it a porous place that can be enjoyed when negotiating on foot or bike, a kind of industrialized, modern version of the romantic network of passages, or "closes," found in the city of Edinburgh. Wong tells me her children learned to ride their bikes along the creek passages and that they are used by many of the kids around here to navigate their neighbourhood.

SOON WE reached L'Amoreaux Collegiate Institute with its distinctive 1973 design by Toronto's Raymond Moriyama, the architect behind other landmark Toronto buildings including the Ontario Science Centre and the Toronto Reference Library. L'Amoreaux is a landmark in its own right as it has a starring role in the music video that the rock band Rush created for their 1982 hit song "Subdivisions."

With passionate Rush fans worldwide rewatching this video for years, L'Amoreaux has lived in the imaginations of people far beyond Scarborough. The video is a remarkable document of early 1980s life in the Toronto suburbs. Dave Glover, the teenage protagonist in the video, was actually a student at the school at the time. The video was shot when this was still a recently built neighbourhood and the school body was overwhelmingly white, a marked difference from today's demographics, just thirty years later.

Neil Peart's lyrics offer a rather dismal characterization of suburban life, however:

> Sprawling on the fringes of the city
> In geometric order
> An insulated border
> In between the bright lights
> And the far unlit unknown
> Growing up it all seems so one-sided
> Opinions all provided
> The future pre-decided
> Detached and subdivided
> In the mass production zone
> Nowhere is the dreamer or the misfit so alone

Since the song was written and the video shot, L'Amoreaux has lost its fringe status, as Rush referred to it. Toronto managed to use the often-bland prefab foundation the suburbs were built on to absorb multicultural populations and build communities, turning the suburbs into a place where growing up isn't so one-sided and isolated in opinion or thought. A city, in other words. The challenge is figuring out how to unleash the potential here – currently suppressed by the income, services, and transportation issues that afflict it.

PAST THE high school Wong led me to McNicoll Avenue, where we walked along the vast open space of the Finch Hydro Corridor, a place that one day could see some form of rapid transit, easily connecting this part of deep Scarborough to the rest of the city. Wong says she chose to stay in Toronto after emigrating from Hong Kong because she could be part of a bigger, mixed city yet have her own community, and she has no time for the urban-suburban divides others dwell on.

"Frankly, I don't like the idea that this is us and that's you," she says. "We're one Toronto of unique communities, but dividing those communities doesn't help anyone. We just need to make sure there's representation at the decision-making level." In 2014 voters in Ward 20 opted for Manna Wong's message of inclusivity of all kinds, so that she won with over 11,000 votes. Yet nearly 10,000 people here still voted for Sam Sotiropoulos, despite, or because of, all that he stood for, so the second battle for the hearts and minds of Agincourt isn't likely over yet.

CHAPTER TWELVE

A CITY PREOCCUPIED WITH DIVIDING ITSELF

IN BERLIN, there is a relentless strip of two-across paving stones zigzagging its way through the city. The path crosses intersections and runs along sidewalks, sometimes stopping at a building or other obstacles, only to start up again on the other side. A casual glance might suggest it's just part of the European hodgepodge of paving materials, but every so often there is an inscription in the pavement reading "Berliner Mauer 1961–1989," telling passersby that this was the site of the Berlin Wall.

What's remarkable about this linear memorial is how normal and everyday it seems now, with Berlin life taking place on either side of it, without much notice that the line is even there marking the former border between East and West and between ideologies that defined half a century of worldwide conflict. It's there if you pay attention, and Berlin does force visitors to confront history, but the city on either side of the strip continues joyously apace despite the tragedy, murder, and Cold War machinations this line represents.

Modern Toronto has had no such strife, but the borders that no longer exist here take on an exaggerated meaning. Where Berlin has figured out a way to move on, Toronto can't seem to let go despite the stakes being so low.

THE INTERSECTION of Victoria Park and Danforth Avenues doesn't call attention to itself much – it's an everyday kind of unremarkable place. But there should be a historic plaque here to mark that it's where three of Toronto's six former municipalities met – East York, Toronto, and Scarborough – before they were dissolved and amalgamated into one megacity in 1997 along with North York, the City of York, and Etobicoke.

The actual meeting point was a few dozen metres south of the intersection itself, but it's as close as Toronto gets to "Four Corners," the site in the American southwest where Colorado, Utah, Arizona, and New Mexico meet, one of those places where you can physically move from one arbitrary spot loaded with symbolic meaning to another arbitrary spot. The plaque would be a memorial to a place that does not exist anymore: the Municipality of Metropolitan Toronto.

Created in 1953 when the suburbs surrounding the old City of Toronto were beginning to grow rapidly and a need to coordinate all the growth was quickly becoming critical, smaller municipalities and quite a bit of rural landscape were combined under one regional "metro" government that looked after things such as police, transit, and public works, while each of the six individual municipalities looked after other matters that catered to each city's individual needs, allowing for different political and civic cultures to develop. Some might even argue that different existential ways of thinking developed about what a city should be.

The idea of what "Toronto" is can be quite distinct in different parts of the city, although the geography is relatively close together and other political and cultural connections are plentiful.

"DOWNTOWNERS HAVE a different understanding of local government," says Zach Taylor. "Fundamentally, the politics of postwar suburbs were about service delivery, while the old city was about people." Taylor taught at the Cities Program at the University of Toronto's Scarborough campus (he's since taken a position at Western University in London) and ran a mapping project called "Big City Politics" with his students that looked at voting patterns using geographic information system or GIS data – who votes for what, and where. They found that political ideas that resonate on one side of Victoria Park don't necessarily play out on the other.

What makes the differences at the municipal level of government, unlike those at the provincial or federal levels, is that ideas are formed around a particular kind of identity politics that relates to lifestyle rather than more ephemeral notions of ideology or intergovernmental and international relations.

It's the identity of everyday life: what happens on the sidewalk out front or where the driveway meets the rest of the city. However, the attention paid to municipal governance is the inverse of its actual effect; it keeps everyday life running, yet has the lowest voter turnout of the three levels of government.

A useful characterization that's often employed to explain this dynamic goes something like this: if the federal government ceased to function, it might be a month before we notice; if the provincial level closed up shop, we would notice in a week or two; but if the municipal government disappeared we would notice in a matter of hours. The water would stop running. Electricity would flicker. Garbage would pile up. Snow would drift across the streets. Ambulances and fire trucks would not respond, and so on.

Municipalities in Canada need to deliver these services – it's their provincially mandated primary and critical function – but like their global counterparts, more of them are also increasingly getting into a headier kind of big-picture thinking called "city building." Few would question, at least in Canada, that at the federal level the government's role is "nation building." How it's done is up for debate, certainly, but all but the libertarians would agree that government has some role to play in this country that relies on institutions to continually define what it is.

City building is not yet a universally accepted term in Toronto, though, and is oft criticized as being overly ambitious and a distraction from the government's core service-provision concerns. Opponents of this kind of active governing may also suggest city building is a left-wing or socialist project, but there's strong drive in cities around the world to address broader city issues that cut across the political spectrum and have as much to do with creating a robust civic life in the city as with filling in the potholes.

In London, both Boris Johnson, on the right, and his predecessor Ken Livingston, on the left, have been mayors who embraced city building, for example, building bike superhighways that snake their way through the capital and (even if a financial and design boondoggle) commissioning a contemporary Routemaster bus that evokes the old London jump on, jump off double-deckers, a move Johnson thought would help boost the civic identity.

In New York City, centre-right billionaire Mike Bloomberg oversaw three terms of ambitious city building, turning most of Broadway, the most famous street in America, over to pedestrians and cyclists, at the same time as Toronto fought over individual bike lanes in neighbourhoods. Bloomberg also banned artificial trans fats from New York restaurants, a nanny-state kind of move but part of his downright progressive effort to change the city.

Mayors are municipal rock stars and some operate with a swagger that is the policy wonk equivalent of moving like Jagger. In Chicago, Richard Daley bulldozed the waterfront airport he wanted removed under the cover of night and under dubious legal circumstances. Daley's successor, Rahm Emanuel, has spent tens of millions of dollars creating a riverwalk along the Chicago River, in his words, "returning the river to the people," and is one of his legacy projects, along with the Chicago Architecture Biennial he founded, with lofty aims to be the architecture capital of North America.

During the 2015 Canadian federal election when the niqab became a dog-whistle political issue, scapegoating Muslims in Canada as well as the Syrian refugees who were on their way, it was, in part, Canadian mayors who stood up and said it was both distracting and divisive. In particular, it was Alberta's big-city mayors, Naheed Nenshi in Calgary and Don Iveson in Edmonton, who took leadership roles on the issue, making public statements that became national news. These two mayors stepped into a national role that wasn't listed on their job descriptions because there was a void that needed to be filled. That's city building, and nation building too.

These mayors and others like them, regardless of their political leanings, knew they had to think big because cities have become drivers of economic and cultural growth, and they need to be on the cutting edge of policy to compete, a trend that will continue with increased urbanization. Globally, de facto city states are absorbing the immigrants migrating to the countries they're located in, and often lead the way in areas of public health, public education, and cultural change.

Denver has been on the ground floor of Colorado's marijuana decriminalization, a change that has affected the city profoundly. In 2015 the Mile High City hosted a "Marijuana

Management Symposium," inviting officials from jurisdictions across the country who saw change coming to their own municipalities to travel to the city and hear about how they're dealing with it. The state didn't require them to do this, but the city decided to take a leadership role.

Toronto, despite all its petty antics and parsimoniousness, has quietly performed a similar kind of duty for some time under the radar. The Toronto District School Board has long been the sponge that absorbed the children of Toronto's celebrated immigrant population and turned them into Torontonians and Canadians, teaching English and instilling institutional Canadianness on them. The Toronto Public Library and its one hundred branches constitute the busiest urban library system in the world, fuelling the city's intellectual and social life. Toronto Public Health began HIV/AIDS education on the streets and in the bathhouses of Toronto in the 1980s when higher levels of government were yet to acknowledge the existence of this plague, and before same-sex marriage was legislated across Canada, Toronto city hall began issuing gay-marriage licences.

The city led the way and it's at these points that the big thinking and service delivery have always met; this is not a new thing. But Toronto is a city still reluctantly coming around to the idea that it is, or can be, one of the great ones, so there is constant resistance to city-building talk and a fear of thinking big. When there isn't an active push toward city building, the void will be filled with the rhetoric of division, geographic or conceptual, leaving lots of room for hefty wedges to be driven between residents of the Toronto.

"We need a better leadership class," says Taylor. "I don't know who they are, but at every level we've developed a politics based on divisions." It's those politics of division that make Victoria Park and the Danforth so interesting. Many people look wistfully back at the Metro era in Toronto politics as a golden time. Throughout the Ford years there were calls from people opposed to his mayoralty to "de-amalgamate" the city and return to the decentralized Metro model, a time held up as utopian, although the cost would be enormous and there appears to be no political will to do so.

Often Vancouver will be cited as an example of a city that works, but Taylor calls it "jewel-box politics" where the small-ish older city of around 600,000 was never amalgamated with suburbs such as Surrey, Richmond, or Burnaby. "Imagine if all of Vancouver amalgamated – the same would happen there," he says.

Although Taylor says the age of amalgamation is over, the toothpaste, as they say, is out of the tube in Toronto, and the civic teeth have become accustomed to being brushed with it. If Toronto is going to figure out how to make this place work, Victoria Park and Danforth is a good place to start thinking about how to do that. The former Metro borders often run through ravines, out of sight and out of mind, but this meeting point is one of the busiest and most visible.

The landscape at our "Three Corners" may not be the rugged high desert of the American Four Corners, but it does have a bank, gas station, and Danforth Shoppers World, the latter, built in 1962, deserving a plaque of its own as one of Canada's earliest enclosed shopping malls. There was once an Eaton's department store here – the first outside of a downtown centre – and the plaza lent its name to the now-ubiquitous Shoppers Drug Mart chain, when founder Murray Koffler opened a pharmacy here – the chain's very first – that same year.

THIS CORNER is what a lot of Toronto looks like. There are low-rise residential areas nearby, the large Crescent Town apartment neighbourhood is a block north, and independent retail shops along Danforth are plentiful. The Victoria Park subway station is newly renovated and ravines are close by too. It's Toronto. Some people walk here. Some drive. Bicycles even roll by. Some own their homes; others rent. People go about their business, city life carries on, and unless you already know, it's impossible to tell which corner here was located in Scarborough, East York, or Toronto, although some people hold onto those old fading lines on the map dearly.

In the fall of 2013 I wrote about this intersection, a place where the differences between the old cities disappear, in my *Toronto Star* column. The local MPP at the time, Michael Prue, wrote a letter to the editor, taking issue with my suggestion that we focus on the similarities rather than the differences on each side of the street.

"East Yorkers – by and large – still resent the forced amalgamation of the borough," he wrote, recalling his previous role as the former mayor of East York in the Metro era. "We were debt-free, had a thriving municipal government, and hundreds of volunteers who gave up their time and talents to make our municipality unique. Watching the recent shenanigans at city hall only reinforces our sense of loss. And yes, if a referendum were held to de-amalgamate, many, if not most, would seize the opportunity to take back that which was so brutally removed."

It was a remarkable letter for an MPP whose current riding included parts of the old City of Toronto and East York to write, revealing how bitterly he held onto the lost amalgamation fight of nearly two decades before. There was also no sense in his letter that East York itself would have not evolved had it remained its own municipality and that it wouldn't be facing many of the same growth pressures the whole city faces today.

Everybody longs for a jewel box. The letter also revealed how deep and strong the politics of division are here: that an MPP would rush to divide the very people he represents, rather than looking for the strengths, connections, and common cause in a system that isn't about to change soon. It seemed an effort in nostalgic vanity rather than a way forward. For his part, Prue was defeated in the provincial election in 2014.

However, not all politicians are so focused on division – for example, look at Paul Bocking.

I MET Paul Bocking at busy Victoria Park and Danforth, the beginning of Ward 35, Scarborough Southwest, where he ran for city council in 2014. A refreshing thing about talking to people who are new to politics is their lack of cynicism, cynicism being something that may be at the root of the current leadership class's division fetish.

"I was shy about canvassing at first, fearing people would slam the door, but people were overwhelmingly nice and polite," said Bocking of his first experience running for office. However, not everyone was as nice, and a candidate is often a lightning rod for rage. "I had the misfortune of knocking on the door of a man who made his passionate hatred of me very clear," he said. "And probably like most candidates, I met hundreds of prematurely curmudgeonly, scowling white men aged 35 to 65, who made no effort at politeness when I visited their houses."

New candidates like Bocking whom I met made the city seem exciting again, full of issues and problems to be sure, but not mired in old hang-ups. Many of them could also talk about service delivery and city building in the same breath, as they aren't mutually exclusive, unless you have something to gain by couching them that way. There are problems and they need to be fixed, but they need not divide the city.

A RESIDENT of Ward 35 for four years, Bocking was working on a Ph.D. in economic geography at York University and was also an occasional teacher with the TDSB while campaigning.

"I taught at Birchmount Park Collegiate a couple of years ago. The concerns of my students around rising TTC fares and cuts to frequency of bus routes got me interested in running."

Bocking wanted to meet at the three corners because it was the beginning of the ward, but also because Danforth Avenue, after it crosses the old border into Scarborough, doesn't have enough streetlights on one side of the road. "Toronto Hydro says they don't need more lights," he says. "It's quiet here at night, though, very different. People aren't comfortable."

Although it's all technically one city now, a close reading of the Toronto landscape reveals the former municipalities in subtle ways: vestigial street signs from the old cities endure; vernacular bits of infrastructure particular to each city, like the kind of streetlamps and the cut of the curbs, are different; but even more fine-grained are places like Danforth here, as urban on one side of Victoria Park as on the other, but the automotive-inspired built form is taking its time catching up to the more urban ways residents use this part of the city. Formerly a mixed industrial area, Danforth as it meanders northeast into Scarborough is an interesting strip now with lots of potential, lined with automotive-related businesses and quite a few empty storefronts.

As it is now, the street is reminiscent, if a bit more spread out, of what Ossington Avenue was like a decade ago before it became hipster ground zero. Then it too was a place to get a car fixed, find a new bathtub fixture, and perhaps sing karaoke in a Vietnamese dive bar with the windows blacked out.

When I first moved to Toronto in 2000 I took the Queen streetcar out to visit a friend who lived on Foxley, a street just off Ossington. The trip seemed far out then, although that seems like a ridiculously narrow notion of what a long trip in Toronto means now. She told me to go one stop beyond Ossington and get off at Dovercourt Road and backtrack. She wasn't exactly imploring me to do so over concerns for my safety – although there had been a handful of gang-related shootings on the strip that marked it as a place where things like that happened – but simply because it was a shabby walk.

There's shabby and there is shabby chic, and Ossington had not yet evolved to the latter, which, arguably, it is now. Danforth Avenue is still the first kind of shabby, and it still seems "far out" to a lot of people who don't live near it, but those two things will change in the near future and this will probably be the first part of Scarborough that Toronto's ravenous real estate market discovers as the next hot neighbourhood.

All it takes is a little activity that catches the notice of the rest of the city for a neighbourhood's geography to morph to something more proximate in their imagination. So much of this is based on perception – just ask the Junction neighbourhood on Toronto's west side, or Leslieville in the east – they're not referred to in the same geographic way they were even a decade ago when both were considered "out there," depending on where one was standing. Geographic change came fast, though.

In Robert Fulford's excellent 1995 book on Toronto, *Accidental City,* he writes about making the journey to Olga Korper's new gallery on Morrow Avenue, just off Dundas as it starts to curve north toward Bloor Street and Roncesvalles Avenue. He recounts getting into a cab and going to what were then the wilds of undiscovered Toronto, and how much of a pioneer Korper was, moving out of the usual downtown gallery district, a sensibility that seems quaint now but continues to repeat in other parts of the city. At some point some lazy writer will say "Scarborough is the next Brooklyn," if they haven't already, and the change will continue.

"The ward is generally working class, there aren't really any wealthy neighbourhoods, but there are some middle-class areas," says Bocking. "Also a large base of Bangladeshi, Tamil, Filipino, and Chinese families, and British, Italian, and Maritime seniors." The housing here is a mix of post-war bungalows, some still occupied by the original owners, and tower neighbourhoods like the one on Teesdale Place at Pharmacy Avenue, a block east of Victoria Park.

Teesdale Place is built on the banks of Taylor Creek, where multi-use trails connect west to the Don Valley. The city-owned Dentonia Park Golf Course is here too, providing an affordable golf option for people who can't meet country club prices. The towers of Teesdale are also connected to Victoria Park Station by a long walkway, and when a subway train leaves the station the sound of it rattling along echoes up dozens of storeys.

Here Bocking mentioned the South Asian Women's Rights Organization working out of the Teesdale apartments, which is engaging people around issues such as a $14 minimum wage and local hiring and employment policies, issues he campaigned on. Many living here were professionals in Bangladesh or Pakistan but can only find work at places like Tim Hortons or driving cabs, another old Toronto story that's become something of a cliché, but it's here you can find parking lots with offduty cabs parked by the towers, the human side of the trope.

It's lush here, by Teesdale. Like others found in the ravines, the Dentonia golf course blocks continuous access along Taylor

Creek, something that could be corrected with a simple public right of way as there are parks on either side of it, with Ward Woods continuing along the creek upstream, deeper into Scarborough.

This ward is triangle-shaped, with Victoria Park and Eglinton Avenue forming the western and northern borders and the diagonal GO and VIA railway corridor along the south. Taylor Creek meanders through the middle of the ward past Warden Woods, but the trail here doesn't continue through Pine Hills Cemetery, and the waterway eventually slips north of Eglinton toward its headwaters north of Highway 401.

Also dividing it is the last leg of the Bloor-Danforth subway corridor, with Warden and Kennedy Stations wholly inside of Scarborough, often forgotten by some local politicians who have claimed Scarborough does not have a subway of its own.

AS WE head north along Pharmacy by Teesdale, the faded ghostly traces of bike lanes that were removed in 2011, along with those on nearby Birchmount Road and Jarvis Street downtown, are visible. The current councillor, Michelle Holland, ran her first 2010 council campaign in part on removing the Scarborough lanes, even producing a flyer playing on this wedge issue during the worst of the bad old days in the rhetorical "war on the car."

Although it doesn't take long to see cyclists here, with kids from the apartment buildings illegally riding the sidewalk instead of in traffic, a flyer put out by Holland in 2010 vilified the previous councillor, Adrian Heaps, as having "MADE TRAFFIC WORSE," claiming that his support of more bike lanes would increase traffic congestion, and that he "supported Mayor Miller's attack on motorists in our city." In her flyer she promised to remove the "unnecessary" Pharmacy and Birchmount bike lanes and relegate new lanes to side roads, stating, "No More Bike Lanes on Busy Streets in Scarborough."

The street is as busy as ever. Bike lanes don't change that, but they do make it safer for the people who ride them. Traffic is bad in Toronto and as more people move here it will get worse: additional lanes won't make it any better, because it's been shown that bigger roads just attract more traffic, not less. But going after bike lanes is an easy scapegoat because driving in Toronto is no longer anybody's idea of fun, and tapping into the rage will get drivers emotionally invested in an election.

Holland's husband is Lorenzo Berardinetti, the Liberal MPP for the provincial riding of Scarborough Southwest, and both are part of a rather powerful informal lobby of Scarborough Liberals who are behind the Scarborough Subway, another civic conversation that doesn't always hinge on facts and rationality.

"A couple of days after signs went up, I saw on the major street adjacent to my home an impressive wall of signs for the incumbent councillor," said Bocking of the daunting emotional task it was to run against a power incumbent. "For the following week, I tried to avoid riding my bike down this stretch of Pharmacy Avenue."

BOCKING **AND** I walked Danforth Road as it veers diagonally across the street grid, away from confusingly named Danforth Avenue, as if it's Scarborough's answer to Broadway paying little heed to Manhattan's grid. He said the film industry should be encouraged to locate here in this patchwork of older industrial buildings and open land amid the postwar residential streets and new infill. There's retail here too, some in strip malls and older, pre-war buildings, but it's struggling. There are traces of old spur railway lines snaking their way around the area as well, evidence of a mighty industrial past, and some of the former industrial buildings are now houses of worship, the cheapest and biggest space around.

Planners tend to frown on this kind of sacred adaptive reuse, because once a congregation moves in, the area becomes less desirable for other industrial tenants, who don't want to deal with the parking and pedestrian issues that houses of worship bring. Not far north of here is the "Golden Mile" along Eglinton Avenue, so named in the 1950s because it represented a prosperous commercial and industrial future when it was opened by none other than Queen Elizabeth II early in her reign. Back down on Danforth there are busy places like The Newfoundlander Tavern and Mama's Boys Burgers, but a number of storefronts are empty, their customer base sucked away by the big-box stores that now line the Golden Mile, so it remains a Broadway in waiting.

Bocking and I walked the breadth of Ward 35 for two hours along Danforth, slowly in the heat, stopping for bottled water at a convenience store in lieu of a fountain, an amenity harder to come by in the inner suburbs even though there are people who walk here everyday and could use a drink. The unplanned mix of uses continues until Danforth meets Eglinton Avenue by Brimley Road, where the streets create a triangle of sorts.

At first glance nobody would call this area vibrant: it doesn't look like the downtown streets that are celebrated in Toronto for the life and variety of commercial establishments along them. Toronto has many extended and continuously interesting sidewalk strips in the old city that are the envy of so many cities that wish they could create just one, but get outside of downtown to places like Danforth and Eglinton, and the same downtown patterns emerge where many least expect them. They just look a little different.

The inner suburbs of Toronto are blessed with versatile retail blocks that can be used by waves of entrepreneurs for all kinds of purposes too, but here they're in the form of the ubiquitous strip mall, a place where Canadian dreams can be made. All along Eglinton, plazas straddle both sides of the street, intermittently in either direction from the Danforth Road intersection. A few have names, such as Liberty Plaza, but those are almost irrelevant: they're just plazas, like a block downtown is just a block. Neighbourhood destinations.

There are a few recognizable chains in these strip malls, such as H&R Block and banks, and familiar institutions, for instance, a Toronto Public Library branch, but the rest are independent retailers selling just about everything: silks, jewellery, haircuts, passport photos, cheeseburgers, eyeglasses, rotis, flowers, burritos, and books. There are butcher shops, travel agents, music schools, pharmacies, Irish pubs, British pubs, Caribbean pubs, Sri Lankan restaurants, bakeries, wool shops, barbers, and some places that defy categorization.

If these blocks were downtown they would be beloved stretches and people would flock to them and they'd be constantly written up, but because they're behind a few rows of parking, they're often dismissed as being just another boring part of the suburbs. Watch how people use the strip malls, though. Some people drive to them, but a lot also walk from neighbouring houses and apartment buildings, adapting to the car-centric landscape that can often be dangerous or, at the very least, unpleasant, when not surrounded by a ton of metal.

Not all see these as places where Canadian dreams are made; former mayor Mel Lastman once said, "Strip plazas have got to go. These things are a holy mess. Their time is over." It's a feeling shared by many who think the mess is ugly, but the mess is economic freedom and produces the kind of organic urbanism that urban thinker Jane Jacobs revered and for which down-towns used to be famous.

Rents are cheaper, so space is affordable to people with little start-up capital. Downtown, the rent alone is often a prohibi-tive barrier, and explains why we get repeating landscapes of Starbucks cafés and other big businesses that can afford to establish themselves on the city's expensive high streets. The strip malls have become the places where mom-and-pop stores can open. If they were part of an institutional framework they would be called "economic incubators," but those are sexier and better funded. Nonetheless, the strip malls are where some of the most exciting sidewalk economy is taking place.

The strip malls and what they represent is why talk of de-amalgamation is so troublesome in Toronto: the city trades on a reputation these strip malls and surrounding areas gives it bragging rights to. We're proud of being one of the most mul-ticultural places on earth, but that multiculturalism happens more in the inner suburbs than it does downtown. As Zack Taylor said, the era of amalgamation in Canada is likely over, but not so in other places. Paris is planning to join the central city that all the tourists see with the ring of less wealthy inner suburbs around it that are rarely visited, to, as the *New York Times* reported in February 2015, "redress a century's worth of urban decisions that have exacerbated the country's gaping cultural divide."

The newly created municipality will be called the "Metropolis of Greater Paris" and will have a population of almost seven million people, three times the amount that live in the central city now, and it's hoped the inequality that caused riots in tower blocks in years past could be alleviated by sharing some of the core's wealth. Although Paris has a larger population, Toronto has a similar situation, with tower blocks and apartment concentrations in the inner suburbs that have been missing out on the city centre's *Sesame Street*-style urbanism of opportunity and prosperity. Paris is moving ahead in a spirit of goodwill and inclusiveness and Toronto, despite already being set up to connect itself together in deeper ways, is stuck arguing about bike lanes, with sitting politicians writing letters calling for the city's break-up and a return to a glorious, if Balkanized, past.

It's self-defeating and energy sucking. To be sure, things like local governance and community decision-making can be improved, but when living in a house divided, only a masochist wouldn't try to find constructive ways to fix that division. As Bocking found at the door, these are neighbourhoods that are worth keeping central to the very idea of Toronto.

"In the midst of thousands of usually brief encounters, there were some beautiful connections that I will never forget," Bocking said. "Meeting my former students, the president of a local mosque who invited me to join his family for dinner, a Portuguese family who shared boiled crabs in garlic juice, the Greek man who plied me with ouzo during our political discussion, his long-time neighbour, a retired plumber, who showed me his rose garden and picked me a ripe tomato that I then made a mess of eating on his immaculate driveway."

IN A time when cities are becoming as influential as countries, it's foolish to divide Toronto simply because of how things were built and over small differences in lifestyles. Great cities are places where economic and cultural elements percolate together and unplanned things happen. More ingredients mean more possibilities. This doesn't mean people in Toronto have to go out to eat in the suburbs more or that people in North York should buy groceries on College Street – although they can if they want – but that focusing on what we've all got in common, such as figuring out how strip malls and downtown streets work, would help Toronto get around inflated barriers.

Toronto has people who win elections through divisions, a reason why it needs city-building projects as much as Canada did from Confederation onwards, knitting together the fabric of the country through both transit ways and the emotional and symbolic ties to hold it together. Fixing Toronto's transit problem may be to the city what building the CPR was to the country.

Canada is an invention, and none of that nation building happened organically or accidentally – it took a concerted effort to fill the void. Toronto has the same kind of space to fill but, in the end, voters in Ward 35 picked the incumbent Holland (who reverted from "Berardinetti" to her birth name in 2016), in a landslide victory with nearly 12,000 votes, with Bocking coming in second with 2,700 votes, a respectable showing for a first-time candidate in a ward where the Berardinetti name represents something of a minor but prominent political dynasty in the Scarborough Liberal heartland.

"Ward politics are really empowering for long-time homeowners that have deep roots in a neighbourhood," said Bocking. "It's disempowering for everyone else. I think this leads to a certain duality between groups and areas focused primarily on immediately local concerns, like how the sidewalk snow plow cuts into their lawn, or that guy's annoying fence, and people that move around more, and are more likely to be concerned about TTC fares."

Downtown, suburb – Toronto argues so much with each other it's as if a low-simmering culture war is ongoing. Who lives where seems to matter, even if it's difficult to tell just who's from where by looking at them. The homes residents live in might be a little different, but are they that unlike each other?

Berlin had a murderous wall running through it and the city has been knitting itself back together for twenty-five years now, yet Toronto remains ready to slip into old notions of "us and them" whenever it's urged on by leaders with something to gain by keeping them apart.

CHAPTER THIRTEEN

OUTLIERS AND BEDBUGS ON THE SCARBOROUGH BLUFFS

"DON'T COME in," came a raspy woman's voice from within the apartment. "I've got the bedbugs." The door was ajar and Parthi Kandavel had pushed it open a little further with his knock, enough to get a glimpse of the piles of garbage bags inside and to let the ripe smell out into the hallway. "Just leave your stuff on the table."

Kandavel slowly closed the door and we walked back down the hall. We didn't say anything to each other for a while, and then there was nothing to say about it.

We were in a TCHC public housing tower just off Kingston Road by the Rosetta McClain Gardens and high atop the Scarborough Bluffs. Kandavel was showing me some of the hidden poverty in the area where the reality of Toronto's affordable housing crisis can be seen, and smelled. The squalor of the apartment and its contents stuffed into those garbage bags in what appeared to be an effort to deal with the bedbugs was in sharp contrast to the sunny day outside where kids played and the birds chirped.

It's the only tall tower in the neighbourhood and, from the outside, looks like any other residential mid-century modern apartment building, with a location in one of the most beautiful spots in Toronto by the spectacular bluffs that run for a dozen and a half kilometres along Toronto's Lake Ontario shoreline. These are Toronto's most dramatic natural features, apart from the ravines, which, by their nature, are hidden from view below grade. And, like a ravine property, not much real estate is valued more in Toronto than a place on the bluffs, although the spectre of sliding into the lake, as houses on the California coast do on occasion, is always there as the bluffs continue to erode in places.

That such poverty is hidden in beautiful places is a reason these troubles have remained outside of Toronto's civic narrative for so long, and the human inclination to play ostrich when something doesn't affect us directly is strong. Unless the door is pushed open, deliberately or not, it's easy not to see it.

Kandavel got to know the building when he was running to be the trustee for Ward 18, Scarborough Southwest, on the Toronto District School Board. Few people opened the door when Kandavel canvassed its floors, so we left the building and he took me across the street to a narrow, paved laneway that led down a steep ravine lined by a thicket of trees on either side. The lane is easy to miss and there's little to suggest a public right of way is here, and no grand welcome for the glory that lies below. The entrance is just east of Wynnview Crescent, a short dead-end street with well-tended front gardens and cute little houses that could be anywhere in middle-class Canada but is a world away from the apartment we got a glimpse of across the street. At the bottom of the ravine the road ends at an overlook in the bluff face, with a tremendous view of the lake and bluffs themselves rising up from the blue water to the east and west.

"Coming from an island off an island, I feel a connection to water," said Kandavel while surveying the lake. Kandavel was born on the Velanai off the northwest tip of Sri Lanka, a place that saw considerable violence during the twenty-five years of the Sri Lankan civil war that began in 1983. The lake here, as in so many places along the bluffs, has a deep azure colour on sunny days that makes it seems quite sea-like, almost tropical. Almost.

Lake Ontario is a cold, deep lake and although it is quite swimmable, its chill can be felt when standing near it. Other Torontonians who feel a connection to water have to work at it here, because despite the long shoreline Scarborough enjoys, access to the beaches below the bluffs is often hard come by, and in many places breakwalls have been constructed to prevent erosion, limiting direct access to the lake.

KANDAVEL ROAMED the city above that shoreline a lot when he was running for the Ward 18 Toronto District School Board trustee position in 2014, concerned about the hidden poverty in the ward as it affects the quality of education of students, as so many other extracurricular things do. With his affection for large bodies of water the ward was the right place to run: the triangularly shaped district straddles the lake from the edge of the Beach neighbourhood in the old City of Toronto, and runs nine kilometres east.

Running all the way north to Eglinton, a considerable distance in the western part of the ward, it's a lot of ground for one person to cover. In Toronto, school board wards encompass two city council wards, in this case Wards 35 and 36.

Of the three positions voters decide on in municipal elections – mayor, councillor, and school board trustee – the trustees are given the least attention, and even voters up on their local council race might have only slight information about who the trustee candidates are. With so much territory to cover, Kandavel was taking me around in his car to see the breadth of it, as doing it on foot would be a days-long hike.

Kandavel described this part of Scarborough as "eclectic," and indeed it's a place of dramatic contrasts, both in topography and wealth. Kandavel said it ranges from working-class neighbourhoods in the northern part of the ward, to multi-million dollar homes south of Kingston Road along the bluffs, not too far east of the TCHC building we visited.

We took a brief detour into the lush grounds of the Toronto Hunt Club, a private golf course on the bluffs, close to the R. C. Harris Water Treatment Plant in the Beach. The lake view from the links is fantastic but Kandavel wanted to share some Scarborough history: the year he moved to Scarborough with his parents at the age of six in 1988, after a stint in England on the way to Canada from Sri Lanka, Prime Minister Brian Mulroney hosted the likes of Margaret Thatcher and Ronald Reagan here during a Group of Seven summit.

Hardly visible from the street, the Hunt Club was a good place to host world leaders in the days before global summits required kilometres of concrete and metal fencing, locking down whatever city it's being held in. This is old Scarborough too, a part of Toronto whose history is often overlooked, as are leafy neighbourhoods like those around the Hunt Club.

Established by officers at Fort York in 1845, the club has been at this site since 1895, although all hunt-related activity was transferred elsewhere by the 1930s. Signs along Kingston Road on either side of the Hunt Club tell would-be bluffers that there is "no access to the bluffs," so the streets are quiet and the neighbourhood retains the quaint feel of the Beach neighbourhood, with quirky houses and a cottage feel. A series of laneways and passages makes for an interesting walk east of the Hunt Club along the waterfront trail as it weaves in and out of the streets south of Kingston. A few peeks of the bluffs and lake are possible here and there between the houses and where there are small parks that do indeed give some bluff access, although there are fences and signs that warn people to stay away from the unstable edge.

IN BLANTYRE Park, north across Kingston Road from the Hunt Club, the neighbourhood character changes to a combination of working- and middle-class housing, although this neighbourhood, judging by some of the replacement houses and major renovations, and its proximity to the Beach neighbourhood itself, is on an upward, middle-class trajectory. Here residents tended to answer their doors.

"People sometimes think I'm a real estate agent asking if they want to sell their house," said Kandavel, of his experience at the door when he was canvassing. Every Torontonian who owns a ground-level house will have a steady parade of real estate agents at the door cold-calling to inquire if they want to sell, an ambulatory version of the office-bound agents in David Mamet's *Glengarry Glenn Ross*.

"Ninety-eight per cent of the people were very friendly, they respect on a fundamental level that I'm out here on the street. At the door I can get a good sense of how many seconds I have to give my spiel."

That spiel included telling residents he's a teacher himself, the third generation in his family, and that he wants schools to increase physical education and address bullying more directly. On top of those issues he had the added challenge of getting people to understand why school issues matter in an election to people who don't have kids. Test scores helped with that.

"Sixteen of twenty-two schools in this ward are below provincial average," he said, although he was also quick to point out that scores are only a small part of a good education. However, as they do affect property values, people without kids might feel compelled to look closely at who they're voting for, apart from a general interest in the well-being of future generations. It's a useful issue to bring up when many people have little understanding of why they're voting for a trustee and what they do. In recent years some TDSB trustees had elevated their office into the headlines with questionable expense habits, including the incumbent Kandavel was running against, Elizabeth Moyer. The school board also reprimanded Moyer in May of 2014 for having breached the trustees' code of conduct when an independent investigation found that she had sexually harassed two executive staff members during her tenure on the board. Political drama need not stay confined to the mayor's office.

WHEN I walked with Kandavel as he knocked on Scarborough doors during his campaign in 2014, people who answered were generally engaged, one man telling him something needed to be done about the teacher unions, another woman saying she was glad Rob Ford had dropped out of the race so that more time could be spent on issues like the schools. When he brought up the need to get kids to exercise more, Kandavel would repeatedly make a joke about "the kids and their iPads" and do a swiping motion with his finger. It was effective; most would laugh, as did the woman who came to her door with a cigarette in her mouth that had an inch and a half of ash precariously dangling from the tip. "Oh ya, those iPads," she chuckled. "Got to get them outside exercising."

Other people had a voter's natural skepticism when a stranger showed up at the door asking for their time. It's fascinating watching candidates build up energy just before each knock for a mini-performance staged every couple of minutes where they have to then react to the voter's mood or questions or anger, as if they were a stand-up comedian responding to hecklers, albeit politely. It's a unique and relentless kind of retail politics that mixes the details of daily life people bring to the door with them with whatever ideas can be wedged back through the doorway in twenty seconds.

Watching it unfold reminded me of being a paperboy in the late 1980s when I would knock on doors once a week to "collect" the money I was owed. Perhaps like politicians at the doorstep, I always got the sense that people didn't want to see me there, asking for $2.10 for a week's worth of *Windsor Stars*, so I had to charm them a bit, show them I was just a kid in the neighbourhood providing them with a service they wanted, not just the bearer of bad news. The brief glimpse into their lives, houses, and the moments I interrupted were fascinating and gave me a deep reading of the street I lived on, details I'd have otherwise missed out on if I didn't have an excuse to knock. The smells, the state of dress, what was on the TV, and over-heard conversations all amounted to an understanding of the neighbourhood that I've only replicated by working on oral history projects, which gave me another excuse to knock.

Candidates on foot get this kind of invaluable local reading on what matters to people, and what their lives are like, one that doesn't much happen at the mayoral level where there's just too much territory to cover, but most certainly does at council and trustee level. These politicians are the people who have the most visceral understanding of the domestic life of the city.

"People are looking for anchors, some sense of connection that they share in the whole," Kandavel said. To demonstrate, he took me to see the Scarborough cenotaph found in the median where Kingston Road and Danforth Avenue meet, a wedge of land that isn't easy to get to as both roads are busy and there's no crosswalk. It has stood there since it was erected in 1931 and has plaques memorializing the wars Canada has fought in with the names of the people who didn't make it back to Scarborough etched on them. Coming partially from a first-generation immigrant family myself, the connection to place and country these kinds of markers provide are a way into a history that "we" didn't necessarily participate in, and they become our memorials as much as those of the people with direct family connections to them, a remarkable but subtle kind of assimilation, one Kandavel certainly felt.

He had parked across the street from the cenotaph in the back lot of Chick 'n Burger a half block east, an old-school roadside greasy spoon that advertises "Hamburger w/ Fries $3.99" and "World Famous Chicken Burgers." "Parking is for customers only," said a woman leaning out of the doorway, eyeing us warily as we walked toward the street.

"We're just going to see the cenotaph," Kandavel answered, pointing across the way.

"Oh the cenotaph, all right then, no problem," she answered, her demeanour changing from suspicion to encouragement and even a nod of solidarity.

Anchors like this memorial matter and connect people to each other and the city, as do issues like property values, test scores, and all the other political discussions on Toronto streets, but there are also things that don't much get discussed on the doorstep.

"People don't want to talk about race," he said, when I asked if these were issues that came up at the door in light of race increasingly becoming a central issue in Toronto over the last few years, from Mayor Ford's racist comments, to the treatment Olivia Chow received during the election, to police carding of black males and Black Lives Matters activism.

"We're a small conservative place," he said, distilling down the essence of Toronto into five simple words, a city that for all its much-vaunted multiculturalism and cosmopolitanism has an incredibly hard time discussing how race actually plays out on the streets and in the hallways of power in Toronto. Some have argued that the veneer of a multicultural peaceable kingdom that Toronto has projected for the last forty or fifty years actually serves to stifle the necessary conversations on race, because it suggests everything is okay or at least better than in many other places.

Further east along the Bluffs, Kandavel took me into the Scarborough Village neighbourhood south of Kingston Road. One of the wealthiest areas in all of Toronto, it's a kind of Rosedale on the lake: big house, large yards, and a deep pocket of money most Torontonians overlook. Unlike the Rosedale neighbourhood's stately Victorian and Edwardian homes, the houses here are all postwar builds, although some aspire to old-money vibes with faux historic trims.

The neighbourhood surrounds Sylvan Park, an uneven cleft in the bluff wall where ravines cut their way down to the lake. It's an unheralded part of the city, a forested and wild place with narrow dirt paths making their way to the beach below.

At the bottom of Gates Gully, a long ravine that runs up to Kingston Road, a large and striking Corten steel sculpture called *Passage* by artist Marlene Hilton Moore is installed near the water. The design, based on both the rib cage of a fish and the ribs of a canoe, is an homage to the late artist Doris McCarthy who lived 57 metres above this place on the adjacent bluff in a house she called Fool's Paradise.

In 1998 McCarthy donated her home and a $500,000 endowment to the Ontario Heritage Trust, stipulating Fool's Paradise be used as an artist's studio and retreat after her death, which came in 2010. Earlier, in 1986, she had already donated seven acres of ravine land to the Toronto and Region Conservation Authority, and the main trail that runs up Gates Gully was later named after her.

McCarthy had purchased the property in 1939 and named it after what her mother called her new property, as she thought the extravagant purchase was silly, but McCarthy was ahead of the real estate curve, even at a time when this area was quite rural and removed from the city.

To some this area is still remote from the downtown, about as far from city hall as Rob and Doug Ford's Ward 2 is, give or take a few kilometres as the crow flies. Like the ward where Ford Nation was spawned, this place "out there" was home to another outlier in Toronto politics, David Soknacki, a mayoral contender who tried to match populism with ideas.

WHILE OUT canvassing, Kandavel brought me to this neighbourhood to see the full socio-economic spectrum of the neighbourhood, and specifically to knock on Soknacki's door and chat with the would-be mayor himself. But nobody answered the door at his or any of the houses nearby; the entire neighbourhood was quiet, as if everyone was away on summer holidays. Often rich neighbourhoods feel the least lived-in.

In many ways Soknacki was an interesting eastside counterpoint to the Fords on the west side. All were from the suburbs and are wealthy and conservative, although where the Fords might be seen as far right, Soknacki is a centre-right small-c conservative.

Unlike the Ford brothers who inherited their family business, Soknacki started his own spice trading company in 1986. From 1994 to 1997 he was a councillor in pre-amalgamation Scarborough and then from 1999 to 2006 he held Toronto's Ward 43 council seat. During his time on Toronto council he served as deputy chair of the budget committee under Mel Lastman, and later as chair of the committee itself under David Miller, his "budget chief," as the position is known, one of the most powerful council positions.

Miller's Soknacki appointment was seen as a gesture to the centre and centre-right of his council, and a sign the mayor wasn't the left-wing zealot his opponents made him out to be. Though a fiscal conservative, Soknacki is also conservative in the Red Tory tradition. While a councillor, he led the push to establish a Poet Laureate of Toronto post and was far from a slash-and-cut conservative, even raising taxes while budget chief.

He retired from politics in 2006, then began his comeback in early 2014, when he registered to run for mayor on a city-building platform, proof that expansive urban policy can transcend the left-right dichotomy.

And there was lots of policy. The tall and lanky Soknacki was the nerd candidate, an image his campaign ran with. He insisted on talking policy during the campaign rather than focussing on whatever direction the prevailing political winds were blowing at the time. There were facts and figures. Studies. Ideas.

He came out with enthusiastic support for the Scarborough light rail plan rather than the Ford-supported subway. "We should never rewrite transit plans that are already paid for, designed, and engineered," Soknacki said, when he released his full platform, going further to say he didn't have an oversized stunt transit map at his press conference like other candidates did because it was up to professional planners and transit engineers to draw the lines.

During the election there was a flurry of these kinds of transit maps, each with their own scheme of new routes, be they subway or light rail, all suggesting different trajectories through Toronto. Most were lines drawn quickly on a map, without the deep study transit planning usually entails. Soknacki also said he would look at the police budget, usually an untouchable part of city policy as it, among other things, risks of being seen as soft on crime.

He talked about reducing rental tax rates on commercial and industrial buildings and reducing pedestrian deaths, resisting the war on the car rhetoric even though he was from one of the most car-centric neighbourhoods in the city. He was also civil, the Wayne Gretzky of Toronto politics, skating around others while they engaged in the dirty fisticuffs of attack politics.

Urbanists and other left-of-centre folks, people who publicly expressed how much they missed David Miller's progressive mayoralty or who might naturally be attracted to an overt NDP candidate like Olivia Chow, were excited by Soknacki. A campaign about ideas! *Finally.* But it's a narrative that failed to be heard among the populism and bluster of a long campaign where the Fords set the tone.

"I still meet people at parties who learn that I was David's manager and then they start this excited spiel: 'I so wanted to vote for David, but we had to get rid of Ford . . .' It's the same speech, over and over, word for word," says Brian Kelcey. "Lack of enthusiasm wasn't our problem." Kelcey is an urban public policy consultant and managed Soknacki's campaign. Previously, he had spent time in the Mayor of Winnipeg's office as a budget advisor and has been involved in municipal and provincial politics in various other capacities. He was recruited to the Soknacki campaign by conservative campaign consultant Jim Ross.

"I assume it was because David and I have a very similar philosophy on city politics," said Kelcey. "We're both mostly socially liberal, and we're both fiscal conservatives. But we're also both strong urbanists, and both of us took pride in working constructively with all sides in our respective tours of duty in different city governments." Ideas may not resonate with voters, but the nerd image did. Like Rob Ford, Soknacki came by his persona naturally.

"For the record," said Kelcey, "David is so unique a guy that even his nerd credentials are eccentric; he's more like a sober, season-one version of Gordon Clark on *Halt and Catch Fire* than he is a Sheldon Cooper on *Big Bang Theory*. Still, that 'nerd candidate' phrase helped to humanize his unusual political identity, it gave our (geek-rich) team some needed cohesion, and it even helped to define his core constituency, all at once."

Kelcey pointed out that being seen as a policy wonk can be a liability but that nerds are now a "positive political personality." A summer campaign rebrand ran with "the cuddly nerd thing" and one team member proposed Soknacki actually campaign at ComicCon, the massive comic book fan expo at the convention centre that is a bit of a nerd mecca.

Kelcey said the real "disease" that killed their campaign was the hatred potential voters had for both Rob and Doug Ford and that without either of them on the ballot they'd have likely been polling at 20 per cent in September, enough to be in range for a win come October. "But the ballot question for those same voters was 'which candidate will get rid of the Fords,' not 'which candidate is best to replace them,' so even some of David's biggest fans were locked in to voting for Tory or Chow," said Kelcey.

"The problem with our strategy wasn't that we weren't capturing the imagination of voters. The problem was that we weren't capturing actual votes. Our long-game thinking was working on some metrics, insofar as David's name recognition rose from 16 per cent on day one of the campaign to over 80 per cent by September with growing favourables, bringing him to a place where he could compete with the celebrity candidates who'd all started with 80 per cent plus name recognition in January."

Kelcey is finishing a book about municipal politics called *Mayoring: Success and Survival in the Second-Hardest Job in Politics* that has a global view but is informed by his participation in both Winnipeg and Toronto politics. The Soknacki campaign was modelled after other successful come-from-nowhere mayoral races such as Naheed Nenshi's in Calgary, David Miller's in Toronto, and Bill de Blasio's in New York.

Kelcey also points out that famous, big-name mayors such as Ed Koch in New York and Richard Riordan in Los Angeles were able to rise from 0 to 6 per cent polling to ultimately win. Yet, in September 2014, Soknacki dropped out of the campaign just as some late-game momentum seemed to be helping his low polling and fundraising. The money just wasn't there to keep the campaign going, and debt builds quickly.

Kelcey said that Soknacki was a somewhat more difficult come-from-behind candidate in that his success in the spice business meant he had lots of international contacts but lacked a strong local network. "David Miller made the point to me that people forget he (Miller) was a Bay Street lawyer before he ran for council, and so he started with a network that he could fundraise from," says Kelcey, of the former mayor.

Many municipal politicians create a network with a run for a school board trustee position, and cynics will say it's the place where the electorally ambitious go to boost their name recognition, playing a political long game, making their way up inside politics rather than doing something big in civilian life before jumping in with some name recognition. In August 2015, the new chair of the TDSB, Shaun Chen, stepped down from his position and took a leave of absence as a trustee to run in the fall federal election as a Liberal candidate, a move that wasn't a surprise, although he was less than a year into the role. Not all agree with the cynical view of trustees of course, especially school-board candidates themselves. "There's so much you can do in the role of trustee," said Kandavel. "You can help create a sense of community, neighbourhood, and connect with parents."

With name recognition from his previous run in 2010, Kandavel was able to win the crowded TDSB Ward 18 ballot, beating nine other candidates with just under 7,000 votes. The incumbent, Moyer, came a close second with about 350 fewer. Two other candidates were able to get more than 4,000 votes, so the vast ward was by no means a sweep.

It's an interesting area in that it's a microcosm of the entire city in one corner of Scarborough: rich and poor; cozy neighbourhoods; fast and wide arterial roads; apartments and houses; and a topography that is sometimes far from beautiful, but also stunningly so in places. The divides between downtown and suburb don't make a lot of sense here, and Kandavel is optimistic about the rather wild political roller coaster the city has been on during the previous four years, where divides in the city were both encouraged and cultivated. "This is just Toronto coming of age," he said. "We'll reconcile our seemingly deep differences, but it'll take some time. It'll take some work."

CHAPTER FOURTEEN

THE END OF TORONTO?

WE WERE halfway into the Highland Creek Wastewater Treatment Plant when we were asked to leave by a kind but determined City of Toronto employee. We were looking at the sedimentation ponds, idyllic-looking pools with mechanical skimming machines on top. It's an essential function of any city to deal with its waste, but this is not a tourist attraction, although there was a small sign at the gate reading "Visitors" that suggested an open invitation to come inside.

In some places there is indeed such a thing as infrastructure tourism, and visitors to the United Kingdom will tour the great civil engineering works of Isambard Kingdom Brunel, master of Victorian bridges, tunnels, and railways. Even in Toronto, taking one of the Saturday tours of the R. C. Harris Water Treatment Plant in the Beach was a rite of urban-appreciation passage in the city until 9/11 security concerns ended public visits to it, and on Doors Open in May, an annual weekend where public and private properties are opened up for tours, people will line up to see the inside of all sorts of public buildings that otherwise might be thought boring.

The Highland Creek facility hasn't yet received the evocative treatment Ondaatje gave the Harris plant, but I still reluctantly followed Amarjeet Chhabra through the sewage plant gates on a sunny warm day at the beginning of summer. She wanted to show me the source of one of the contentious issues in the eastern end of the Toronto waterfront. Being around politicians is an adventurous experience: how they approach any encounter is different from how most people do it.

They act with a forthrightness and a sense of entitlement to their way that gives them the boldness necessary for everyday campaigning, where inserting themselves into all sorts of situations is required. They'll say hello to strangers on the street, look them in the eye while smiling, and assume a quick sense of familiarity. Being shy isn't good for their future job prospects. They'll also join conversations on porches, approach tables in restaurants, and even here, along Lake Ontario, walk into a sewage treatment plant.

When we were stopped by the plant employee, I instinctively started to head back to the gate at the first signal that we weren't supposed to be there, but Chhabra pressed our civic interlocutor with more questions. What did he think about the plant itself? What were his thoughts about its relationship with the neighbouring communities? What about the biosolids? Still friendly, but aware we weren't just a couple of overly curious sightseers, he smiled again and asked us to leave, so we did.

"It's beauty and the beast," said Chhabra, of the plant and its location. She wanted to show me this place because the biosolids it produces, as fine a colloquialism for civic turds as there ever was, are trucked out through the nearby residential community, and many residents would rather see the on-site incinerators updated so the waste doesn't have to pass by their homes. It was an issue she heard a lot about when she ran for council here in Ward 44 in 2014.

Like many conflicts across the city between industrial and residential uses, it erupted years after the industrial site was established, which was long before either the modern community was built, or before it became the kind of neighbourhood that complains about a sewage plant. It's an inevitable arc in Toronto neighbourhoods, whether involving the island airport, increasing rail capacity on the GO Train line to Barrie, or dealing with what the city flushes down the toilet. Opened in 1956, with numerous expansions later, the plant is a big complex spread over a number of acres along Lake Ontario by the mouth of the creek that lends it its name. Its moment of grace is the rather artful Brutalist concrete building and exhaust stack that dominates what is otherwise a bucolic, near-rural landscape. It's worthy of some romanticization by the city's authors, certainly, but for now the literature of this place is written in the technical language of environmental assessments and planning documents.

The plant is not an unpleasant place to be around, even if there is a faint smell of something a little off in the air now and then. Sewage plants aren't what they used to be: the trees are thick, there's ample fauna in the air and on the ground, and trails lead through a jungle of ferns and bushes down to the lake. It's right along here that the mighty Scarborough Bluffs give way to a much more tame shoreline closer to the ground.

When the plant was first built Scarborough was largely a rural place, dotted by farm villages and a few larger enclaves, but the plant was far from any major settlements. Although most of Scarborough has been developed since then, the land around the plant has remained an oddly exurban place and a bit feral, with a few houses scattered in the scrubland along the adjacent railway corridor, appearing more township than suburb. Yet the proximity of other residential neighbourhoods just a little farther away have resulted in pressure to fine-tune Toronto's urban fabric here.

In the broadest of strokes, the way the city works now has evolved from the fast progress of mid-century development that filled up all available land to a more civic-minded approach where the concerns of people here are at least listened to. Such concerns today, like those around the biosolids, are similar to the kinds of issues people in the older parts of the city have had for decades.

COMMUTERS SPEEDING eastward out of Toronto by train follow the railway line that hugs the Lake Ontario shoreline for about four kilometres, beginning at the mouth of Highland Creek and extending to the Pickering border, where it then curves back inland on the way to Oshawa, Montreal, and beyond. The lake is an azure blue if the skies aren't grey, a hue that doesn't seem possible after all we've heard about Lake Ontario over the decades.

Scarborough is full of surprises, and one of them is that the lake is beautiful here. After getting kicked out of the sewage plant, we walked east along the waterfront trail. "You don't need to go anywhere expensive to get away," said Chhabra, looking at the cottage country in Scarborough's backyard. She's right; this part of southeast Scarborough is a gem. The paved path along the water is crowded on warm summer evenings when people promenade and selfie themselves with the lake as backdrop, something that wasn't possible in the not so distant past, before what was a rough bit of the Scarborough shoreline was turned into the Scarborough Riviera by the Toronto and Region Conservation Authority with a series of massive but elegantly constructed concrete breakwalls that created a linear park.

This new "Port Union Waterfront," named for the adjacent neighbourhood, begins on a bridge above the mouth of

Highland Creek where regular GO trains rumble by on the old railway bridge. Once they pass by, the dominant sound here is of lapping waves and birds. Some of those trains even stop at the Rouge Hill GO station a little further east, which has an exit right onto the trail so that people living in the GTA can, in fact, take the train right to a beach in Toronto, something other cities would celebrate but such a new experience here that Toronto is only getting used to it.

People in this corner of Scarborough are ahead of the curve, though, already using it. The waterfront trail now connects to the one that runs up Highland Creek and into Scarborough's interior, and ends at Rouge Park beach, where Toronto itself ends in a rather beautiful spit of shifting sandbar at the mouth of the Rouge River, with the Pickering nuclear plant in the eastern distance. Here another old truss bridge carries the trains in and out of the city over the Rouge and a smaller adjacent bridge allows the trail passage into Pickering. It's the edge of the city, but still deeply connected to it.

This all could be the beginning of Toronto, but in political terms, it's the end, as it's the forty-fourth of forty-four wards and twenty-five kilometres from city hall. In 2014, Chhabra was up against Ron Moeser, the incumbent with the second-worst attendance record in city hall during the previous four years, and although poor health was cited as the reason he missed so many meetings, he waited until the last day possible to register for re-election, six weeks before the election itself. It's a sneaky but allowable tactic that many incumbents employ, making it difficult for challengers to figure out who or what they have to campaign against, and one of the built-in advantages to incumbency on top of name recognition.

At one debate Chhabra called his council attendance the "elephant in the room" but since city hall doesn't live viscerally in the minds of the general population unless the mayor is doing something exceptional, the individual presence of councillors matters even less. In this sense, city hall has much in common with the Canadian senate: out of sight, out of mind.

Other issues Chhabra said people here talk about are lack of social services in the area; less funding to local organizations, as compared to other parts of the city; and a general disillusionment with the never-ending transit debate – all similar to grievances heard in other outer wards. "People want to see a shovel in the ground," she said, as we walked outside the plant. "They just want something built."

Transit talk in Toronto will turn nearly everyone into a cynic, but this part of Scarborough in particular is a long way from the planned Scarborough Subway route and will receive little if any benefit from it. Arguably, the Transit City light rail proposals that reached further into Scarborough, all the way to Malvern a few kilometres north of here, would be a fairly short bus ride away, making other parts of the city easier to get to. It's here at the edge that the size of Scarborough is most evident. *Scarborough* is a name so often tossed off, as if referring to a neighbourhood somewhere in the east end of the city, making it easy for the idea that one subway line there could solve some transit problems.

If you were to fold Scarborough over to the west, as if the city were a paper map, it would cover all of Toronto, North York, and most of Etobicoke. Scarborough is massive. Anybody wanting to govern this city has to contend with its Los Angeles scale, as a distributed city with relatively high density in nodes downtown and elsewhere, separated by vast territories of relatively lower density. The Toronto-Los Angeles comparison is one that keen observers are beginning to use rather than Toronto's traditional counterpoints like New York or Chicago, which are, perhaps, the cities some people wish Toronto could be, rather than the one it is.

Chhabra first gave Toronto's big house a shot in 2006 when she entered a competition called "City Idol," a fun riff on the *Canadian Idol* and *American Idol* television shows and started by long-time Toronto civic activist and organizer David Meslin. It was an effort to get more people representative of the city's demographics involved in local politics. So true to the television model was Meslin that he got a cease-and-desist letter from CTV at one point. During four well-attended events at various venues during that election cycle, more than one hundred potential candidates were vetted and voted on as if they were pop stars, but instead of tunes they talked policy. It was wonky showbiz at its best and, eventually, four winning candidates were picked and given some support to run in that fall's council election, including Toronto writer and activist Desmond Cole, who has gone on to become a critical voice in Toronto.

None of the City Idols won that year but Chhabra, then in her mid-twenties, had run in Ward 43, Scarborough East, and received some early local exposure. Later, she worked for a labour union, and in 2013 re-entered politics by way of the nomination race to be the NDP candidate in the provincial riding of Scarborough-Guildwood.

In that race she was controversially beaten by star candidate Adam Giambrone, a former downtown city councillor whose nascent mayoral campaign in 2010 was ended early by an adultery scandal that clashed with his squeaky-clean image, a turn of events that seems cute after the wild Ford years. Giambrone was a parachute candidate who did not live anywhere near the riding, and there was more than a whiff of great white hope when the Ontario NDP picked him in a nomination process that Chhabra disputed with a legal action.

The irony in the 2013 provincial election was that both Giambrone and the Liberal challenger who beat him, Mitzie Hunter, were both once supporters of the Transit City plan to provide intelligently-planned transit to Scarborough rather than the politically-conjured subway: Giambrone in his role as former mayor David Miller's hand-picked Toronto Transit Commission chair, and Hunter in her capacity as CEO of Civic Action, a civil society group that advocates for city issues. John Tory himself was CEO of it before elected mayor, and some have argued that he too abandoned some of his Civic Action principles to get elected.

All of them eventually supported the subway, and in 2013 Giambrone and Hunter even campaigned on it, the latter even putting "SUBWAY CHAMPION" on her election signs. Such is the state of Toronto politics, where transit has always been a political football, free from evidence-based decision making, bouncing recklessly down the field, only to be punted again.

Ward 44 itself is a diverse landscape, with Highway 401 bisecting it like an extremely wide concrete belt. Most of the ward is relatively new, built in the last three or four decades, although like a lot of Toronto, smaller communities were absorbed as the city grew, so that the ward includes older villages like West Hill, Port Union, and a curiously quaint bit of two-lane blacktop along Old Kingston Road, once the main road between Toronto and points east before Highway 401 was built.

Here Scarborough feels like a small Ontario town, with occasional farmhouses and former roadhouses tucked into the newer developments that enveloped it, like ghosts from the not-too-distant past. There's a restaurant on Old Kingston, just after it dips in and out of the Highland Creek ravine, called Ted's. It's a diner like many another, but it's been here since the mid-1950s, a constant presence in a built environment that has continuously changed.

"Everyone goes to Ted's," says Chhabra. "Go there if you want to know what's going on." These kinds of places exist all across Toronto, giving a small-town vibe within the bigger city. They're good in that they can give people a sense of familiarity and a quaint urban scale, but they also feed the illusion that Toronto is still just a dusty burg instead of a city of nearly three million people with all the things that come with metropolitan life.

The area includes large swaths of typical postwar developments, the earliest neighbourhoods having generous yards, larger than most in Toronto, built when land was still plentiful and the pressure on maximizing the value of each lot wasn't as great. There are massive parks here too, along Highland Creek as it meanders through a large part of central Scarborough, its dominant watershed. The creek runs below the University of Toronto's Scarborough campus (UTSC), an ever-growing place established in 1966 with a space-age concrete campus designed by the same architect as the CN Tower.

Perched on the edge of the Highland Creek Ravine, it's the kind of place where deer will occasionally be spotted grazing on the school's lawn, having wandered up one of the trails from the creek where, if visited at the right time, the salmon migration upstream can be observed down below. On those days a *Wild Kingdom* film crew would not be out of place there.

Although still technically a satellite of the university's downtown St. George campus, UTSC has an orbital pull of its own and a diverse student body that doesn't necessarily see downtown at the centre of things but rather just another, albeit large, node in the city. Chhabra mentions there are issues around illegal rooming houses near the campus because the demand for student housing is high. Many of the more than ten thousand students who attend courses here, as did Chhabra herself, a former biology student, will stay in the area, creating an underappreciated layer of intellectual capital and creative potential yet to be fully realized, as in downtown where the student and university presence has been part of the city for a century and a half.

On the east side of the ward along the Toronto-Pickering border Rouge Park is planned to become Canada's first urban national park, although infighting among various levels of government has delayed its creation. It's a massive park and its watershed extends right up into the Oak Ridges Moraine north of the city. But the lower portion is in Ward 44, in which Toronto's only campground is located, where outdoors lovers can be lulled to sleep by the hum of cars and trucks passing by on the 401 next to it, a sound not unlike the white noise of ocean surf. But the vastness of the green spaces such as the Rouge, or along Highland Creek, are an uncelebrated Scarborough landscape in which Torontonians can experience settings ranging from very urban to near-rural or wild without ever leaving the city itself, a characteristic that doesn't fully factor into the city's identity.

JUST NORTH here by the Toronto Zoo are some of the Rouge Park trailheads. I've gone on long walks here with my dog, parking by the zoo or further south along Twyn Rivers Drive. The trails along the edge of the Rouge Valley offer a panoramic view, as Grand Canyon as Toronto gets but with the high-tension power lines of the Gatineau Corridor, like electric intravenous tubes, feeding Toronto.

Shorter trails can be accessed at various other points along the Rouge, with lesser-known ways in such as the informal path at the end of Island Road, a residential street in the older part of Port Union, tucked in just south of the twenty-odd lanes of the 401. The path leads down into the marshland of the lower Rouge and deep into the reeds where the ground becomes unstable underfoot, changing from solid to near liquid. Remote Toronto, wild Toronto, the edge of Toronto, but still Toronto. Yet if you ask around, most residents, even long-time ones, have never seen or been to this territory.

On warm and dry weekend days in the summer when people with the means to do so will be crawling north in countryside traffic jams to cottage country, my dog and I might only pass around twenty people on the main trails here. All are well marked – this is not the back country – so it's remarkable to be so alone, considering we're in a metropolitan area of millions of people.

The lack of people let me and others do things normally reserved for empty countryside, like let dogs off leash, even where not technically allowed. If a poodle is off leash in the forest and nobody is around to see, does anybody care? Nope. In parks like the Rouge it's possible to feel far away from the city, then, suddenly be back in the city in minutes. Frank O'Hara, an archetypal New Yorker, wrote of this mix of urban and pastoral in his 1957 poem *Meditations in an Emergency*: "I can't even enjoy a blade of grass unless I know there's a subway handy, or a record store or some other sign that people do not totally *regret* life." The subway may not be handy in this corner of Scarborough, but the city here is evolving faster and becoming more interesting a landscape than most realize. It's the place to watch, every bit as much as the downtown skyline.

Ultimately, in 2014, Scarborough voters in Ward 44 returned Ron Moeser to city hall, but with just 26 per cent of the 42,037 votes cast here, only 600 votes more than his nearest challenger, environmental scientist Jennifer McKelvie. Chhabra came in fourth, with 11 per cent of the vote. Like many wards, the votes here were split among a few strong candidates, so the incumbent's win was by no means a majority, yet the status quo was held up. Mayorally, Ward 44 threw 45 per cent of its support behind Doug Ford, with John Tory receiving 40 per cent and Olivia Chow coming in far behind at 15 per cent.

Although not in line with how the majority of the city went, Ward 44 supported Doug Ford for mayor, as nearly all Scarborough wards did, half of Etobicoke's, a third of North York, and all the old city of York. Ford Nation remained a force here at the end of Toronto, and across the city.

JOHN TORY became mayor of Toronto with 40 per cent of the vote in 2014, but Doug Ford, even without his brother's natural charisma, was still able to take 34 per cent of the city, with Olivia Chow coming in third, at 23 per cent. The democratic repudiation of the Fords that was long awaited, that so many in Toronto and elsewhere absolutely longed for, didn't happen. After all the drama the city went through on this political roller coaster, 330,000 people in Toronto wanted to "stay the course," as Rob Ford was so fond of saying. With just under one million people casting a vote in that election, it's not a number that can be ignored, and deep inequality behind why many of them voted the way they did must become a central part of the city's civic conversation.

On the surface Toronto has returned to normal. The city tends not to make international news anymore unless Drake, the Blue Jays, or the Raptors do something exceptional. Toronto has continued to appear on "best of" lists, whether as a place to live or a place to invest. The condos keep going up, and the housing bubble seems less a fragile balloon than a concrete fortress, never to burst and forever growing. The mayor is an affable if a bit boring fellow, perhaps what the city desired, or needed, after four years of political turmoil. It's easy for Toronto to return to a sense of oblivious normalcy, as if the Ford era never happened.

The friendly mayor himself has brought a timid approach to governing Toronto. The Scarborough Subway, with even more dubious ridership numbers than before, remains a priority project for him despite the chance to stop it, or change it, before it becomes a white elephant costing billions of dollars. Property tax in Toronto is the lowest in the region, but there's a deep unwillingness to raise it or even talk about the true cost of running the kind of city people here want.

A once-in-a-lifetime chance to tear down an underused section of the Gardiner Expressway in the West Don Lands was squandered. Steady leadership, but, yes, relentlessly timid, with an aversion to the kind of initiative and city-building vision that a young and quickly growing city like Toronto desperately needs.

There are even more critical questions on whether the crises Toronto faces are being tackled boldly enough. The headlines still tell of a city that could go either way: the public transportation system is at capacity everyday; aggressive driving results in the deaths of people simply walking around their city routinely; the affordable-housing wait list is nearly one hundred thousand people long, and existing stock is still crumbling – and that inequality keeps growing.

The mayor does talk about these things, to his credit, but bold action, free from the politics that resulted in the Scarborough Subway, is rare. Even the issue of police randomly carding young people of colour, one that had civic leaders coming out in droves to denounce, the mayor took forever to address, barely saying it was a problem at first. He's a conservative's conservative, but even conservatives who run other big cities around the world know they need to think big and act courageously for their citizenry. There's still time to grow into that role, though.

It's hard to make change in a city the size of Toronto, and it's hard to be an underdog. Only the two would-be school board trustees of the twelve candidates I walked with won their races. Although underdogs themselves, the issues, geography, and people they cared about remain vital. Until cancer forced him to take leave from his city council position before it ultimately took his life, Rob Ford remained the biggest threat to John Tory's re-election in 2018. Although the Ford era may be over (for now), this city is at risk of ignoring the conditions that brought him to power. Toronto and other cities with similar dynamics would be foolish to forget them.

ACKNOWLEDGEMENTS

It takes a village to write a book about a city.

There are many people who made this project possible over the last two years. Thanks to Doug Pepper and Scott Sellers at Penguin Random House for coming up with the idea for this book and commissioning me to write it during the wildest days of the Ford era. Early editorial direction and encouragement from Martha Kanya-Forstner and ongoing editorial guidance from Tim Rostron were essential and appreciated. Lynn Schellenberg's keen eye during copyediting made the text here much sharper. Thanks to all of them for following this project as it went from a little book about a gonzo election to a much broader peripatetic look at Toronto at this moment in its history.

Research time was afforded by some of the publications I write for. My editors at the *Toronto Star* let me write early, much shorter, versions of segments of this book. Many thanks to Janet Hurley, Dianne De Fenoyl, Mary Vallis, Irene Gentle, Wendy Metcalfe, Julie Carl, Kate Robertson, Tania Pereira, Ariel Teplitsky, Kathryn Lascarious, Sabrina Melchiori, and Amber Shortt, all kind, smart, and humane editors who make the *Star* a great paper to contribute to. Thanks also to Matt Blackett and my colleagues at *Spacing* magazine for letting me go AWOL from publication duties save for the essays I wrote there that were explorations of the themes expanded on here. Also Denise Balkissoon and her publication *Ethnic Aisle* let me consider the role ravines play in the multicultural life of this city.

Other folks were the cheerleaders and angst-absorbers I relied upon. First, I owe a great debt to Carol Off for suggesting I might be a good person to write a book about Toronto during this peculiar and critical time, and for her continuing support. There's nobody in Canadian media with more integrity than her. My literary agent, Samantha Haywood, is the best person you could ever hope to have in your corner. Many more individuals were helpful along the way, including: John Lorinc, Matt Galloway, Stephen Otto, Michelle Kasprzak, Anna Bowness, Ian Boyko, Andrea Addario, Elizabeth Bowie, Liz Clayton, Alfred Holden, Lisan Jutras, Melissa Taylor, Pamela Robinson, Ken Rosenberg, Daniel Rosenbluth, Todd Irvine, Dale Duncan, Simon Reader and certainly my family: Pat Cameron, Chuck Micallef, and Danielle Micallef.

Perhaps none of this would have happened without Ivor Tossell and me talking each other into going to that early Ford Fest in 2010, a gadfly habit that continued throughout his mayoralty. Ivor's thoughts and ideas on all things Toronto and Ford have been appreciated.

Much love to Robert Ruggiero who delicately manoeuvred around a mercurial writer and project that demanded endless amounts of time and emotional labour.

ABOUT THE AUTHOR

Shawn Micallef is weekly columnist with the *Toronto Star*, co-founder of *Spacing* magazine and an instructor at the University of Toronto. He is a frequent commentator on urban issues and is known for his passion for the city – its geography, architecture, culture, and people. Follow him @ShawnMicallef.